AAAS Atlas of
population
&environment

**Published in association with
the AAAS by The University of
California Press**
University of California Press
Berkeley and Los Angeles,
California
University of California Press, Ltd.
London, England

**© 2000 American Association for
the Advancement of Science
(AAAS)**
International Directorate
1200 New York Avenue, NW
Washington DC, 20005, USA
Telephone: 202-326-6650
Fax: 202-289-4958
Internet: http://www.aaas.org/
international/

*Cataloging-in-Publication data
is on file with the Library of
Congress.*

Cloth edition ISBN:
0-520-23081-7

Paperback edition ISBN:
0-520-23084-1

AMERICAN ASSOCIATION FOR THE
ADVANCEMENT OF SCIENCE

AAAS Atlas of
population
&environment

Paul Harrison
Fred Pearce

FOREWORD BY Peter H. Raven

UNIVERSITY OF CALIFORNIA PRESS
BERKELEY LOS ANGELES LONDON

AAAS Atlas of population &environment

Executive editor
Victoria Dompka Markham
Director, Center for Environment
and Population (CEP)

Senior AAAS advisor
Richard W. Getzinger, PhD
Director, AAAS International
Programs Directorate

Principal contributors
Paul Harrison
Fred Pearce

Principal researcher
Lars Bromley

Other contributors
Philip Lightowlers
Maggie Thurgood

Project editor
Helen de Mattos

Research editors
Jane Lyons
Christine Hawkins

Research assistants
Carrie Miller
Liz Dew

Reviewers
Gayl D. Ness, Professor Emeritus of
Sociology, University of Michigan
(UM), and Director, UM Population
Environment Dynamics Project
Geoffrey Lean, international
environmental writer and journalist

Case studies
L.J. Gorenflo, The Nature
Conservancy
Holly Strand, World Wildlife Fund

Cartography and diagrams
Lars Bromley
David Burles
Simon Blyth

Design
Price Watkins

Consultants
Uwe Deichmann
Prashant Hedao

Color separations
Swaingrove

Software donation
Environmental Systems Research
Institute, Inc. (ESRI)

Printed in Hong Kong

Prepared in cooperation with the
AAAS International Directorate by
Banson
3 Turville Street
London E2 7HX, UK
banson@ourplanet.com

ABOUT AAAS
AAAS is the world's largest
federation of scientists and
engineers, with nearly 300 affiliate
organizations and more than
140 000 scientists, engineers,
science educators, policy makers,
journalists and interested
citizens worldwide. AAAS
publishes *Science*, one of the most
prestigious and frequently cited
scientific journals. The Association
also undertakes program activities
to expand international scientific
cooperation on global issues,
advance science education, and
shape policy issues grounded in
science and technology.

Contents

Introduction

P opulation and environmental issues are, in and of themselves, extremely complex; linked, they create a whole new set of dynamics which add to that complexity. In conceiving this *AAAS Atlas of Population and Environment*, the AAAS International Programs Directorate wanted to bring together population-environment linkages in ways that make them easily accessible to policy and decision makers, students and the general public. Our hope is that in presenting the issues clearly, the debate surrounding population-environment dynamics and our understanding of the issues will broaden in the coming years.

In origin, atlases contained both maps and expository text. It is on this tradition that we have tried to build, providing maps and graphics that quantify and illustrate many of the issues, and text that lays out the broader links between population dynamics and the environment and places them within their historical perspective. This is followed by a series of analyses of individual topics – both ecosystems and human activities such as migration or trade – that bring together what is known about the ways in which people impact the Earth's environment. Lastly the atlas contains six case studies that look at population-environment relationships in selected areas.

None of this could have been done without the help and support of a large number of institutions and individuals. We are grateful to the Summit Foundation, the Turner Foundation and the Hewlett Foundation for their generous support, without which this project would not have been possible. We would also like to thank the World Wildlife Fund (WWF-US) and The Nature Conservancy (TNC) for their contribution of the case studies. Thanks are also due to the many individuals in those organizations listed at the end of the book, whose skills, willingness to share data, advice, encouragement, and above all unfailing good humor, made this publication possible.

Covering all aspects of the population-environment relationship is nearly impossible in any circumstances, let alone in a single introductory volume. However, by drawing on very current research and data as well as the most up-to-date mapping techniques, we have attempted to provide a cogent entry-way to some of the most important concepts and questions facing us at the beginning of the 21st century. In producing the *AAAS Atlas of Population and Environment* we have tried to make that critical link between the scientific data, research and analysis of issues, and policies and public understanding. We hope you will find it useful.

Richard W. Getzinger, PhD
Director, AAAS International Programs Directorate

Victoria Dompka Markham
Director, Center for Environment and Population (CEP)

Foreword

OPINIONS vary widely on the numbers of people that individual areas, or the world as a whole, can support, and objective analyses of the relationships that exist between population and the environment are few and far between. In view of this lack of readily available, clearly presented information, this volume fills an important void. Its graphics, analyses and discussions of individual ecosystems provide the kind of basis that any educated person would like to have in approaching this subject or in acting intelligently in many areas of modern life. It is thus a most welcome contribution to the growing body of literature about the environment, focusing exclusively on what is clearly the key area of concern.

As our numbers continue to grow, with increasing pressure on the environment everywhere, it becomes more and more important to understand in as much depth as possible the many and diverse aspects of this set of relationships. In this volume, you will find them laid out in a way that is graphically appealing, clear, consistent with contemporary thought on the issues and readily accessible to the intelligent lay person. In doing so, the book makes a contribution that is exceedingly timely, one that will lead to further analyses and reflection on the part of individuals, governments and corporations, as the authors have clearly intended.

Although it has long seemed obvious that there is an important linkage between such factors as human population density, rate of growth, consumption and the choice of particular technologies on the one hand, and the state of the environment on the other, the quantitative analysis of such relationships has by no means been adequately pursued, and they are often poorly understood and represented. For these reasons, it is of great importance to make what we do know accessible to both specialist and broader audiences, as a basis for developing theory further and for making the best decisions we can now. Although it is difficult to view the pertinent facts clearly and without bias, it is evident that no relationships are more important for us to understand as we strive to create a sustainable world for the 21st century and beyond. General statements, speculation and intuitive deductions about the impacts of various aspects of human population on the environment are no longer sufficient as a basis for effective action, and additional empirical evidence and analyses are badly needed. This book does not attempt such analyses, but rather endeavors to establish a common base of understanding about what is known in this area. In doing so, it makes an important contribution.

In its opening chapters, this book illustrates the various ways in which population factors, such as rates of growth, absolute growth, consumption, migration and the application of various technologies, affect both in the short term and more enduringly the health of the world's ecosystems. Here, Paul Harrison presents an overview of exceptional clarity concerning the relationship between population dynamics and the environment. This treatment does not represent original research, but rather is a presentation of contemporary thinking and data. The extensive use of graphics makes every page a rich source of easily understood facts and figures about the central relationships that this book explores.

The balance of the book presents an extensive series of analyses of individual habitats throughout the world, considering in depth what is known about the ways in which they are impacted by pressures associated with population. This is a feature that will provide useful insights in many areas and for many different people.

One of the most difficult aspects of providing sound analyses of these relationships in the past has been the difficulty of linking the social and natural sciences. Here, however, we find the issues presented in a multidimensional fashion, demonstrating the cross connections between human and natural environmental factors in determining a particular outcome. In such an area, the AAAS, which brings together the wide array of all the sciences, has a comparative advantage, and is particularly suited to undertake interdisciplinary studies.

Where do we stand in our efforts to achieve a sustainable world? Clearly, the past half century has been a traumatic one, as the collective impact of human numbers, affluence (consumption per individual) and our choices of technology continue to exploit rapidly an increasing proportion of the world's resources at an unsustainable rate. Ehrlich and Holdren's IPAT relationship, discussed in the second chapter of this book, lies at the heart of understanding the population-environment relationship and needs to be understood both in terms of the amount of resources necessary to produce each unit of consumption, and also the amount of waste or pollution generated in the process. At any event, during a remarkably short period of time, we have lost a quarter of the world's topsoil and a fifth of its agricultural land, altered the composition of the atmosphere profoundly, and destroyed a major proportion of our forests and other natural habitats without replacing them. Worst of all, we have driven the rate of biological extinction, the permanent loss of species, up several hundred times beyond its historical levels, and are threatened with the loss of a majority of all species by the end of the 21st century.

As George Schaller, the noted conservationist, has put it, "We cannot afford another century like this one" (i.e., the 20th century). As the new millennium begins, human beings are estimated to be consuming directly, wasting or diverting more than 40 percent of the total net terrestrial photosynthetic productivity, and to be using about 55 percent of the world's renewable supplies of freshwater. Median World Bank estimates, however, have the human population increasing by another 50 percent over the next half century, before leveling off at perhaps 10 billion people by the year 2100. Trends over the past decades, which indicate a slowing in overall population growth, support these projections, but it is clear that our population will not, in fact, reach stability unless we find effective ways to continue to address growth and to achieve goals that we have selected.

At the same time, levels of consumption are rising throughout the world, even though it has been estimated that if everyone in the world were to live in the way we do in the United States, it would require three more planets comparable to Earth to support them. The notion that development will eventually lead all of the world's people to achieve standards of consumption comparable to those enjoyed in our country, using the technologies we have available now, is clearly inaccurate; and yet it implicitly underlies many of our actions, thoughts and aspirations. We live in a world in which the World Health Organization considers that half of us are malnourished at some level, taking into account vitamins, minerals and calories, and one in which one in four people survives on less than a dollar per day. It is not a world in which conditions will be improved by wishful thinking, but only by concrete action, based on the kind of understanding that this book will help to make possible.

The realization that the peoples of the world, rich and poor, are interdependent, and that the rich have a responsibility to help the poor and that they will need to do so in order to be able to achieve overall stability, is a relatively recent one, coming into focus with the formation of the United Nations following the Second World War, and especially with the 1972 Stockholm conference on the global environment. Much has been written about these matters over the past few decades, and when the nations of the world came together at the Earth Summit in Rio de Janeiro in 1992, it was hoped that effective action could be taken to address the complex needs involved in building a sustainable world, and particularly the ways in which social justice was necessary both morally and as a condition of forming such a world. Day by day, this is becoming more important as more and more people make larger and larger demands on relatively static types and amounts of resources.

In view of the complex relationships presented in the pages of this book, it evidently is not feasible to estimate the Earth's carrying capacity for people as an absolute. Rather, it is the complex relationship between population density, consumption and choice of technology, together with the choices that we make about the quality of life, that will determine the number of people that an individual area, or the Earth as a whole, can support sustainably. The diversity of our planet is decreasing rapidly, and has done so dramatically for the past 400 generations, since crop agriculture and the domestication of animals provided the means for building villages, towns and cities, and gave rise to the complex human societies in which the manifold activities that we call civilization take place. The question that the relationships presented in this book bring into focus is one of choice: what kind of world do we wish to have and to leave for our children and grandchildren, all those who come after us. Human populations will attain sustainability, but will it be sustainability marked by dull, monotonous, unhealthy landscapes, or one in which the biological and cultural riches that we enjoy in the early years of the 21st century will be maintained and enhanced, sources of material and spiritual enrichment for everyone?

In making the many choices involved in constructing the world of the future, we must go far beyond the mechanical calculations of an Adam Smith to the vision of a Gandhi, who said, "The world contains enough to satisfy every man's need, but never enough for our greed". It is absolutely necessary to adopt a spiritual approach if we want the world of the future to be a nurturing one, filled with variety of all kinds; but it is not sufficient to have such an attitude to understand what we must do to achieve this goal. In order to do so, we must understand the relationships that are so well presented in the present volume in a way that will inform the debate for years to come.

One puts down this book feeling a debt of gratitude to the authors, editors and those who prepared the illustrations for the enlightenment and feeling of rational hope that they have conveyed by laying out the realities of the all-important population-environment relationship so clearly, comprehensively and well. In order to build a better, more prosperous and healthier life for our children and all those who will come after us, we all badly need the kind of clarity of understanding that this very welcome book represents. Given that understanding and our commitment to deal effectively and well with our own future, we shall certainly be able to succeed beyond our most optimistic assumptions.

Peter H. Raven
Director, Missouri Botanical Garden

Part 1: Overview

THE SCALE OF OUR PRESENCE

THE THEORY OF POPULATION-ENVIRONMENT LINKS

POPULATION AND CONSUMPTION TRENDS

NATURAL RESOURCES AND WASTES

THE STATE OF MAJOR ECOSYSTEMS

POLICY RESPONSES

The scale of our presence

HUMANS are perhaps the most successful species in the history of life on Earth. From a few thousand individuals some 200 000 years ago, we passed 1 billion around 1800 and 6 billion in 1999. Our levels of consumption and the scope of our technologies have grown in parallel with, and in some ways outpaced, our numbers.

But our success is showing signs of overreaching itself, of threatening the key resources on which we depend. Today our impact on the planet has reached a truly massive scale. In many fields our ecological "footprint" outweighs the impact of all other living species combined.

We have transformed approximately half the land on Earth for our own uses – around 11 percent each for farming and forestry, and 26 percent for pasture, with at least another 2 to 3 percent for housing, industry, services and transport[1]. The area used for growing crops has increased by almost six times since 1700, mainly at the expense of forest and woodland[2].

Of the easily accessible freshwater we already use more than half. We have regulated the flow of around two thirds of all rivers on Earth, creating artificial lakes and altering the ecology of existing lakes and estuaries[3].

The oceans make up seven tenths of the planet's surface, and we use only an estimated 8 percent of their total primary productivity. Yet we have fished up to the limits or beyond of two thirds of marine fisheries and altered the ecology of a vast range of marine species. During this century we have destroyed perhaps half of all coastal mangrove forests and irrevocably degraded 10 percent of coral reefs.

Through fossil-fuel burning and fertilizer application we have altered the natural cycles of carbon and nitrogen. The amount of nitrogen entering the cycle has more than doubled over the last century, and we now contribute 50 percent more to the nitrogen cycle than all natural sources combined. The excess is leading to the impoverishment of forest soils and forest death, and at sea to the development of toxic algal blooms and expanding "dead" zones devoid of oxygen[4].

By burning fossil fuels in which carbon was locked up hundreds of millions of years ago, we have increased the carbon dioxide content of the atmosphere by 30 percent over pre-industrial levels. We have boosted methane content by 145 percent over natural levels[5].

Through mining and processing we are releasing toxic metals into the biosphere that would otherwise have remained safely locked in stone. We are producing new synthetic chemicals, many of which may have as yet undetermined effects on other organisms.

We have thinned the ozone layer that protects life on Earth from harmful ultra-violet radiation. Most scientists agree that human activities are contributing to global warming, raising global temperatures and sea levels.

These processes affect the habitats and environmental pressures under which all species exist. As a result, we have had an incalculable effect on the Earth's biodiversity. The 484 animal and 654 plant species recorded as extinct since 1600 are only the tip of a massive iceberg[6].

We have become a major force of evolution, not just for the "new" species we breed and genetically engineer, but for the thousands of species whose habitats we modify, consigning many to

The scale of human activities

The scale of human activities can be represented partly by observing population density, both over the globe and over time.

POPULATION DENSITY, 1998
Per square kilometer

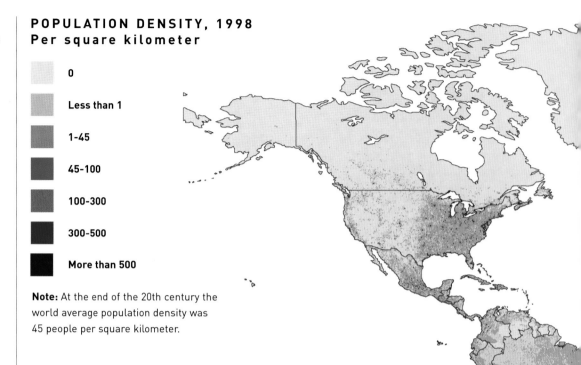

- 0
- Less than 1
- 1-45
- 45-100
- 100-300
- 300-500
- More than 500

Note: At the end of the 20th century the world average population density was 45 people per square kilometer.

Population density per square kilometer

- Less than 1
- 1-45
- 45-100
- 100-300
- 300-500
- More than 500

EXPANSION OF THE HUMAN POPULATION
1700

1800

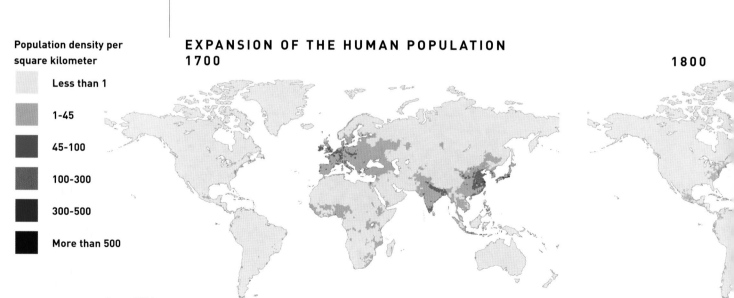

Source: RIVM.

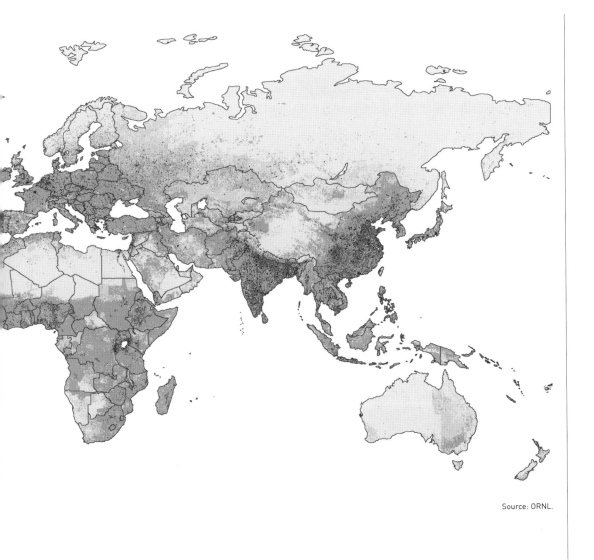

Source: ORNL.

1900

extinction; compelling others to evolve and adapt to our pressures. We have become a force of nature comparable to volcanoes or to cyclical variations in the Earth's orbit.

The scale of our activities depends on our population numbers, our consumption and the resource or pollution impact of our technologies – and all three of these factors are still on the increase. The maps on the previous pages illustrate the increasing spread and density of the human population over the last three centuries.

As we enter the third millennium, the destiny of the planet is in our hands as never before, yet they are inexperienced hands. We are modifying ecosystems and global systems faster than we can understand the changes and prepare responses to them. All the factors in this vast equation affect each other constantly. In a globalized world the elements of human activity interact with each other and with local and planetary environments.

In this unprecedented situation, the need to be fully aware of what we are doing has never been greater. We need to understand the way in which population, consumption and technology create their impact, to review that impact across the most critical fields, and to find ways of using our understanding of the links to inform policy.

The theory of population-environment links

DOCUMENTATION of population-environment linkages has all too often consisted of a simple listing of population trends side-by-side with environmental trends, on the assumption that one is the direct cause of the other.

Effective measures for dealing with how human populations affect the environment require a good understanding of the way things interact. We need an overarching theory of population-environment linkages, but so far there is no consensus on what such a theory would look like.

Research into the links between population factors and the environment is relatively young and undeveloped, and still riddled with controversy. The subject is complex and demands a broad and deep knowledge of demography, economics, and social and environmental sciences, which few possess. Family planning and environmental politics are contentious areas, and personal views on these often color scientific research and theories.

Most theorists agree that overall human pressure on the environment is a product of three factors: population, consumption per person and technology. Population is the total number of people, consumption relates to the amount each person consumes, and technology determines how many resources are used and how much waste or pollution is produced for each unit of consumption.

The best known standpoints often emphasize a single one of these factors as the dominant cause of our rising environmental impact. For some, this is inexorable population growth. For others, it is polluting technology. Still others stress excessive consumption, policy and market failures, or common ownership of key environmental resources.

A SYSTEMS APPROACH

All of these viewpoints are correct some of the time. None of them is correct all of the time. A comprehensive theory must include all factors, and recognize that their relative importance may vary at different times and in different places.

In every human interaction with the environment – even in the simplest societies – the three major elements are in play. They can be linked in the famous formula introduced by Ehrlich and Holdren:

I = P x A x T, or

Impact = Population x Affluence x Technology[1]

More explicitly, environmental impact is the product of population, multiplied by consumption per person, multiplied by the amount of resources needed, or wastes created, while producing each unit of consumption.

Ehrlich used the formula to show that population growth was the dominant factor in environmental damage. In reality, at various historical times, different elements have been uppermost. The

The IPAT formula

The IPAT or IPCT formula is necessarily a simplification. The technology element can usually be broken down into two separate elements: the amount of resources used to produce each unit of consumption, and the amount of waste or pollution generated for each unit of resources.

The impact measured in the IPAT formula is not true environmental impact, but takes the amount of resources used or pollution produced as a proxy for environmental damage. In many situations an extra factor has to be added to arrive at the true damage: the sensitivity of the environment. So a fuller formula would read:

I = P x C x Tr x Tw x S

Tr refers to the technology of resource use, Tw to the technology of waste management, and S to the amount by which the environment changes in response to a given amount of resource extraction or pollution. In practice, S is hard to quantify.

ABUNDANCE...

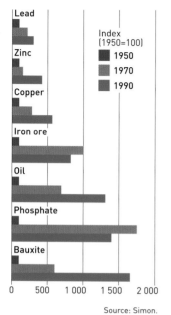

Source: Simon.

CATASTROPHE...

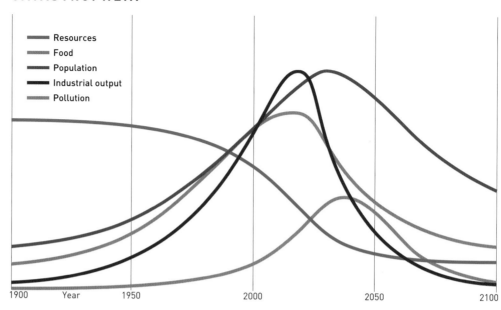

Resources
Food
Population
Industrial output
Pollution

Source: Meadows et al.

Abundance: Julian Simon's chart from *The Ultimate Resource 2*, shows how known mineral reserves have increased with time, despite higher use and growing populations.

Catastrophe: The business-as-usual scenario from *Beyond the Limits*. As resources are assumed to run out, industrial output and food production drop, leading to a collapse of human populations.

increase in arable area in many parts of Africa up to around 1980, and the deforestation that went with it, was mainly driven by population growth. There was little rise in consumption of agricultural products per person, and little improvement in yields. By contrast, the dramatic rise in human output of chlorofluorocarbons from the 1940s onwards was due overwhelmingly to the introduction of a new technology.

Of course, the impact also depends on the sensitivity of the environment, and this is not always predictable. It has certain thresholds which, if crossed, lead to rapid depletion and degradation. Resources such as fisheries, forests and groundwater have a maximum sustainable yield, beyond which they will be unable to replenish themselves. Sinks for our wastes, such as soils, rivers, lakes, oceans and atmosphere, have critical loads for various pollutants, beyond which important aspects of their productivity will degrade.

Sometimes the environment may successfully evolve as human pressures increase. At other times it may change suddenly when human pressure exceeds certain thresholds. When erosion strips soil close to bedrock, yields fall abruptly. If global warming melts the polar icecaps, major ocean currents may cease or shift direction, producing faster climate change.

Although the IPAT model as it is written assumes independence of each of the PAT elements, the authors recognize that these are not independent in the real world, rather they interact with each other. In the 1980s, for example, slower population growth appeared to facilitate faster growth of consumption in developing countries. Higher income levels tend to improve environmental technology – wealthier nations have a greater willingness and ability to pay for environmental quality.

Reality is still more complex. There are many other factors which affect each element of the "pressure" side of the equation. Population change, for example, is determined by fertility, mortality and migration. Each of these, in turn, is affected by a host of other factors, from patterns of breastfeeding and the status and education of women, to child health, availability of contraception, the distribution of land and income, and the opportunities for migration.

This complexity is best viewed using a systems approach, which helps to overcome the polarization found in the most prominent views of population-environment linkages.

The systems approach has two key differences from conventional approaches. It does not focus on a single factor, but instead builds in as many potential factors as possible; and it does not see human impact on the environment simply as a one-way street. There is feedback. Changes in the environment have an impact on human welfare. This is primarily as a result of:

- resource depletion or degradation and the resulting shortages and scarcities;
- loss of a valued amenity such as natural wilderness areas or beautiful landscapes;
- impacts on human health and fertility.

These environmental problems in turn produce a human response – often driving us to alter our behavior so as to reduce the problems.

There have been several attempts at producing diagrams showing these complex linkages and feedbacks, but the number of factors and cross-links involved in the real world makes them extremely complex[2]. One of the most successful attempts to produce a dynamic model of the population-environment relationship is the study of Mauritius by the International Institute for Applied Systems Analysis (IIASA)[3].

When attempts are made to quantify linkages in order to attempt projections, radical simplification is usually necessary. The *Beyond the Limits* studies by Meadows and colleagues, for example, modelled all resources through the behavior of a single fictitious non-renewable Resource, and all pollution through a single fictitious Pollutant which affected human health and agricultural yields[4].

The interactions and uncertainties when studying whole ecosystems or the whole Earth are so great that quantitative forecasts are virtually impossible. All that can be offered are "what if" scenarios that show the possible consequences of a range of trends.

CRISIS VERSUS ADAPTATION

The systems approach helps resolve another conflict in the theory of population-environment linkages, over the way in which humans respond to environmental problems of their own making.

On one side is the "Malthusian crisis" approach, exemplified by Ehrlich and the *Beyond the Limits* studies. In this approach, the pressures of resource demands and pollution loads can build up and are predicted to reach crisis level if business continues as usual. Unless drastic action is taken, catastrophe follows: economy and society collapse, death rates rise and populations fall. We do not achieve adaptation by choice or plan – it is forced on us by nature. However, Malthusian scenarios usually suggest that catastrophe can be avoided – as long as humanity heeds the warning signs and takes the necessary steps in time[5].

On the opposing side is what might be called the "economic adaptation approach", fervently championed by economist Julian Simon. In this scenario, humans adapt to the problems that our development produces, for the most part smoothly and without grave setbacks. In the process we gain increased productivity and efficiency, and improved human welfare. Simon saw population growth as an asset, producing more brainpower to deal with any specific problem[6].

A more sophisticated adaptation approach was put forward by Ester Boserup in her classic book *The Conditions of Agricultural Growth*. Boserup suggested that population growth was the principal force driving societies to find new agricultural technologies[7].

Unlike Simon, Boserup did not claim that the process ran smoothly. She acknowledged that population pressure could cause serious resource shortages and environmental problems, and it was these problems that drove people to find solutions. Nor did she claim that things were always better after the adaptation.

They could often be worse. For example, when hunter-gatherers with growing populations depleted the stocks of game and wild foods across the Near East, they were forced to introduce agriculture. But agriculture brought much longer hours of work and a less rich diet than hunter-gatherers enjoyed. Further population growth among shifting slash-and-burn farmers led to shorter fallow periods, falling yields and soil erosion. Plowing and fertilizers were introduced to deal with these problems – but once again involved longer hours of work[8].

The major flaw with both the adaptationist and the Malthusian approaches lies in their claim to universality. In reality, both may be true of different civilizations at different historical periods, and a comprehensive theory must be able to account for both approaches.

Malthusian crises in history

History has seen Malthusian-type crises when whole civilizations failed to adapt to the consequences of their own pressure on the environment and suffered total or partial collapse. Salinization drove farming out of southern Mesopotamia. Deforestation may have brought the Maya and Easter Island civilizations to an end. In medieval Europe the extension of farmland into marginal areas brought soil erosion and declining yields. Poor harvests led to malnutrition, lowering resistance to disease and culminating in the Black Death.

Societies can collapse if, for one reason or another, they are unable to adopt the technology that might save them. When the climate cooled in 15th century Greenland, the Viking settlers could have survived by abandoning their livestock-based economy and adopting Inuit lifestyles, but the leap was too great and their communities died out.

In one way or another these are all failures of adaptation: failures to change technologies or ways of managing resources in time to prevent the collapse of a key resource.

The pressure-state-response model

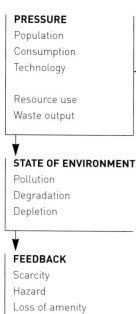

PRESSURE
Population
Consumption
Technology

Resource use
Waste output

STATE OF ENVIRONMENT
Pollution
Degradation
Depletion

FEEDBACK
Scarcity
Hazard
Loss of amenity

FILTERS
Science
Monitoring
Political system
Legal system
Market system
Property system

SOCIETAL RESPONSE
Price shift
Changes in:
behavior
culture
technology
resource management
Policy measures:
regulation
taxation
subsidy

HUMAN ADAPTABILITY AND ITS LIMITATIONS

Humans, by nature, are adaptable. That is why we have been so successful as a species. Through the course of our history, we have radically changed our cultures, our technologies, our consumption patterns, and the number of children we have. In modern times we have changed all of these at unprecedented rates.

Adaptation is possible even in apparently extreme situations. In the 1930s the Machakos area of Kenya had almost no tree cover and rapid soil erosion. Enforced colonial soil conservation programs achieved little. But from the late 1970s onwards indigenous methods of soil conservation were introduced, and there was a massive wave of tree planting. Soil erosion diminished, crop yields rose and fuelwood availability increased – all this at the same time as population continued to grow rapidly. This success story depended on farmers being able to respond freely to market demand, and having *de facto* ownership of their land so that they could benefit from their own tree planting and terracing efforts[9].

Nonetheless, much of sub-Saharan Africa, at least during the period from 1970 to 1990, was trapped in a Malthusian-type scenario. Rapid population growth was increasing pressure on the land, yet agricultural technology was not adapting fast enough, leading to deforestation, soil erosion and, in many places, stagnant or falling yields. For dryland Africa the technologies and crop varieties still do not exist to allow crop yields to keep pace with population growth, leaving migration as the only way to relieve the pressure for many marginal groups. Of course in many countries inadequate governance, market imperfections and endemic conflict made the task of adaptation all the more difficult.

A systems approach sees our interactions with the environment in terms of pressure, state, feedback and response. The *pressure* is the particular human activity, such as carbon dioxide (CO_2) emissions or fish catches, causing an impact. The level of pressure is determined by population, consumption and technology, and by the level of resource use and waste output these generate. The *state* is the resulting condition of the environment – in these cases the atmospheric concentration of CO_2 and global mean temperature, and the size of fish stocks.

Changes in the environment act as feedback when we notice a problem – a resource shortage, an effect on human health, a new hazard or the loss of an amenity, such as the disappearance of a species or wilderness area.

How we respond to the feedback depends on various filters through which we process environmental information: our level of monitoring and scientific understanding, the form of ownership or management of the resource, the freedom of the market to respond to scarcities, and the biases in the political or legal system that determine an adequate response.

The *response* is the policy or action taken to deal with the environmental problem, such as regulations regarding fuel efficiency, carbon taxes or fishing quotas. Our responses, in turn, change the pressures we load onto the environment, completing the cycle[10].

Failures of adaptation can occur at many points in the cycle. In general, feedback works very well in free markets with privately controlled resources like mines or land. In these cases the people affected are able to take direct action to remedy their problem. Where farmers and entrepreneurs have the freedom and incentive to respond to shortages, they can shift to other resources or change their technology very swiftly. This is why the world, by and large, has not faced any constraining scarcity of key inputs – the raw materials required for producing energy or food, for example.

Even in these situations, technology does not automatically keep pace with growing population and consumption pressures so as to reduce environmental impact or keep it constant. Fuel efficiency is constantly improving in cars, for example, but not fast enough to counteract the growth in car ownership and the mileage driven.

Feedback does not work at all well in the case of commonly owned or non-owned resources – such as groundwater, fishing stocks, and the oceans and atmosphere which we use as sinks for our liquid and gaseous wastes. As Garrett Hardin pointed out, lack of ownership or management arrangements encourages individuals to overuse commons for their own private advantage, even if this means degrading the resource. Each user gains the full advantage of their overuse, but suffers only a very small share of the losses it causes. This is the well-known "tragedy of the commons"[11].

In traditional societies, if shared resources seemed to be under threat, users often agreed on rules for their management. But in modern societies the people affected are often unable to take direct action, and must channel their demands through the political and legal systems.

Effective feedback depends on information about the environmental change and its effects passing a long sequence of filters, any of which can act as a blockage or a bottleneck. An emerging problem must first be recognized as a problem, yet many environmental changes are slow, hard to identify and require monitoring. The people affected must be able to make their voices heard in the political and legal system. Yet large sections of society may be unable to do so in countries without effective democracy, a free and investigative press, high levels of literacy and access to an affordable legal system.

Finally, there must be a good scientific understanding of how to remedy the problem. All environmental impacts are extremely complex. They involve the interaction of many different agents and elements, and often the outcome can be unpredictable. Oversimplistic solutions can often lead to further problems. The systems approach allows us to see the Malthusian and adaptationist outcomes as special cases occurring under different conditions.

The human response to environmental change can be effective and timely when:
- the impacts are perceived and properly understood;
- those affected can act directly or compel the political and legal system to act;
- the science is good and the measures are well-chosen.

Under these circumstances, the economic adaptation model applies. However, our responses may be delayed, inadequate or misguided when:
- we do not perceive the problem or properly understand its causes;
- blockages and bottlenecks prevent the smooth flow of information;
- market or democratic imperfections prevent appropriate action;
- the appropriate technology or management techniques or institutions have not yet been properly developed.

When the delays and mistakes are serious enough, severe environmental damage can occur. Sometimes, if a critical resource is involved, this can lead to the collapse of societies and steep population drops. In these situations the Malthusian model applies. However, such cases happen rarely and only under extreme circumstances.

In today's world we have a mixture of these two patterns. In our use of privately controlled resources, we generally adapt well and the supply of key inputs like food, minerals or energy is maintained. In our use of commonly owned or non-owned resources or waste sinks, we do not as a rule adapt well.

In one area after another, problems have not been effectively dealt with until they have become highly visible and had a strong impact on very large numbers of people. In one area after another we have exceeded the maximum sustainable yield or the critical load of pollutants: marine fish, coral reefs, acid deposition, greenhouse gases, the ozone layer.

The oceans and atmosphere are crucial to the stability of all ecosystems on Earth, and determine the productivity of all the natural resources on which humans depend. Yet these are non-owned resources, and we have been in the habit of allowing problems to mount to critical levels before acting. They are also resources where gradual change can suddenly become catastrophic. It is possible that in this case a Malthusian situation – a situation of failed adaptation – could arise for the whole human race.

Population and consumption trends

W HEN people think of the human impact on the environment, they often think in terms of total population numbers and population growth. These elements are important, but they are only two of the demographic factors that have an environmental impact. Population density and distribution, determined by migration and urbanization, are also important, as is population composition in terms of age and household size. All of these impact on consumption levels and trends.

POPULATION NUMBERS AND GROWTH RATES

Along with consumption and technology, our sheer numbers affect the total burden we place on the environment. Rough estimates suggest that the population of the entire world 2 000 years ago may have been around 300 million. Over the whole of the next millennium, the period of the Dark Ages in the West, this rose by as little as 10 million.

The acceleration of human expansion can be seen dramatically in the time it took for each milestone of a billion to be reached. Our first billion, passed around 1804, took perhaps 200 000 years to reach. The second billion took only 123 years and the third, reached in 1960, a mere 33 years. Since then we have been in overdrive, adding a billion every 13 or 14 years. We passed the 6 billion mark late in 1999[1].

Rates of population growth are also significant. Together with the growth in consumption levels, these affect our ability to adapt our technology and institutions to environmental challenges. The faster the growth rates of population and consumption, the faster we must be able to adapt if we are to prevent an increase in environmental damage – and the more likely it is that we will not adapt quickly enough.

Human population has grown in a flattened S-shaped curve, rising very slowly at first, then gradually building up speed and entering a sharp upward hike. Although we are still on the riser of that steep slope, the growth rate has slowed considerably and the curve will begin to level out in the next few decades.

The growth rate was very slow up to 1500, averaging less than 0.1 percent per year. The agricultural and industrial revolutions of the 18th century spurred growth to 0.4 or 0.5 percent per year up to the beginning of the 20th century. After the Second World War, further advances in agriculture and medicine spread to developing countries. World population growth rates of around 1 percent a year between 1920 and 1950 rose to an all-time peak of 2.04 percent in the later 1960s.

Since 1965-70 the growth rate has slowed considerably. In the early years of the 2000s, it is running at a projected 1.2 percent, but there are sharp differences between regions. Developed countries are growing at only 0.2 percent a year, while Africa's rate is 2.36 percent a year, with other regions ranged in between.

The absolute increase in numbers per year continued to rise for three decades after the peak growth rate had passed because the rate was being applied to a much larger overall total. Annual additions grew from 67 million people a year in the 1960s to a peak of 86 million a year in 1985-90. But these too have now begun to slow, to a projected 75 million a year in 2000-05. However, this is still equivalent to adding almost a new Germany every year, or a new United States in less than four years.

Fertility and mortality

Put simply, the human population spurt came about because death rates fell faster than birth rates. Antibiotics, immunization, clean water and improved food availability produced instant improvements in infant and child mortality. Reproductive habits and entrenched cultural values about family size take much longer to adjust.

The total fertility rate (TFR) for a given year expresses the number of children the typical woman will have over a lifetime, if patterns in that year persist. In almost all countries, total fertility rates have been moving downwards.

Fertility is the most important factor in determining future population growth over the long run. A TFR of about 2.1 is needed to keep population stable over time. By 1995-2000 no less than 61 countries had fallen below this replacement level. Between them they housed 44 percent of the world's population. Many developing countries had lower fertility than the United States – for example, China (with a TFR of 1.8), Thailand (1.74), Republic of Korea (1.65) and Cuba (1.55)[2].

Some 23 countries had very low fertility rates, below 1.5 in 1995-2000. The average fertility rate for Western Europe was only 1.7, while in Eastern Europe it was 1.36. The lowest rates of all were found in Southern Europe, where Spain, Italy and Greece had rates below 1.3. Spain was lowest of all with 1.15.

In all these countries population will eventually start to decline unless fertility rates rise sharply. In Southern Europe this is already occurring; in Western and Northern Europe it is expected to begin in the next 15 to 20 years.

Mortality does have some effect on future projections. In most regions a continued decline in infant and child mortality is expected, along with a rise in average life expectancy.

But in sub-Saharan Africa, rising mortality is a factor. Here AIDS has cut life expectancy at a time when it would otherwise have been increasing. In the 29 African countries hardest hit by AIDS, life expectancy at birth is currently estimated at only 47 years – without AIDS it was expected to reach 54. In Botswana, where one out of every four adults is infected, life expectancy was only 41 years in 1995-2000, right back to the level of 50 years earlier. Because of this, by 2015 Botswana's population will be 20 percent smaller than it would have been without AIDS[3].

Population projections

The United Nations Population Division has had a remarkable record of accuracy in its predictions since 1950. But at the turn of the millennium we are entering uncharted waters.

The Population Division has had to revise its projections significantly downwards in the 1990s. The latest medium projection, produced in 1998, expects world population to reach 8.9 billion in 2050. This is a massive 1.1 billion less than was expected in the projection made in 1990[4].

On the current medium projection 97 percent of the future increase will occur in today's developing countries. Today's developed countries will drop from 20 percent of the total in 2000, to only 13 percent in 2050. Africa will undergo the most rapid growth, increasing from 784 million in 2000 to nearly 1.8 billion in 2050. India will overtake China as the most populous country, rising from just over 1 billion to more than 1.5 billion between 2000 and 2050[5].

The most recent long-range medium projection, based on the previous 1996 projection, had world population rising to 10.4 billion in 2100 and levelling out at just under 11 billion around 2200.

However, these projections depend heavily on what might happen to human fertility in the future, and that is more uncertain today than ever before. In many countries, fertility rates have fallen faster than anyone expected – in some cases to levels not previously seen outside economic depression or war.

Demographer John Bongaarts believes that very low fertility may be at least in part due to birth deferment, and fertility may rise again[6]. However, so many countries now have below-replacement

Rapid fertility decline

It used to be said that cultural factors kept fertility unusually high in some areas, especially sub-Saharan Africa and Islamic countries. But there are now examples from every continent and culture area to show that fertility rates can fall dramatically as soon as good quality family planning becomes widely available. Fertility rates in China, for example, fell from 6.1 to 2.47 in just 20 years between 1965-70 and 1985-90. Kenya's total fertility rate dropped from 8.1 in 1975-80 to 4.4 in 1995-2000. Iran, under a traditional Islamic regime, saw fertility fall from 6.8 in 1980-85 to 2.8 in 1995-2000. These drops are among the fastest ever seen in any country on Earth.

Again, it used to be thought that poverty kept fertility rates high. Yet Bangladesh managed to reduce fertility from 6.44 in 1980-85 to 3.1 just 15 years later, even while infant and child mortality and female illiteracy all remained high.

These success stories all rely on the widespread availability of a choice of family planning methods and usually on improved reproductive rights, female education and health. They contrast markedly with countries from the same regions such as Malawi, Iraq and Pakistan (see page 15).

POPULATION GROWTH RATES, 1990-95

More than 3.5% population doubles in less than 20 years

2.5-3.5% population doubles in 20-30 years

1.44-2.5% population doubles in 30-50 years

0-1.44% population doubles in 50 years or more

–2-0% population could halve in around 35 years

Less than –2%

The map shows annual population growth rates between 1990 and 1995, by census district. These districts vary considerably in size both within and between countries, with sparsely populated districts often being very much larger. Large thinly populated areas with high growth rates can therefore appear more prominent than smaller heavily populated areas with low growth rates, although the increase in actual numbers in the latter will be greater. The world average population growth rate at the end of the 20th century was 1.44%.

THREE VIEWS OF POPULATION GROWTH

How current population growth is perceived depends very much on the data you look at. Popular approaches concentrate on total numbers (chart 1), which are important for our overall impact. These show a curve getting steeper from 1950 onwards, beginning to level out in 2050. We are currently on the steep section.

Annual additions (chart 2) are important as they show the total numbers of new human beings the planet must provide with resources each year. These passed their peak more than a decade ago, at 86 million a year in the latter half of the 1980s. Currently they are running at some 75 million a year.

Population growth rates (chart 3) – which determine the rate at which we must adapt our technology and institutions to avoid increasing environmental damage – hit their highest 35 years ago, between 1965 and 1970, at 2.1 percent a year. In the current decennium they are projected to average only 1.2 percent a year.

Source:UNPD.

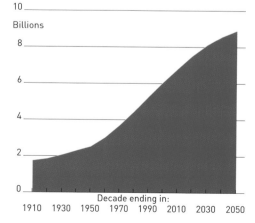

1. Total numbers

Billions

Decade ending in: 1910 1930 1950 1970 1990 2010 2030 2050

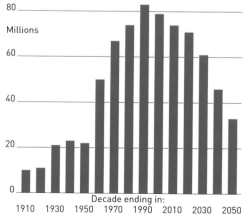

2. Annual additions

Millions

Decade ending in: 1910 1930 1950 1970 1990 2010 2030 2050

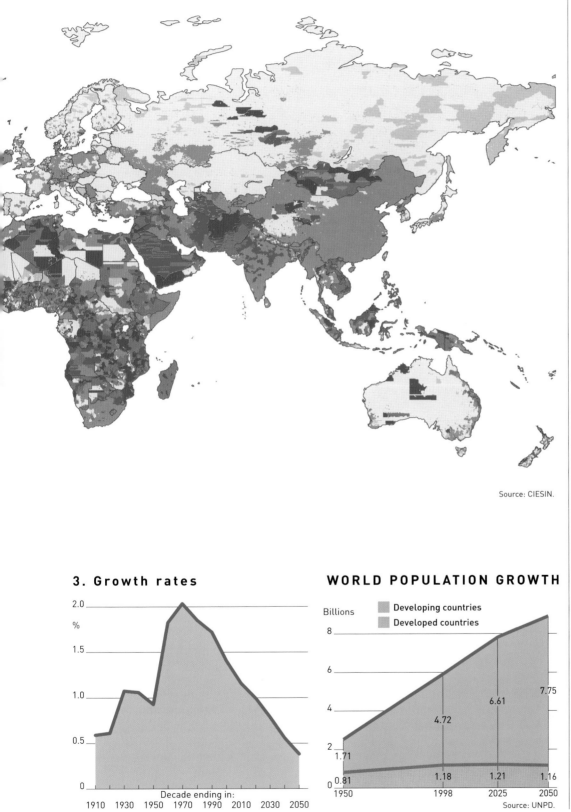

Source: CIESIN.

CONTRASTING FERTILITY

Many countries have seen steep declines in total fertility rates due to serious efforts to ensure access to family planning and other reproductive rights, usually, but not always, along with improvements in mother and child health and female education. Meanwhile other countries in the same region which did not make similar efforts have seen their fertility remain high.

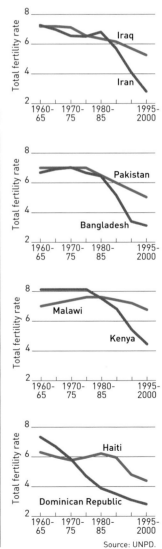

Source: UNPD.

3. Growth rates

Decade ending in: 1910 1930 1950 1970 1990 2010 2030 2050

WORLD POPULATION GROWTH

Billions

Developing countries
Developed countries

1.71
0.81
1950

4.72
1.18
1998

6.61
1.21
2025

7.75
1.16
2050

Source: UNPD.

The 1998 projections from the United Nations Population Division trace three paths, largely depending on how fertility changes. The medium projection assumes that countries with fertility above 2.1 will not fall below that level, and countries with current fertility below 1.6 will rise again to between 1.6 and 1.9. The low projection allows fertility to fall more rapidly, to a floor of 1.6 in most countries, and to remain below that level where it is already below. The high projection assumes eventual stable fertility levels of 2.1 to 2.6 in all countries.

POPULATION PROJECTIONS

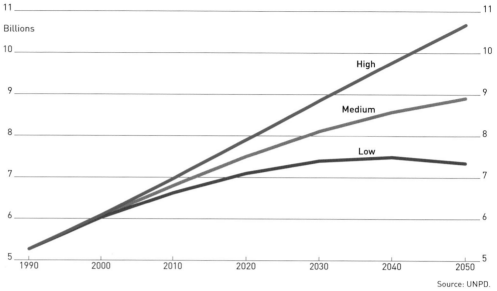

Source: UNPD.

fertility, in so many culture areas, in so many different stages of the economic cycle, that demographers are beginning to believe it may be more than a temporary blip[7]. Surveys in these countries still show that people typically want to have two children, but many pressures prevent them from achieving their goals. They include rising women's employment, rising age at marriage and at first birth, rising rates of divorce and single parenthood, and infertility. Cultural shifts in most developed countries have removed the pressure on people to have marriages for show, and couples in most Western countries can now choose to remain childless without suffering social stigma.

The Population Division's medium projection assumes that countries with low present fertility will see it rise again to between 1.6 and 1.9 and remain there. In countries with fertility currently above 2.1, the assumption is that it will decline towards replacement level (2.1) and remain there.

But as we get further into the next century, this looks more like guesswork than any previous projection. From 2010 onwards, more and more rows in the tables of projected fertility rates fill up with unchanging entries of "stable" fertility levels, in some cases stretching for 40 years up to 2050. Of course some assumption about fertility has to be made, or projection is impossible. It is certain that the reality will be different, but not certain in what direction it may be different.

Most discussions of future populations refer to a time of stabilization or levelling off. But human population has never remained stable in the past, and there is no strong reason to assume it will do so in the future. It is possible that in many more countries fertility rates will in fact fall below 2.1. The Population Division's low projection assumes that fertility will remain low where it is currently low, and in other regions will drop to 1.6. In this case, world population would peak around 2040 at 7.5 billion and would then begin to drop. The long-range low projection, based on 1996 figures, had world population falling further to 5.6 billion in 2100 and 3.55 billion another 50 years later[8].

This scenario is not very probable in the shorter term, because it assumes rapid drops in fertility everywhere in the next couple of decades. But if present success in ensuring reproductive rights continues, and if women everywhere follow the pattern of today's developed countries, it is quite possible that world population may peak at 8 or 9 billion around the middle of the next century and then begin to fall.

It is unlikely but not impossible – for example in a world of constant warfare, insecurity, and deteriorating health and women's rights – that fertility might stick higher, at 2.1 to 2.6. In that case population would continue to rise. The high projection reaches 10.7 billion in 2050 and over 18 billion a century later.

POPULATION DISTRIBUTION

Population distribution in space has a significant impact on the environment by way of population density. The impact of a given number of people may be very different, depending on whether they are focused in a smaller or larger area.

Population distribution is affected partly by different fertility rates in different areas (cities tend to have lower fertility rates than rural areas) and partly by migration.

Most migration occurs within national boundaries. Some of it is forced, by warfare or by severe environmental degradation. The United Nations High Commissioner for Refugees estimates that the number of people internally displaced just by conflict is around 20 to 25 million, with up to 16 million of these in Africa and 6 or 7 million in Asia. Much larger numbers may be environmental refugees, forced to migrate because their home area cannot provide land or work[9].

In conflict situations internal migration may be from one rural area to another. When large numbers move, this can have disastrous environmental consequences. In the exodus from Rwanda into Zaire in the mid-1990s, massive numbers of people were concentrated in small areas, forcing them to plunder forests and local wildlife for food, fuel and shelter.

Slower environmental change or population pressure can also produce rural-to-rural flows. In the Sahel people from the more densely populated semi-arid areas have shifted towards the more humid south, where they have increased rates of land clearance and deforestation. They have also extended northwards into even more arid zones not suitable for rainfed agriculture, leading to accelerated soil degradation.

More commonly, migration occurs from rural areas to urban, as people move in search of better incomes and opportunities, or are driven by the lack of opportunities in their home area. Over the past half century there has been a dramatic shift in the distribution of the world's population towards towns and cities. In 1950 only 29 percent of the world's people lived in urban areas. At the end of the 20th century the proportion was 47 percent, expected to rise to 61 percent by the year 2030. At the turn of the century, urban areas are growing at an average 2.2 percent a year, while rural areas are growing at only 0.4 percent. Approximately half of urban growth is fuelled by migration from rural areas[10].

Some experts believe that urbanization is not all bad for the environment. The shift of populations from rural to urban helps to reduce the pressure of land clearance on forests and other natural habitats. Urban women also tend to have fewer children than rural women. On the other hand, urbanization in developing countries has tended to increase energy use and carbon dioxide (CO_2) output. People shift from fuelwood to fossil fuels, and food and other products must be transported over bigger and bigger distances. Urbanization covers large areas with impervious surfaces such as tarmac and concrete, which increases runoff.

Rapid urban growth can also bring environmental problems for cities themselves. With many cities growing at 4 to 5 percent a year, provision of clean water, sewage, electricity and roads can rarely keep up with population growth.

Lack of sewage treatment leads to water pollution, eutrophication and loss of biodiversity in rivers and around outlets. Water demand may lower river and groundwater levels. As industry and traffic grow, there is an initial rise in urban air pollution, which affects human health and natural habitats around the cities. As incomes grow and with them concern about environmental standards, however, local air and water quality tend to improve as a result of political pressure[11].

International migration also has environmental impacts. After a seemingly inexorable rise in refugees worldwide up to the early 1990s, the end of the Cold War has seen a considerable drop in cross-border refugees, with millions being repatriated to Afghanistan, Cambodia, Ethiopia and other "hotspots". Total refugee numbers dropped from 18.2 million in 1993 to 13.2 million in 1997[12].

But overall international migration has increased steeply in recent decades. In 1965 an estimated 75 million people were not living in their home countries. By 1990 this had risen to 120 million. The majority of these were in developing countries, but migration from developing to developed countries was growing faster than other flows, especially into North America and Oceania[13].

Water for urban dwellers

The International Decade for Drinking Water Supply and Sanitation (1980-90) saw massive efforts to extend services, and registered impressive achievements. In urban areas, the numbers with access to clean water rose from 701 million in 1980 to 1.128 billion in 1990. The numbers with safe sanitation also grew by 425 million[14].

But the pace of population growth meant that the numbers of people without coverage also grew, especially in Africa and Asia. In urban Africa the numbers without clean water grew from 28 million to 31 million, and those without safe sanitation from 38 million to 47 million[15].

AN URBAN WORLD

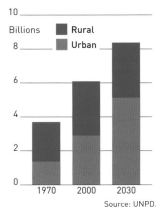

Source: UNPD.

The world is becoming increasingly urbanized, rising from 37 percent urban in 1970 to a projected 61 percent in 2030. Urban areas will see 95 percent of population growth between 1996 and 2030.

Migration from poorer developing to richer developed countries can increase the consumption levels of individual families. However, families adjust to the fertility level of their new host country, and have fewer children than they would have had in their home country.

Tourism can be seen as a temporary form of migration that has environmental impacts through coastal development, increased air flights, pressure on coral reefs, national parks and so on. In the decade from 1988, international tourist arrivals grew at an average 3.7 percent a year, reaching 625 million in 1998. The World Tourism Organization expects this figure to rise to 1.6 billion by 2020[16].

POPULATION COMPOSITION

Population composition – its makeup in terms of age, sex, marital status and so on – is another important demographic factor that affects human impact on the environment, mainly through its effects on consumption.

The most dramatic change in composition is the ageing of the world population. Age distribution can be represented as a building, with each storey representing a five or ten year age group, and the width of each storey determined by the numbers of people in that age group.

In developing countries with high fertility the building looks like a pyramid, with wide floors at the lower, younger levels. As you move upwards into older age groups, each storey gets narrower. In developed countries the shape is more like a bulging urn, with more people in middle age groups than young or old. In the future, in countries where fertility is already low, the shape will be more like that of a skyscraper with a wide upper storey representing the over-80s. As countries develop, their age distribution will come to resemble that of the West.

The UN's medium population projection assumes that life expectancy will continue to advance, reaching an average 81.2 years in developed countries and 75.5 in developing ones by the year 2050. In developed countries today, there is roughly the same number of under-15s as over-60s. By the middle of the century the over-60s will make up 33 percent of the population and will outnumber the under-15s by more than two to one[17]. There will be a dramatic "population explosion" of elderly folk: while the total population is projected to increase by only 40 percent between 2000 and 2050, the numbers of over-60s will rocket by 232 percent[18].

Ageing has consequences for the environment. On average, over-60s consume more per person than under-15s, so the shift is likely to increase average consumption per person. On the other hand, the increasing burden of supporting older dependents and the shortage of young entrants to the labor force may depress economic growth and reduce consumption.

ENVIRONMENTAL IMPACTS ON HUMAN DEMOGRAPHICS

In the past the changes we wrought on the environment typically worked to reduce mortality and increase population growth. But many current changes may raise morbidity and mortality. Antibiotics, for example, lowered mortality rates, but there is concern that the spread of antibiotic-resistant bacteria may reverse this trend. Fertilizer use made great headway in providing sufficiently nutritious diets to lower mortality levels, but the environmental degradation resulting from overuse is deteriorating water quality and so raising mortality levels.

Burning fossil fuels originally enabled a rapid growth in incomes, which improved nutrition, reduced mortality and accelerated population growth. But excess use of fossil fuels is driving global warming, which may increase mortality by enlarging the zones susceptible to warm-climate diseases, and increasing the frequency of heatwaves, storms and flooding. Rising sea levels could lower the productivity of soils in certain areas and lead to increased malnutrition.

CONSUMPTION

The human demand for resources at any given level of technology is always the result of population multiplied by consumption, and in many fields, consumption has grown more rapidly than population. Between 1980 and 1996, for example, the number of cars in the world increased from 320 million to 496 million[19], an annual growth rate of 2.8 percent. Of this, the growth in car ownership

THE AGEING POPULATION

Developing countries, 2000

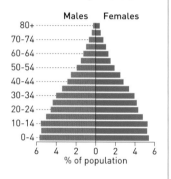

Developed countries, 2000

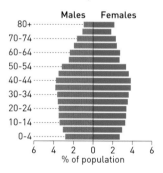

Developed countries, 2050

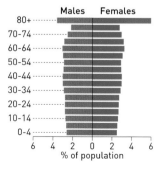

Source: US Bureau of the Census.

per person accounted for 43 percent and population growth for 57 percent. Over this same period the number of television sets in the world grew from 561 million to 1.361 billion[20] – an average of 5.7 percent per year. Of this, the increase in television ownership levels accounted for 70 percent, and population growth for only 30 percent.

As population growth is slowing, consumption growth is emerging as the dominant factor increasing our pressure on the environment. Currently, world population is rising at around 1.2 percent per year. Between 1965 and 1997, average world income per person grew at an average 1.4 percent a year[21]. If economic growth continues this long-term trend, then consumption growth is already a larger factor than population growth in our rising demand.

In the future the role of consumption will become more significant, as in all probability population growth will slow to a halt some time around the middle of this century. This also highlights one of the limitations of the IPAT model. This, and many other population-environment models, assumes that population means an aggregate of individuals. MacKellar et al., and Lutz, show how important alternative views can be[22]. If we count population as households rather than as individuals, the impact of population on CO_2 emissions in the developed world is much greater. This is quite reasonable, since numbers of households in the developed world, unlike those in the less developed world, are growing more rapidly than population, and it is often households rather than individuals that are the real units of consumption. Moreover, Lutz has shown that disaggregating population by age, sex, education and labor-force participation provides a far better picture of population than if we view it as a simple aggregate of undifferentiated individuals. In Lutz's view, people are not merely consumers; they are also producers, and their differences in skill level indicate differences in efficiency and productivity.

Most people's underlying family size desires moderate as countries develop: on average they aspire to replace themselves, no more, and in many cases constraints prevent them even from achieving that. But consumption ambitions are not so moderate. There is a constant increase in expectations as families find that having two or more of everything is more convenient than squabbling over one: two bathrooms, two televisions, two cars, two homes. Increasingly, better-off families with older children may have one car per person.

Yesterday's luxuries become today's necessities. In the 1970s a United States survey asked people what elements were necessary for a good life: 19 percent mentioned a vacation home and 26 percent home air-conditioning. When the same question was put two decades later, the proportions saying they needed these items had almost doubled[23].

HOUSEHOLD SIZE AND THE ENVIRONMENT

The average household size in developed countries fell from around 3.6 in 1950 to 2.7 in 1990. This rapid decline can largely be accounted for by ageing, rising divorce rates, rising age at marriage and increasing childlessness.

Household size in developing countries that still had high fertility actually increased over this period – but in the majority of countries, where fertility dropped, it declined. Since more and more countries now come into the latter category, household size can be expected to decline in developing countries too[24].

Generally, smaller households have higher consumption per person. This happens because each household usually has a dwelling unit with its own heating and lighting, and all basic consumer items from televisions and refrigerators to cars.

A survey in the United States found that one-person households spent an average of US$774 on residential energy, while the increase for each additional person above two in the household was only US$120 to US$160.

A study by the International Institute for Applied Systems Analysis found that between 1970 and 1990, the growth in the number of households in developed regions had more than double the impact on growth in CO_2 emissions than did the growth in population numbers[25].

HOUSEHOLD SIZE

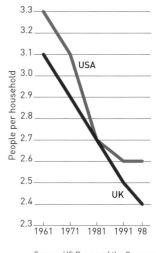

Source: US Bureau of the Census; STATBASE.

Moreover, consumption is not just pursued for need or even convenience. It is an arena where people express social status and power, and for these purposes consumption appears to have no practical upper limit.

TECHNOLOGY

Population and consumption taken together determine the level of human demand for resources, but the way in which demand is satisfied – the chosen technology – is also crucial. It is possible to satisfy demand through sustainable technologies, such as solar power, or through unsustainable ones like burning fossil fuels.

As a general rule almost all technologies that were sustainable when first introduced became unsustainable as human population densities and consumption levels increased. We are currently engaged in a race with time and with our own limitations to find and adopt technologies that can sustain up to 9 or 10 billion humans on a finite planet with sensitive ecosystems.

POPULATION CARRYING CAPACITY

Carrying capacity is a term derived from ecology and range management, where it means the maximum number of animals of a species that a habitat can support indefinitely – that is, without degrading the resource base.

It has been tempting to try to sum up the population-environment nexus by applying this to humans, and there have been many attempts to calculate the Earth's carrying capacity for human populations. The first two estimates, dating from the late 17th century, were surprisingly close to the central range of modern projections: 6 to 12 billion (Gregory King) and 13.4 billion (Leeuwenhook). Some science fiction estimates, based on capturing the total energy flow from the sun, have been as high as a billion billion[26].

More serious recent estimates range from David Pimentel's 1 to 2 billion people in relative prosperity, to the Food and Agriculture Organization's estimate of 33 billion people fed on minimum rations and using every available hectare of suitable land for high-intensity food production[27].

It is not the number of people that makes a difference to the environment: it is our total burden of resource use and waste output. It is possible, useful and necessary to specify the maximum sustainable burden beyond which a given resource will degrade or become unstable, in specific fields. It can be done item by item, say, for ocean fish (where we are near to the maximum) or CO_2 emissions (where we have exceeded it). But there is no way to aggregate these different limits into one overall global figure.

We could adopt the law formulated by German chemist Justus von Liebig, that the population of a species is constrained by whatever survival resource is in shortest supply. However, this is very difficult in the case of humans, because we are such consummate resource-shifters.

Even if this could be done, because the total burden is the product of population, consumption and technology combined, it is not possible to single out the population element separately. A huge range of combinations of population, consumption and technology levels would produce the same range of impact. For every population estimate you would need to specify the consumption level and the technology involved.

Given the complex reality of population-environment interactions, estimating the Earth's carrying capacity for human populations is a forlorn task. We have no choice but to look individually at each area of our resource use and waste output, and at the impact these are having on the planet's diverse ecosystems.

Natural resources and wastes

P OPULATION, consumption and technology impact on the environment by way of two major types of human activity. First, we use resources. We occupy or pre-empt the use of space, and so modify or remove entirely the habitats of many wild species. We extract resources – growing food, catching fish, mining minerals, pumping groundwater or oil. This affects the stock of resources available for humans and for other species in the future.

Resources fall into two main categories. Renewable resources like water or fish are replenished naturally. Non-renewable resources like oil or iron ore have a limited stock that is not replenished, except on geological timescales of millions of years.

Second, we dump wastes – not just those that consumers throw away, but all the waste solids, liquids and gases that are generated from raw material to final product. These affect the state of land, groundwater, rivers, oceans, atmosphere and climate.

Resources have traditionally been the main focus of concern about the impact of population and consumption on the environment. Frequent warnings were issued that we faced massive famines, or that we would "run out" of essential fuels and minerals. More recently it has become apparent that more serious, more immediate and more intractable problems lie in the global threats that derive from our wastes.

NON-RENEWABLE RESOURCES

Ultimately, all non-renewable resources on Earth are limited: if used constantly they must sooner or later run out. So far, however, the threatened exhaustion of non-renewable resources has not happened, thanks to market mechanisms which have ensured successful adaptation.

When shortages of any mineral resource begin to be felt, prices rise. This stimulates more exploration and research, and makes it economical to develop more expensive technology, and to exploit reserves that are more costly to work. Manufacturers find ways of making do with less, recycling increases, and cheaper substitutes are found.

Due to these mechanisms, the projected lifespan of many minerals has remained more or less level or in some cases grown with time, despite dramatic increases in use. In 1989, for example, recoverable reserves of oil and natural gas liquids were enough to cover 41 years of production at current rates. Nine years later they were enough to cover 43 years. Recoverable reserves of natural gas were enough to cover only 23 years of production in 1989; by 1998 this had grown to 57 years. Recoverable reserves of coal did fall, but were still sufficient for more than two centuries of production[1].

Prices are a good indication of impending shortage, and the prices of minerals have declined in real terms over the past four decades. In constant prices, between 1980 and 1996 the price of metals and minerals fell by an average 41 percent, while that of oil fell by 65 percent[2].

Of course, this conjuring trick cannot go on forever. But in modern times the human race has not run into shortages of any key non-renewable resource that has actually constrained the end use to which that resource was put. The mechanism of adaptation, based on free markets, resourceful

CEREAL PRICES

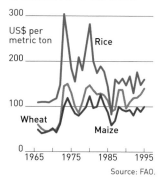

Despite shrinking amounts of land per person and continuing soil erosion, food availability has improved in most parts of the world and cereal prices have not risen since the 1970s. When inflation is taken into account, prices have dropped considerably.

companies, continual research and canny consumers, has worked very well in this sphere, and there is no strong reason to believe it will not continue to do so.

This is not to say that our use of non-renewable resources is problem-free, but the major difficulties arise from the wastes created in producing and consuming these resources. Extracting and processing fossil fuels and other mineral resources on an increasing scale produces water and air pollution as well as solid wastes.

RENEWABLE RESOURCES

Renewable resources like freshwater, soil or wild fish stocks are much more problematic than non-renewable resources, because most of them are vulnerable to human overuse or pollution.

By definition, renewable resources are replenishable by nature – yet replenishment is not guaranteed. Renewal occurs only if they are given the chance to renew. If we exploit them faster than they can renew themselves, they deplete or degrade. The majority of renewable resources, including the most basic ones needed for human survival – land, food and water – are now affected by human overexploitation or pollution.

Food and land

The oldest question about human population and the environment was posed by Malthus. Can agricultural production keep up with potential human population growth? Malthus' answer was no: agricultural production can only increase arithmetically (3+3+3=9) whereas population can increase geometrically (3x3x3=27).

It followed, Malthus argued, that the human population would always be kept in check by the food supply. In reality, the reverse has usually been the case: market mechanisms have worked to expand the food supply in line with demand, and this expansion has more than matched the growth of the human population.

Land availability

Malthus' basic outlook still dominates the popular view, and some recent trends provide material for renewed concern.

In most parts of the world, cultivated land has not been expanding in line with population growth, so the amount of farmland per person has been declining. The area per person has declined only slowly in developed countries, from 0.65 hectares in 1965 to 0.51 hectares 30 years later. In developing countries, where population growth is faster, the area per person fell from 0.3 to 0.19 hectares over this same period[3].

The steepest fall was in Africa, where the extension of the farmed area has lagged far behind population growth. In 1965, Africa had half a hectare of cultivated land per person, but this dropped dramatically to a mere 0.28 hectares in 1995. If expansion continues at the same rate as it did between 1965 and 1995, and the UN's medium population projection is realized, then by the year 2040 Africa will have only 0.15 hectares of farmland per person. This is less than Asia had in 1995, and Asia has fewer problem soils and climates, and far more potential for irrigation. Many parts of Central, Southern-Central and West Africa still have abundant land, but much of this is subject to severe soil, climate or disease constraints. It seems likely that many African countries will run into serious land shortages[4].

Food availability

Overall, cereal production has not been keeping pace with population growth for the past decade. The amount of grain available per person rose fairly steadily from 135 kilos in 1961 to 161 kilos in 1989, but since then has dropped to about 157 kilos[5].

We must be cautious before concluding that we are seeing the harbingers of a coming global food crisis. If these developments were really reducing the ability of farmers to meet market demand then we would expect to see rising food prices and declining food intakes.

Yet neither of these things is happening. On the contrary, allowing for inflation, the prices of most cereals have been on a falling, not a rising, trend. In constant 1990 US dollars, the prices of wheat and maize in 1996 were 40 percent lower than in 1980 and 50 percent lower than in 1960[6].

Nor was there any overall decline in average food intakes per person. Average daily calorie intake in 1998 was 2 790 calories[7], the highest on record, following fairly steady growth from 2 295 in 1963. Average daily protein intake was 74.9 grams, again the highest on record, up from 63 grams in 1961[8].

Improvements were notched up in all developing areas, most rapidly in Asia, but also in Africa, even though average calorie and protein intakes remained low.

How can we explain the simultaneous drop in cereal production per person and the rise in dietary intakes? The simple answer is that people do not live by bread alone: calorie intakes from cereals have been more or less static since 1984[9]. The increase has come rather from meat and fish, oils and other vegetable products. Global meat intake per person grew steadily from 24 kilos per person in 1963 to 37 kilos in 1998[10].

Within the cereal sector it is likely that cereals are being used more efficiently at every stage, with lower losses in storage and processing between harvest and table. Cereals used for livestock feed are increasingly being replaced by soybeans, and soybean production has been growing rapidly[11].

The continued improvement is a sign that markets are by and large matching production with effective demand. People are also adapting their diets as a result of health and environmental concerns. For example, all the 1963-98 increase in meat consumption per person came from pork (up 71 percent) and poultry (up 237 percent). It takes considerably less cereal and land to produce a kilo of chicken or pork than a kilo of beef[12].

Moreover, people's need for dietary energy is, on average, declining. Farming has the highest calorie requirements, followed in turn by heavy industry, light industry, services, and then non-employment. The general trend in all societies is to have higher and higher percentages of people represented in sectors with lower food energy needs.

Barring severe climatic change, it is very unlikely that we face catastrophic food shortages at global level. Research has shown that with relatively modest improvement in regionally specific agricultural practices, the world could feed 10 billion people with current land and technology levels[13].

Persistent problems

The agricultural sector has been very successful in raising food production since 1945 to meet growing populations and consumption levels, but this has often been at the cost of exporting problems to other ecosystems. High levels of fertilizer application have caused water pollution and eutrophication. The expansion of farmland has been to the detriment of wildlife habitat and biodiversity, which has been further harmed by pesticide use.

Population growth is directly implicated in all of these trends. For example, the area of land needed for any given crop is the product of population, multiplied by consumption per person, multiplied by the area needed to produce each unit of consumption. This latter element is the result of farming technology. Where this has been able to increase yield faster than the growth in population multiplied by consumption, the area needed for farming has fallen over time. But where yield has not kept pace, the area of farms and pastures has increased at the expense of forests and other wild habitats.

Unsustainable soil and water management practices have caused land degradation. A major assessment found that by 1990 soils had degraded on 38 percent of the world's cropland, 21 percent of pasture and 18 percent of forests[14]. Productivity has declined significantly on 16 percent of agricultural land in developing countries[15]. One recent estimate suggested that cropland productivity is 12.7 percent lower than it would have been without human-induced soil degradation[16].

Serious problems of food production will also continue in localized areas and in individual countries. These include many countries in sub-Saharan Africa and some individual countries outside Africa such as Bolivia, Haiti and Afghanistan. Many countries that cannot produce enough food

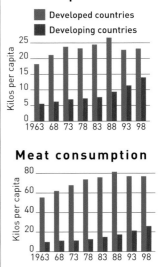

THE CLOSING GAP

Fish and seafood consumption

■ Developed countries
■ Developing countries

Kilos per capita
1963 68 73 78 83 88 93 98

Meat consumption

Kilos per capita
1963 68 73 78 83 88 93 98

Source: FAO.

Fish consumption per person has more than doubled in developing countries since 1963, despite a decline in the per-capita availability of marine fish. Aquaculture has largely been responsible for making up the shortfall, but has also caused massive damage to wetland ecosystems.

Meat consumption per person in developing countries has risen by concentrating on animals such as pigs and poultry, which require less land and resources per unit than cattle and sheep. In developed countries per-capita consumption of both fish and meat has fallen since 1990.

FRESHWATER SCARCITY

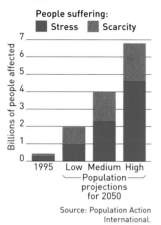

People suffering:
■ Stress ■ Scarcity

Source: Population Action International.

The number of people in countries facing freshwater shortages, around 436 million in 1995, is set to rise steeply over the next half century, but will vary enormously depending on the rate of population growth.

for their own needs can pay for food imports by exporting manufactured goods or services. But many marginal areas, and many poor food-deficit or landlocked countries, especially in Africa, are badly placed to develop competitive industries or services.

There are millions of people who do not get enough food for a healthy, active and productive life. The estimated incidence of malnutrition in developing countries has halved from 35 percent of the population in 1969-71 to 17 percent in 1995-97, but because of the growth in population the absolute drop in numbers, from 917 million to 790 million, has been much more modest[17].

The numbers of malnourished will probably continue to decline slowly, while still remaining unacceptably high. However, malnutrition is not a sign that not enough food is available at global or even national level. It is a symptom of poverty and inequality – the poor lack enough money to buy, or enough good land to grow, sufficient food for the needs of their families.

Reducing the number of malnourished means taking measures to create jobs, redistribute land more equitably, and increase the productivity of small and marginal farms through targeted agricultural training, crop breeding, and soil and water conservation programs. Once the poor's own resources have been boosted, they themselves will grow, or the world market will produce, enough food to meet their effective demand.

Freshwater

We live on a planet whose surface is mainly ocean, but freshwater is a much more limited resource. Some 97 percent of all water is salty, currently useless for drinking or agriculture.

Most freshwater is locked up in ice and snow and in aquifers too deep to tap, and the rest is very unevenly distributed. Equatorial regions and some northern latitudes have a surfeit. Dry areas in between, including much of Africa, have supplies that are too scarce or too uncertain.

Freshwater is crucial for survival, for health, for agriculture, for industry, and for comfort and leisure. But the freshwater resources of any country are limited. There is only so much to go round: the larger the population, the less there is for each person.

In some countries, shortages are already biting. According to Swedish hydrologist Malin Falkenmark, a minimum of 1 700 cubic meters of renewable freshwater is needed per person per year to avoid serious problems. Below this level, a country is in a situation of water stress, when water supply problems may become chronic and widespread. There may be a need for long-distance water transfers, reuse of treated waste water, or supply interruptions in dry periods.

Where supplies fall below 1 000 cubic meters per person per year, a situation of water scarcity applies, and a society will face difficult choices between agriculture, industry, personal health and convenience which will hamper development[18].

In 1995 some 436 million people were already suffering water scarcity or stress. Even these levels of water shortage are causing severe development problems in some areas. There are conflicts among farmers and between farming and urban needs, and heightening tensions between countries dependent on the same resources, such as Israel and Jordan; Turkey, Syria and Iraq; India and Bangladesh; Sudan and Egypt[19]. Saudi Arabia, Israel and the whole of North Africa from Egypt to Mauritania are already withdrawing groundwater faster than it can replenish itself. Yet these countries face population increases of between 52 and 152 percent over the next 50 years[20].

Different population futures make a considerable difference to water futures. An analysis of the UN's 1996 population projections has estimated numbers likely to be suffering water shortage in the future. By 2050, on the medium projection, the number of people in countries suffering water stress or scarcity will have risen to 4 billion[21]. If the UN's low population projection could be achieved, then the total population in countries facing water scarcity or stress would amount to only 2 billion. By contrast, if the world were to hit the high projection, this total would be 6.8 billion.

POLLUTION AND WASTES

Perhaps the most intractable threats to the globe today relate as much to what we waste as to what we consume. Pollution places a mounting burden on local and planetary ecosystems. Ultimately it is exported to the global commons: the oceans and atmosphere, where our understanding of inter-actions is still inadequate. Sustainable management strategies are complex to devise and politically difficult to introduce.

In the process of making the end products we actually use, our machines dig up, churn over, swallow up and spew out gigatons of material. One study found that some 93 percent of materials used in production do not end up in saleable products but in waste, while 80 percent of products are discarded after a single use[22].

The result is a veritable avalanche of materials. In 1995, for example, the world produced 1.42 billion tons of cement – about a quarter of a ton for every man, woman and child on Earth. Some 2.57 billion tons of sand and gravel were produced in the 52 countries for which data are available[23].

Figures on carbon dioxide (CO_2) illustrate how the waste deluge has grown. Back in 1750, the human race produced only 11 million tons of CO_2 from fossil-fuel burning and cement production. A century later this had grown 18-fold to 198 million tons, and in another century a further 30-fold to around 6 billion tons. By 1995 our annual CO_2 output had multiplied by another four times to reach almost 24 billion tons[24].

These material flows have left deepening scars on the planet. The solid wastes that are not incinerated deface or pollute localized areas and water courses. Liquid and gaseous pollutants are more insidious and spread invisibly across the whole globe.

Humans raised the level of CO_2 in the air from 280 parts per million in pre-industrial times to 363 parts per million in 1996. Over this same period we raised methane concentrations by 145 percent. There were no gaseous chlorines in the atmosphere before industrial times. By 1996 there were 2 731 parts per trillion, most of these produced in the 20th century[25].

Significant traces of organic and metallic pollutants are now found in the deepest marine sediments, in the remotest glaciers and icecaps, and in the fat of arctic mammals. Studies of human breast milk have found traces of more than 350 contaminants, including 87 dioxin and dioxin-like compounds and 190 volatile compounds[26].

The rise of pollution and waste is not inexorable. Water and air pollution usually increase in the early stages of economic development, but once a certain income threshold has passed, people tend to value environmental quality more highly and have the resources to pay for protection measures. In most developed countries there have been significant reductions in emissions of lead, sulfur dioxide (SO_2) and particulates (smoke), and widespread improvements in water quality in rivers and around beaches. These are cases of immediate hazard, or easily noticeable local problems, or substances that have been the subject of intense media publicity, where political pressure for change is strong[27].

But even in rich countries waste emissions with less immediate, less visible or less dramatic effects have not been the subject of effective controls. The same is true where the costs are exported over a vast area or over the whole globe, or where remedial action would be costly and might affect powerful business interests or important groups of voters. These include, for example, emissions of the greenhouse gases CO_2 and methane.

Population is always a factor in waste and pollution, along with consumption and technology. The level of production of wastes or pollutants is the product of the number of people, the amount each person consumes, and the amount of waste created for each unit of consumption in the whole process from production and packaging to the consumer and his or her dustbin or sewage outlet.

Several efforts have been made to identify the relative shares of responsibility for rising pollution. Environmentalist Barry Commoner studied examples from the United States between 1946 and 1968. Population growth accounted for only 14 to 18 percent of the increase in synthetic organic pesticides, in nitrogen oxides and in tetraethyl lead from vehicles. It was responsible for only 7 percent of the increase in non-returnable beer bottles and a mere 3 percent of the increase in phosphorus from detergents. In almost every case, technology was the dominant factor. A later study by Commoner of nitrates, cars and electricity in 65 developing countries came to similar conclusions[28].

Waste

In the mid-1990s the rich countries belonging to the Organisation for Economic Co-operation and Development produced 1.5 billion tons of industrial waste and 579 million tons of municipal waste – an annual total of almost 2 tons of waste for every person. The United States alone produced 214 million tons of hazardous waste – almost half a kilo for every dollar of GDP[29].

MUNICIPAL WASTE PRODUCTION AND DISPOSAL, MID-1990s

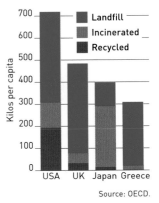

Source: OECD.

In developed countries each person produces five to ten times their body weight in municipal waste per year. There are huge variations: the average Japanese produces 45 percent less waste than the average American. Industrial, mining and construction wastes are many times greater than municipal. The shares going to recycling, incineration or landfill also vary widely.

Clearly, technology is always implicated, and in many cases it may be the prime culprit. However, Commoner chose only cases where technological change was rapid. There are other cases where population or consumption are dominant, such as increased methane emissions from livestock or paddy fields. In more and more cases, technological change is a downward pressure, working to reduce our output of wastes, while growth in population and consumption continues to gear it upwards.

Studies of changes in air pollutants (SO_2, nitrogen oxides, smoke and CO_2) in countries of the Organisation for Economic Co-operation and Development (OECD) between 1970 and 1988 showed technology as a downward pressure in all four cases – mainly through increased energy efficiency in the case of CO_2 and nitrogen oxides, and through cleaner technology in the case of SO_2 and smoke. Population growth was responsible for a quarter of the upward pressure on emissions, while consumption was responsible for three quarters[30].

The state of major ecosystems

ALL ECOSYSTEMS from the local to the global are under threat from the pressures of human resource extraction and pollution, driven by population, consumption and technology.

Ecosystems are important not just from an aesthetic or ethical point of view; they play roles that are crucial to human survival and prosperity. Wetlands purify water and assimilate waste. Forests stimulate local rainfall and prevent erosion and floods. Coral reefs and mangroves protect coasts from erosion. In all their variety, ecosystems both constitute and harbor the biological diversity that makes up the stuff of life.

BIODIVERSITY

Biodiversity is an immense resource, built up over 3.5 billion years of evolution. It embraces not only the number of species on Earth, but the range of habitats and genetic diversity within species as well. It is of enormous importance to humans. Of the 270 000 known plants, some 3 000 are exploited for food, and between 25 000 and 50 000 more are used in traditional medicine. Wild plants are potential sources of new medicines and of material for genetic engineering. Biodiversity is a major attraction for tourism, and not least a lasting source of human aesthetic pleasure[1].

Estimates of the total number of species on Earth vary wildly. Around 1.75 million species have been scientifically described. More than half of these are insects, while vertebrates – including fish, birds, mammals, reptiles and amphibians – make up only 2.5 percent[2].

But the real number is certainly far higher. Most recent estimates fall in the 7 to 20 million range, though a widely acceptable working estimate, used by the United Nations Environment Programme's *Global Biodiversity Assessment* of 1995, is 13.6 million[3].

Most ecologists believe that we are currently undergoing a mass extinction driven by human activities. Since 1600, 484 animal and 654 plant species are known to have become extinct through human actions. But these are only the tip of a vast iceberg. Since most species are as yet undescribed, the majority of current extinctions are going unrecorded – species are dying out before we even learn of their existence[4].

Projections of future losses vary widely, from 2 to 25 percent of all species over the next 25 years. But even the low end of this range is 1 000 times the background rate of extinction[5].

The total extinction of a species is drastic and at present irreversible. But local extinctions are serious, and far more common. Species are disappearing from more and more locations, where they can no longer play the distinctive ecological, economic and aesthetic roles they once filled.

Data on species are far from complete, but countries and taxonomic groups with more complete information have a higher share of species threatened, so it is quite likely that as more data become available, the percentage judged to be under threat will rise[6].

The prospects for the coming decades look gloomy. Forests are the home of between 50 and 90 percent of all land species in the world. If tropical deforestation continues at present rates for the next 30 years, it is estimated that 5 to 11 percent of forest species will eventually be lost[7].

Wildlife habitat is becoming increasingly fragmented by human activities – making way for

Natural extinctions

The Earth's biodiversity has been devastated by mass extinctions in the past. Up to 90 percent of species were lost in the great extinctions marking the end of the Permian and Cretaceous periods. And there has always been an ongoing natural attrition. The average lifetime of a species in the fossil record is 5 to 10 million years. Between one and three species per year became extinct through natural processes in pre-human times.

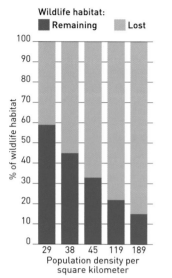

Source: IUCN; WRI.

cities, farms and roads. Fragmentation lowers the size of individual populations, reducing their genetic variability, and making them more vulnerable to extinction. Human barriers also make it difficult for animals and plants to migrate in response to environmental change.

At the same time, global warming will be shifting present temperature zones generally polewards and uphill. Species will have a greater need to migrate but will encounter human barriers blocking their way. Some species which prefer cold temperatures will see their natural habitats disappear completely.

Meanwhile genetic engineering – unless it is rigorously controlled – may introduce new genes which could spread to wildlife with unforeseeable consequences. There is no doubt that genes from existing commercial crops can pass to wild relatives, and even with rigorous control measures, it is unlikely that accidental transfers could be prevented indefinitely[8]. The extent to which this is likely to have negative impacts on the environment and biological diversity is still not known.

When one species dies out, another may evolve to fill the niche it left vacant. The problem now is that most human-induced extinctions happen because we are progressively occupying or polluting more and more niches and habitats, leaving less and less ecological space for other species.

The *Global Biodiversity Assessment* found that the major threat to biodiversity was habitat loss, fragmentation and degradation, due to the need for land for farms, dwellings, industry, services, transport and leisure. Of those species that are threatened, habitat loss affects 44 percent of the bird species, 55 percent of the fishes, 68 percent of the reptiles, and 75 percent of the mammals[9].

Other direct pressures are overexploitation of species for commercial gain, for subsistence or for sport. The introduction of alien species, pollution and climate change are all major threats.

Population is a major indirect cause underlying most of these threats[10]. Population density is closely linked with most forms of habitat loss. A sample of 50 non-desert countries in Asia and Africa where wildlife habitat loss has been estimated showed that the percentage loss tends to be highest where population density is highest. The top 20 percent of countries, ranked in terms of habitat loss, had lost an average of 85 percent of their original wildlife habitat. Their average population density was 189 people per square kilometer. The 20 percent with lowest population density had lost an average of only 41 percent of their wildlife habitat – and their average population density was only 29 people per square kilometer[11].

As always there are many other indirect causes of loss of biodiversity: inappropriate technology, short-term thinking, and failure of markets to factor in environmental costs and benefits.

Governments are gradually moving to give wider areas protected status, but progress is slow. Globally, in 1997, only 6.4 percent of the land area was protected. To protect the full range of species, large areas are needed, but 88 percent of protected areas in 1997 were smaller than 100 000 hectares – a square with sides of about 32 kilometers[12].

FORESTS

In the mid-1990s forests covered about one third of the world's land area – probably around half the original extent before human intervention[13]. We are continuing to lose forests at the rate of some 112 million hectares each decade, an area twice the size of Kenya or France[14].

As with many kinds of environmental indicator, a country's forest cover usually follows a U-shaped curve. It declines during the earlier stages of development, then as population slows in growth and becomes more urban, it stabilizes and may eventually begin to rise again.

So each year, while developing countries are deforesting some 13.7 million hectares – an annual loss of 0.61 percent – developed countries are actually increasing their forested area at the rate of almost 1 million hectares per year[15].

Among developing countries, India and China have almost come to the end of their period of deforestation and have begun to reverse forest loss. Some of the fastest rates of deforestation are found in middle-income developing countries with strong commercial logging interests (Indonesia 2.4 percent, the Philippines 3.5 percent, Thailand 2.6 percent).

Overall, deforestation in developing countries may now be slowing down. According to estimates by the Food and Agriculture Organization of the United Nations (FAO), the annual loss in 1990-95 was 1.7 million hectares a year lower than in the 1980s. Against this, there was massive damage from forest fires in the late 1990s. In 1998 alone more than 6 million hectares were burned in Indonesia, Brazil and Russia[16].

Deforestation data reveal only the net loss of forest converted to other uses. They say nothing about the quality of the remaining forest – its health and biodiversity. Logged-over forests still count as forest, since they can in theory regrow, but destructive logging methods mean that secondary forest is often impoverished. Plantations also count as forest, though they are usually made up of a single species with all competing weeds and shrubs cleared from the ground.

Increasingly, natural forests are fragmented into smaller areas which can no longer support the full range of species. Only three areas of very extensive natural "frontier forest" remain on Earth – in Canada/Alaska, in Russia and in the Amazon basin. Some 39 percent of this remaining extent is threatened, mostly by logging, mining and roads. Some 76 countries have lost all their frontier forest[17].

Perhaps not surprisingly, the more people there are in any given area, the less forest. A number of studies have found a strong correlation between population density and deforestation rates at national level[18].

A recent report by the United Nations Population Fund (UNFPA) divided developing countries for which data exist into two groups of 37, according to the speed of deforestation. In the group suffering faster deforestation – with an average loss of 1.8 percent of forests per year in 1980-90 – population density was 89 people per square kilometer. In the group with slower deforestation population density was just 34 per square kilometer, and the average deforestation rate was only 0.5 percent[19].

The reason for the link with population density is straightforward. The land needed for farming depends on the total population, the consumption of agricultural products per person, and the amount of land needed to produce each unit of consumption. If population or consumption increase, and yield improvements do not compensate fully, then the farm area must expand.

Land is also needed for dwellings, industry, roads, leisure and so on. These are partly a function of population, but also depend on many other things such as standards of residential space, the share of people living in high-rise buildings, the size of gardens, or the level of car ownership. Generally, non-farm land requirements per person rise in line with income.

Of course, many other factors drive deforestation today, from government policies on timber royalties and protected areas, to the numbers of landless people.

COASTAL ENVIRONMENTS

A very high proportion of human population and activity is located on or near coasts. Coastal areas have always been important for trade, sea transport and defence, and contain some of the densest concentrations of human population and activities on Earth today. Nearly two fifths of the world's population live within 150 kilometers of a coastline. In rapidly developing regions such as China, tens of millions of people have moved to coastal cities in search of work in the last two decades[20].

A recent assessment found that over half the world's coastlines are at risk from coastal development and just over one third are at high risk. Nearly three quarters of the world's marine protected areas are similarly threatened[21]. In addition, human activities over a vast inland area have an impact on the coast and coastal water. Much of the water pollution and sediment eroded from whole watersheds is transported to the sea.

Coral reefs

The world has an estimated 255 000 square kilometers of near-surface coral reefs, which constitute one of the richest resources of biodiversity on the planet. The Great Barrier Reef alone has more than 700 species of coral, 1 500 species of fish and more than 4 000 species of mollusc. The

CHANGES IN FOREST AREA, 1980-95

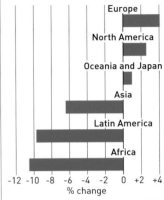

Source: FAO.

Between 1980 and 1995 Africa lost 10.5 percent of its forest cover, Latin America 9.7 percent, and Asia 6.4 percent. But developed areas managed to increase their forest cover; Europe by around 4 percent.

Mangroves

Mangroves are estimated to cover 18 million hectares of the Earth's tropical coastlines, around one quarter of the total. Mangroves host unique species, and are important nurseries for commercial marine species.

No comprehensive survey has yet been made, but it is estimated that around half of all tropical mangroves have been destroyed. The Philippines, Puerto Rico, Kenya and Liberia have lost over 70 percent. The major direct pressures are cutting for fuelwood and timber; habitat conversion for coastal development or aquaculture (often shrimp farming); and damming of rivers which alters water salinity. Population growth and concentration, as well as tourism and resource consumption in and around coastal areas, are important direct and indirect causes of these pressures.

net primary productivity of reefs is higher even than that of tropical forests, and 20 times higher than that of the open ocean[22].

Reefs are a major source of livelihood, providing 20 to 25 percent of the fish catch of developing countries, and serving as a major tourist attraction in many countries dependent on tourist income. Overall, reefs have been calculated to provide resources and services worth about US$375 billion per year.

Yet reefs are among the most seriously threatened habitats on Earth. The status of world reefs has never been comprehensively evaluated, but it is believed that around 10 percent have already been degraded beyond recovery, and another 30 percent are expected to degrade seriously within the next two decades[23]. A recent study estimated that 58 percent of the world's reefs are potentially threatened by human activity, almost half of these seriously so. In Southeast Asia, which has a very high level of coral and fish diversity, more than 80 percent are potentially at risk[24].

The threats to coral reefs are many. Overfishing pushes fish stocks below their maximum sustainable yield. Destructive fishing practices like cyanide poisoning or dynamite blasting kill or damage many species. In many areas reefs are directly plundered for specimens of fish, shell and coral, and even construction materials. Tourist divers and their boats damage corals.

Water pollution from industry, sewage and fertilizer, and sediment eroded from deforested or badly farmed areas, all wash into the sea, reducing light levels and physically smothering corals. Finally there is evidence that episodes of coral bleaching – when corals lose their symbiotic algae – have been rising in severity and frequency as sea temperatures increase with global warming.

As with all environmental damage, these pressures have many indirect causes ranging from technologies for fishing, construction, agriculture and sewage, to changes in incomes and shifts in tastes and leisure habits.

Population factors are important indirect causes. Rising population contributes to increased demand for fish and construction materials. The speed with which urban population growth outpaces improvements in sewage treatment affects levels of water pollution. The rising demand for food of growing populations increases the pressure to use more fertilizer on farmland, much of which gets leached out by rain and washed into rivers, lakes and seas.

MARINE ENVIRONMENTS

Human response to any environmental problem depends on how visible it is, how good our data and our understanding of its causes are, and how directly the problem impacts on people in a position to do something about it.

Of all ecological zones, marine environments are the least visible, the least studied and the least understood. Because of this they are probably the most at risk. The sea's surface is reflective and few venture below it to check what is happening. Baseline data of pristine conditions have not been compiled, and most marine species have yet to be described. Changes due to human activity are therefore hard to document.

But we do have reasonably good data about fish catches, and these reveal disturbing trends in the ecology of the oceans. Assessments made in 1999 found that 44 percent of major fish stocks are already exploited to their maximum sustainable yield. Another 16 percent are overfished, which means that future catches will fall unless remedial action is taken. And 6 percent are depleted, with falling production. Only 34 percent still have room for growth in production[25].

Fisheries pass through a sequence of phases over time. From an undeveloped phase, they enter a developing phase where catches increase rapidly, and then a mature phase where the maximum sustainable yield is reached. If the maximum sustainable yield is overshot, a senescent phase follows when yields are stagnant or declining. According to a 1997 assessment, as recently as 1960 only a very small percentage of fisheries were mature, none were senescent, and half were still undeveloped. By 1994, 35 percent were senescent, showing declining yields, 25 percent were mature, and only 40 percent were still in the developing phase[26].

These phases correspond to states of the underlying ecology and the human response to growing shortages. At the maximum sustainable yield the population of the target species is plentiful and can be sustained indefinitely. But good resource management is in short supply, so the maximum sustainable yield is usually overshot and the target fish population begins to decline. Collapses have hit major fisheries. The Peruvian anchovy fishery collapsed in the 1970s. Catches of cod, hake and haddock in the Northwest Atlantic were at their peak in 1965, at 2.27 million tons. After this they declined and levelled off at around 1 million throughout the 1980s, but in the 1990s they fell precipitously, reaching 126 000 tons in 1997[27].

Fishers are now shifting rapidly across the spectrum of species and areas, altering the underlying ecology in ways that we can only catch glimpses of. Many of our preferred fish are top-level predators. As these are overfished, their prey may have population explosions, which in turn reduce populations of the fish they feed on and so on down the food chain. Recent research by Daniel Pauly and colleagues shows that the fishing effort since 1950 has been moving down the food chain at the rate of about one whole level per century. But this shift does not bring respite for the top predators, as they are left with little to eat[28].

Fish increasingly fail to grow to full size, and may not reach reproductive age. There has been a very considerable drop in the average size of fish caught, from about 100 centimeters in the early 1980s to just over 40 centimeters in 1997[29].

In the absence of effective fishery management at national, regional and global levels, it is likely that the ecology of the oceans will be even more drastically altered by human intervention.

Fishing is not the only source of ocean problems. Alien species from ships' ballast tanks are being spread to areas where they compete with indigenous species. "Red tides" – planktonic blooms of toxic marine algae which can kill fish and cause amnesia, paralysis and death in humans – are on the increase.

There are now around 50 known "dead zones" with no or low oxygen. Most of these have appeared over the last half century, and are blamed on excess influx of nitrogen and phosphorus from farming and sewage. The dead zone in the Gulf of Mexico is 4 144 square kilometers and has doubled in size since 1993[30].

The direct causes of these marine trends are complex. Species are being overexploited through overfishing, collecting and resource extraction. Ecosystems are being physically altered by coastal development, blast fishing and so on.

Ocean pollution is rising inexorably. Although dumping at sea is now better policed and oil spillages are less common, more than three quarters of marine pollution originates on land, where marine-related controls are absent. Pollution from runoff and rivers includes sewage, industrial effluents, fertilizers, pesticides and herbicides. Air pollution is the source of one third of marine pollutants. Some of the most harmful organic molecules accumulate at the boundary layer between sea and air where the early stages of many species develop as plankton, causing mortality, deformity and chromosomal abnormalities[31].

Finally, atmospheric and climatic changes threaten the sea. Rising temperatures have been implicated in coral bleaching, while the thinning ozone layer allows in higher levels of ultraviolet radiation which depresses the productivity of phytoplankton, the basis of almost all life at sea[32].

Behind these direct causes lie indirect ones. Fishing is driven by the level of demand for marine products. The demand, in turn, is determined by the absolute size of the human population, the level of income, and the proportion available to spend on fish.

It is not just the total level of demand, however, but the way in which it is being met that does the harm. The technologies of modern fishing – radar, sonar, global positioning systems – allow a terrifying efficiency in tracking down and catching every last stock. Modern net designs practically vacuum the sea and sea bottom clean of living organisms. There is a very high level of by-catch of unwanted species, or juveniles that would be illegal to land. These amount to about one quarter of the catch, and are simply discarded at sea.

Misguided fishery policy based on short-term political advantage has been a major factor preventing timely adaptation. In most countries the fishing industry has been subsidized for electoral

Shifting ground in fishing

Fishermen respond to the decline in a target species by moving to other fishing areas or other species of fish, and the sequence starts again.

Area shifting has been seen in Atlantic fisheries for favored species like cod, haddock and hake. When Northwest Atlantic fisheries began to decline after 1965, fishing effort shifted to the Northeast and Southeast. As the Southeast in turn showed signs of decline, attention was turned to the Southwest[33].

Species shifting has been seen in the case of whaling. As humpback whale populations declined in the first decades of this century, whalers began to take more blue whales. As these, in turn, declined, sperm and fin whales bore the brunt of the catch. When these too were overhunted, blue and minke whales were targeted. Eventually every whale species was so severely hit that commercial whaling had to be halted[34].

RAPID RESPONSE

CFC production

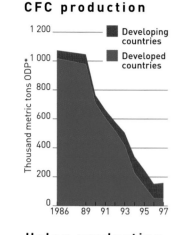

Halon production

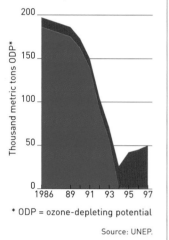

* ODP = ozone-depleting potential

Source: UNEP.

The Montreal Protocol on Substances that Deplete the Ozone Layer was in place in 1987 and, as a result, by 1997 production of CFCs had been slashed by 85 percent and halons by 75 percent – although halon production in China has increased considerably since 1993.

reasons, creating excess capacity. This artificially lowers the price of marine fish and thereby increases the demand. Even after scientists start warning that maximum sustainable yields are being exceeded, politicians rarely act decisively or adequately for fear of alienating voters in fishing constituencies. As a result, collapse of fisheries with massive job losses becomes more likely.

ATMOSPHERE AND CLIMATE

Perhaps the most dramatic and threatening of all the signs of our deepening environmental impact are the changes we are working in the Earth's atmosphere, altering its composition and chemistry, and affecting the Earth's climate.

Ozone

The most immediate threat is the thinning of the ozone layer. Ozone losses pose serious threats to human health, by increasing rates of skin cancer, and by affecting biological productivity in plankton and some plants.

Although ozone losses have not progressed as far as was predicted in the mid-1990s, they are still serious. Total column ozone losses between 1979 and 1994-97 averaged 5 percent all year round in southern mid-latitudes. In northern mid-latitudes losses varied from 2.8 percent in summer to 5.4 percent in winter/spring[35].

The immediate cause was human emissions of ozone-depleting chemicals. The role of population and consumption in their growth was extremely small. The major cause was technological change – the introduction and rapid spread of chlorofluorocarbons (CFCs) from the 1930s on. Between 1940 and 1970 production grew at 20 percent a year, far outstripping the growth of population and consumption combined.

The ozone problem gave us one of the most encouraging examples of rapid response to a perceived environmental problem. The seminal paper documenting the ozone thinning was published in 1985. Within just two years the world had an international treaty to limit and reduce production of ozone-depleting chemicals.

By and large the treaty has been working well. Global production of CFCs fell by 85 percent between 1987 and 1997. As a result, atmospheric concentrations of ozone-depleting chemicals peaked in 1994 and are now slowly declining, though illegal production and trade in CFCs are growing problems[36].

Global warming

In the case of ozone-destroying chemicals rapid response was possible because producers were few, CFCs were not central to our industrial way of life, and economical substitutes were already available. Prospects for similar rapid response on the major greenhouse gases are much less rosy.

Over the past century, the global mean surface air temperature has increased by between 0.3 and 0.6 degrees centigrade. Linked to this warming, the sea level has risen by between 10 and 25 centimeters. Atmospheric concentrations of carbon dioxide (CO_2) have increased by more than 20 percent, and methane by 145 percent over pre-industrial levels[37].

The climate models used by the Intergovernmental Panel on Climate Change (IPCC) predict that over the coming century average world temperature will rise by 1 to 3.5 degrees centigrade and sea level by 15 to 95 centimeters over 1990 levels. The central estimates suggest a warming of 2 degrees and a sea-level rise of 45 to 50 centimeters by 2100. The rate of warming will be faster than any seen over the whole of human history.

The potential impacts are grave. The range of certain diseases and their insect carriers will increase. The range of malaria transmission will spread. If the upper range temperatures are reached, the number of malaria cases could increase by between 10 and 16 percent by the latter half of the 21st century[38].

Extreme weather events such as droughts and floods may increase in frequency. Between 200 and 250 million people currently live below the annual storm surge level on the coasts, liable to

POPULATION TRENDS AND CO₂ EMISSIONS*

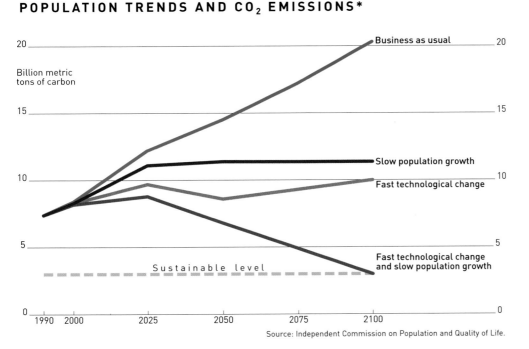

Source: Independent Commission on Population and Quality of Life.

Future CO_2 emissions can be considerably reduced, compared to the business-as-usual scenario, by more rapid shifts to low-carbon and renewable energy sources, and by slower population growth.

* This figure expresses CO_2 emissions as elemental carbon. 1 ton elemental carbon = 3.664 tons CO_2

annual flooding. Sea-level rise combined with population growth could double this total by 2020[39]. The impacts of climate change could have far-reaching consequences for social stability.

The historical record shows that major shifts in climate can occur over very short periods when major ocean currents are affected. The Gulf Stream which warms Western Europe, for example, is driven partly by the sinking of cold saline waters in the Arctic. Increased melting of the Arctic ice cap is now reducing Arctic salinity, which could result in a reduction or shutdown of the Gulf Stream.

For each of the gases that cause global warming – such as CO_2, methane and nitrous oxide – emissions are the product of population, multiplied by consumption per person, multiplied by emissions per unit of consumption. In the case of methane emissions, the population element is very significant. Rice paddies and livestock are among the most important human-induced sources. Between 1961 and 1985 population growth accounted for 69 percent of the increase in livestock numbers in developing countries, whereas changes in meat and milk consumption per person accounted for only 31 percent. As so often happens, technology – the productivity of livestock – worked to reduce the livestock numbers needed for any given level of production[40].

In the case of CO_2 emissions, population was a lesser but still significant element, accounting for just over one third of the increase in emissions between 1965 and 1989[41]. Again, however, at issue is the unit of analysis. If population is counted as households rather than as individuals, its unit contribution to CO_2 will be much greater.

All projections of future global warming made by the IPCC depend on assumptions about population, consumption and technology. The technology element is the result of two factors: energy efficiency (the amount of energy used per dollar of GDP) and carbon intensity (the amount of carbon emitted per unit of energy used). Carbon intensity depends on the share of energy production due to fossil fuels, and on the relative shares of gas, oil and coal in fossil-fuel use (gas produces the least carbon and coal the most).

The IPCC has produced several alternative scenarios, but each scenario varies several factors at once, making it impossible to get an idea of the potential impact of different policies affecting population, or consumption, or technology.

However, a study for the Independent Commission on Population and Quality of Life used the IPCC's raw data to develop policy-oriented scenarios which showed the potential impacts of changes in economic growth, technology and population growth taken separately. Although these factors do interact, the exercise provides at least a rough idea of the possible gains[42].

The IPCC used three population projections – medium-low (7.8 billion people by 2050), medium (10 billion) and medium-high (12.5 billion). The central IPCC scenario (IS92a) projected direct greenhouse gas emissions equivalent to 14.5 billion tons of carbon by the year 2050. Applying the low population projection while leaving everything else unchanged would result in emissions of only 11.4 billion tons of carbon. The "savings" of 3.1 billion tons are equivalent to half the total emissions from fossil fuels in 1990, and more than twice the level of 1990 carbon emissions from deforestation.

Thus population measures could have a very large potential impact on global warming. Achieving the low population projection rather than the medium could, over the next 50 years, have more than twice the impact on greenhouse gas emissions as halting all deforestation at today's rates. It would be equivalent to more than doubling today's energy efficiency, or replacing more than half of today's fossil-fuel use with renewable energy.

However, this reduction would not be enough. To achieve the level of emissions that the IPCC suggests is sustainable, we would also need to achieve rapid shifts in energy efficiency and in the transition to renewable energy. The Independent Commission on Population and Quality of Life study suggested that a combination of slow population growth and fast but achievable technological change could bring total greenhouse gas emissions down to the more or less sustainable level of 3.2 billion tons of carbon equivalent by 2100. A further study, done by the International Institute for Applied Systems Analysis in 1997, found a similar level of benefit from slower population growth[43].

These studies omit possible feedback effects – for example, slower population growth might result in faster economic growth. Nevertheless they show clearly that measures to slow population growth could make a major contribution to reducing future growth of greenhouse gas emissions.

There are many other policy opportunities available which would not only reduce greenhouse gas emissions, but also bring other benefits. They include energy efficiency measures which would save money, or shifting tax and subsidy regimes so that "bads" like fossil-fuel use are discouraged, and "goods" like renewable energy are encouraged.

The sinks and reservoirs for greenhouse gases can also be boosted, for example by increased tree planting or improved forest management. These would bring other benefits in regulating local climates, slowing soil erosion and reducing flooding.

Policy responses

IN ONE ecosystem and one planetary cycle after another, our impact already exceeds what is sustainable in the long run. We risk not only damaging the diversity and beauty of our natural environment, but endangering the resources and environmental services on which our welfare and survival depend.

The challenge ahead is decisive. It depends critically on what happens to population, consumption and technology, and all the political, social and economic factors that influence them.

Over the next half century, world population is projected to grow by one half. Consumption per person, if it continues at the rate of recent decades, will roughly double. So the overall scale of the world economy, the sum of our demand for products and services, is likely to multiply by around three times. If our current level of efficiency in resource use and waste output were to remain unchanged, then our environmental impact by 2050 would be three times greater than today, even if we did not cross any dangerous thresholds relating to oceans and atmosphere.

Determined action will be needed to bring our impact down to sustainable levels. It will be needed on all three elements – population, consumption and technology – and on all the policies, institutions and values that affect them.

POPULATION

The days when the fertility of hundreds of millions of women could be regarded as a useful instrument of environmental policy are over. Women and their partners make their own decisions about how many children to have.

Nevertheless, governments can help to create the conditions where having fewer children will make sense, and where people have the means to reach their desired fertility. And if fertility can be reduced, there will usually be environmental benefits.

Considerable progress has been made in the past decade in reducing fertility and slowing future population growth rates. The greatest scope for further progress lies in those countries and areas where fertility is still high – in the northern parts of South Asia, much of the Middle East, and sub-Saharan Africa. While more than 60 percent of Asian and Latin American women were using some form of contraception in the late 1990s, the figure for Africa was only 20 percent[1].

By and large the countries where there is scope for faster progress are also countries that are likely to face severe human and environmental problems from rapid population growth – land degradation in sub-Saharan Africa, water shortages in the Arab world, and land shortages in South Asia.

Provision of good quality family planning with a choice of methods can have a considerable impact on women's fertility, but the greatest effect is achieved when this is combined with a broad range of measures to improve mother and child health, women's literacy and education, and women's rights more generally. These measures are win-win solutions. All of them are valuable in their own right. Improving human welfare will always be the primary rationale for pursuing them – but the environmental spin-offs come as an added bonus.

CONSUMPTION

The consumption factor is perhaps the toughest one to tackle. The poor of the Earth desperately need to increase their incomes. In 1997 the poorest 2 billion people in the world had average real incomes of only US$1 400 – less than a quarter of the world average and a mere 6 percent of the high-income country average[2].

But even in countries with middle and high incomes people have come to expect steadily increasing prosperity. No politician can hope to get elected on a platform of reducing consumption: leaders who preside over periods of slower economic growth often fail to get re-elected.

A more realistic approach is to divert consumption into channels with lower environmental costs, while ensuring that people still enjoy the end products or services they need for dignity and comfort. The balance of taxes and subsidies can be shifted so as to make environmental "bads" like excessive car or fossil-fuel use less attractive to consumers, and environmental "goods" such as energy-saving technology more attractive.

The Internet, by enabling more people to work from home or shift information and services electronically rather than physically, is reducing the resource requirements of industry and especially services. Changes in culture and values, such as the movement for a simpler, more environmentally friendly lifestyle, are also having an impact on consumer behavior[3].

TECHNOLOGY

Inevitably, the heaviest burden will fall on the technology element of the equation. If, as is quite likely, the scale of the world economy trebles by 2050, then technological changes will have to reduce the environmental impact of our activities by two thirds – just to prevent the present rate of damage from increasing.

Since our impact is already unsustainable, the Club of Rome has proposed a Factor Four improvement in resource efficiency (that is, a 75 percent reduction in resource use per unit of production)[4].

However, in the long run that would produce an impact only 25 percent below the present unsustainable level, and may be too modest a target. More probably we need something approaching a Factor Ten reduction – that is, we would reduce by 90 percent the amount of resources and wastes produced for each unit of consumption, while eliminating poverty and maintaining reasonable standards for all. To reach this target by 2050 would require a 4.5 percent reduction per year. To reach it by 2100 would require a 2.3 percent reduction per year.

Though these rates are higher than those achieved in fuel efficiency over recent decades, we know that at times of technological breakthrough or crisis much faster rates of change are possible. For example, the achievable density of transistors on integrated circuits doubles every two years, an annual increase of 41 percent. Refrigeration technology shifted very rapidly away from the use of chlorofluorocarbons, with an average reduction in CFC production of at least 23 percent a year between 1986 and 1995[5].

A wide range of policies is needed to encourage environmentally friendly technology. Many policies are specific to each different field or area and most are beyond the scope of this atlas. More general approaches include:

- shifting taxes from social or environmental "goods" (such as employment) to environmental "bads" (such as carbon use);
- tightening regulations on pollution;
- setting minimum targets for improvements in resource use or waste emissions;
- raising the share of wastes required to be recycled;
- government sponsorship or subsidy of research and development of leading-edge technologies that are not yet economic.

All of these measures would go some way to ensuring that the pricing of goods and services reflects the true environmental costs, thereby encouraging more environmentally sound approaches to consumption and technological development.

POPULATION-ENVIRONMENT LINKS

Because the population, consumption and technology equation is a multiplication sum, actions that reduce any one component in isolation are necessary. However, there is also a range of measures for tackling population and environment jointly.

There was a time when international conferences avoided all explicit linking of population and environment. Conferences in the 1990s, from the United Nations Conference on Environment and Development in 1992 onwards, were much more willing to acknowledge the interaction. Yet the areas of population and environment are still seriously underfunded in development assistance, and the United Nations Environment Programme is one of the most impoverished UN agencies.

At the national level there is still ground to be made up. Although most national development plans, national sustainable development strategies and national environmental action plans make some mention of population, it is usually simply a token gesture: the potential contribution of population measures to easing environmental stresses is not usually acknowledged.

At local level there have been many successful integrated programs which encouraged communities to pursue sustainable approaches across the board from environment to population. Efforts to incorporate environmental elements into population and reproductive health programs, and vice versa, have been less successful. The best results for the environment are achieved when these programs focus on doing their core activities as well as possible. Burdening them with extra responsibilities may jeopardize this.

Finally, research into population-environment linkages at every level from village to planet can help to inform policy. International studies of global environmental problems, such as the Intergovernmental Panel on Climate Change reports, should include scenarios showing the potential impact of slower population growth.

INSTITUTIONS

A number of blockages and bottlenecks can slow our adaptive response to environmental challenges and make disastrous Malthusian outcomes more likely. Various steps can be taken to remove these blocks.

Environmental science and monitoring must be adequately funded. At a minimum we have to know what is going on, and understand the processes and interactions involved. Market imperfections that worsen environmental problems must be removed – starting with the wide range of subsidies in many countries that encourage activities like fossil-fuel burning or overfishing.

Democratic imperfections need attention too: in less developed countries the people most affected by environmental change, who are usually the poorest, need better access to the political and legal system and to the media. In developed countries state funding of political parties and strict limits on election spending will reduce the influence of business and labor lobbies on government. Freedom of information must be strengthened to allow concerned citizens full access to important environmental data, whether held by governments or private companies.

Finally we need a shift in values towards nature conservation and lower resource use. This is happening spontaneously as environmental problems mount, not just in rich countries but in many developing countries.

If we can mobilize the full range of policy responses, then we can move towards a sustainable relationship with the environment within the next 50 years. The timing is critical: even a decade's delay could trigger threshold effects with incalculable consequences.

Endnotes

The scale of our presence

1. Crop and pasture area: FAOSTAT.

2. Turner (ed.), *The Earth as Transformed by Human Action*, Cambridge University Press, UK, 1990.

3. Vitousek et al., *Science*, 277: 494, 1997.

4. Moffat, *Science*, 279: 988, 1998.

5. WRI, *World Resources 1998-99*, 1998.

6. UNEP (Heywood, ed.) *Global Biodiversity Assessment*, 1995.

The theory of population-environment links

1. Ehrlich and Holdren, *Science*, 171: 1212, 1974.

2. See, for example, Harrison, *The Third Revolution*, Penguin Books, 1993, and Ness, *Population and Strategies for National Sustainable Development*, Earthscan, 1997.

3. Lutz, *Population-Development-Environment. Understanding their Interactions in Mauritius*, IIASA, 1994.

4. Meadows, Dennis et al., *The Limits to Growth*, Potomac Associates, Washington DC, 1972; Meadows, Donella et al., *Beyond the Limits*, Earthscan Publications, 1992.

5. Ibid.

6. Simon, *The Ultimate Resource 2*, Princeton University Press, 1996.

7. Boserup, *The Conditions of Agricultural Growth*, Allen and Unwin, 1965, expanded and updated in *Population and Technology*, Blackwell, 1980.

8. Ibid.

9. Tiffen, *More People, Less Erosion*, John Wiley, 1994.

10. OECD, *Environmental Indicators*, 1994; Schulze and Michael, *A Conceptual Framework to Support Development and Use of Environmental Information in Decision Making*, EPA, Environmental Statistics and Information Division, undated, http://www.epa.gov/indicator/frame/contents.html.

11. Commoner, *Chemistry in Britain*, 8(2): 52; Hardin, *Science*, 162: 1243, 1968.

Population and consumption trends

1. Durand, *Historical Estimates of World Population*, University of Pennsylvania Population Studies Center, mimeo, 1974; UNPD, *World Population Prospects: The 1998 Revision*, 1999.

2. UNPD, *World Population Prospects: The 1998 Revision*, 1999.

3. UNPD, *Briefing Packet: 1998 Revision World Population Estimates and Projections*, 1999.

4. UNPD, *World Population Prospects: The 1998 Revision*, 1999.

5. UNPD, *World Population Projections to 2150*, 1998.

6. Bongaarts, *Science*, 282(5388), 1998.

7. UNPD, Proceedings of Expert Group Meeting on Below Replacement Fertility, 1997.

8. UNPD, *World Population Projections to 2150*, 1998.

9. UNHCR, *The State of the World's Refugees: A Humanitarian Agenda*, 1998.

10. UNPD, *Urban and Rural Areas 1950-2030 (The 1996 Revision)*, 1997.

11. WRI, *World Resources 1996-97*, 1996.

12. UNHCR, *State of the World's Refugees*, 1999.

13. Zlotnik, *Population and Development Review*, 24(3): 429, 1998.

14. WHO, *The International Drinking Water Supply and Sanitation Decade: End of Decade Review*, 1992.

15. Ibid.

16. World Tourism Organization, *Tourism 2020*, 1998.

17. UNPD, *World Population Prospects: The 1998 Revision*, 1999.

18. UNPD, *Population Ageing 1999*, ST/ESA/SER.A/179, 1999.

19. World Bank, *World Development Indicators 2000*, 2000.

20. UNESCO, *UNESCO Statistical Yearbook*, 1998.

21. World Bank, *World Development Report 1998/99*, 1999.

22. MacKellar et al., Population, number of households and global warming, *POPNET* (Population Network Newsletter), 27: 1, 1994; Lutz, *Population-Development-Environment. Understanding their Interactions in Mauritius*, IIASA, 1994.

23. UNPD, *Human Development Report 1998*, 1998.

24. Bruce et al., *Families in Focus*, Population Council, New York, 1995.

25. MacKellar et al., *Population and Global Warming*, IIASA, 1997; MacKellar et al., *Population and Development Review*, 21(4), 1995.

26. Cohen, *How Many People can the Earth Support?*, W.W. Norton, 1996.

27. Ibid.

Natural resources and wastes

1. World Energy Council, *Survey of Energy Resources 1989* and *1998*, 1989 and 1998.

2. World Bank, *World Development Indicators 1999*, 1999.

3. FAOSTAT, June 1999.

4. Ibid.

5. Ibid.

6. Ibid.

7. FAOSTAT, September 2000.

8. Ibid.

9. Ibid.

10. Ibid.

11. Brown et al., *Vital Signs 1998*, Worldwatch Institute, 1998.

12. FAOSTAT, July 1999.

13. Smill, How many people can the Earth feed?, *Population and Development Review*, 20(2): 255, June 1994.

14. Oldeman et al., *World Map of the Status of Human-induced Soil Degradation: An Explanatory Note*, GLASOD, Wageningen, Netherlands, 1991.

15. Scherr, *Soil Degradation*, International Food Policy Research Institute, Washington DC, 1999.

16. Oldeman, *Soil Degradation: A Threat to Food Security?* Report 98/01, International Soil Reference and Information Centre (ISRIC), Wageningen, Netherlands, 1998.

17. FAO, *Food, Agriculture and Food Security*, 1996; *The State of Food Insecurity in the World 1999*, 1999.

18. *Ambio*,18(2), 1989.

19. Groundwater data from WRI, *World Resources 1998-99*, 1998.

20. Postel, *Dividing the Waters*, Worldwatch Paper 132, Worldwatch Institute, 1996.

21. Gardner-Outlaw and Engelman, *Sustaining Water, Easing Scarcity: 2nd Update*, Population Action International, 1997.

22. Quoted in Weizsäcker et al., *Factor Four*, Earthscan, 1997.

23. WRI, *World Resources 1998-99 Database Diskette*, 1998.

24. Ibid.

25. Ibid.

26. Lyons, *Chemical Trespass*, WWF-UK, 1999.

27. World Bank, *World Development Report 1992*, 1992.

28. Commoner, *Chemistry in Britain*, 8(2): 52; Commoner, in *Consequences of Rapid Population Growth in Developing Countries*, proceedings of United Nations expert group meeting, August 1988, ESA/P/WP.110, United Nations, 1989.

29. OECD, *Environmental Indicators*, 1998.

30. Harrison, *The Third Revolution*, Penguin Books, 1993.

The state of major ecosystems

1. UNEP (Heywood, ed.), *Global Biodiversity Assessment*, 1995.

2. Ibid.

3. Ibid.

4. Ibid.

5. Ibid.

6. IUCN, *1996 Red List of Threatened Animals*, *1997 Red List of Threatened Plants*, 1996 and 1997; Oldfield et al., *World List of Threatened Trees*, World Conservation Press, UK, 1998.

7. UNEP (Heywood, ed.), *Global Biodiversity Assessment*, 1995.

8. Conway, *Our Planet*, 10(5), UNEP, 2000.

9. UNEP (Heywood, ed.), *Global Biodiversity Assessment*, 1995.

10. AAAS (Dompka Markham, ed.), *Human Population, Biodiversity and Protected Areas: Science and Policy Issues*, AAAS, 1996; Cincotta and Engelman, *Nature's Place*, Population Action International, 2000.

11. Harrison, *The Third Revolution*, Penguin Books, 1993. Data from McNeely et al., *Conserving the World's Biological Diversity*, IUCN, 1990 (habitat loss), and WRI, *World Resources 1990-91*, 1990 (population density). Countries with large areas of desert were excluded as population density is misleading in these cases. The correlation between loss of original habitat and log population density was r=0.74 (p<=.0001).

12. WRI, *World Resources 1998-99*, 1998.

13. Bryant et al., *The Last Frontier Forests*, WRI, 1997.

14. FAO, *State of the World's Forests 1999*, 1999.

15. Ibid.

16. Ibid.

17. Bryant et al., *The Last Frontier Forests*, WRI, 1997.

18. Mather, *Geography*, 72(1): 1, 1987; Palo and Mery, *18th IUFRO (International Union of Forestry Research Organizations) Congress Report*, Ljubljana, 1986.

19. Data source: *World Resources 1994-95 Data Diskettes*. The link between population density for 1980 and deforestation rates in 1980-90 was statistically very significant (r=0.52, p < .0001). The probability of this link arising by chance was less than one in 10 000.

20. Cohen and Vitousek, *Science*, 278: 1209c.

21. Bryant et al., *Coastlines at Risk*, WRI, 1995.

22. Estimate of reef extent from Spalding and Grenfell, *Coral Reefs*, 16: 225-230, 1997; Bryant et al., *Reefs at Risk*, WRI, 1998.

23. James et al., *State of the Reefs*, International Coral Reef Initiative Executive Secretariat, Background Paper, May 1995.

24. Ibid.

25. FAO, *State of World Fisheries and Aquaculture 1999*, 1999.

26. FAO, *Review of the State of World Fishery Resources*, FAO Fisheries Circular No. 920, 1997.

27. FAOSTAT, July 1999.

28. Daniel Pauly et al., *Science*, 279: 860, 1998.

29. Ibid.

30. Lubchenko, *The State of the World's Oceans*, 10 Years after Exxon Valdez Symposium, Anchorage, Alaska, March 1999.

31. UNEP, *GESAMP: The State of the Marine Environment*, 1990.

32. Hader et al., in *Environmental Effects of Ozone Depletion: 1994 Assessment*, UNEP, 1994.

33. FAOSTAT, July 1999.

34. UNEP, *Environmental Data Report 1989-90*, 1989.

35. WMO, *Scientific Assessment of Ozone Depletion 1998*, 1998.

36. WRI, *World Resources 1998-99*, 1998.

37. IPCC, *Summary for Policymakers: The Science of Climate Change*, IPCC Working Group I, 1995.

38. Watson et al. (eds.), *The Regional Impacts of Climate Change*, IPCC, 1997.

39. Misdorp and Hoozemans, *Global Vulnerability Assessment Atlas*, Netherlands Ministry of Transport and Water, July 1999, http://www.mimnenv.nl/projects/netcoast/gva/intro.htm.

40. Harrison, *The Third Revolution*, Penguin Books, 1993.

41. Ibid.

42. Harrison, *Carrying Capacity in Relation to Production and Consumption Patterns*, Independent Commission on Population and Quality of Life, Paris, 1994. Data were derived from William Pepper et al., *Emissions Scenarios for the IPCC: An Update*, mimeo and data diskette available from William Pepper, fax: +1 703 934 9740.

43. MacKellar et al., *Population and Global Warming*, IIASA, 1997.

Policy responses

1. United Nations Population Fund (UNFPA), *The State of World Population 1999*, 1999.

2. World Bank, *World Development Indicators Data Diskettes*, 1999.

3. Durning, *How Much is Enough?*, W.W. Norton, 1992.

4. Weizsäcker et al., *Factor Four*, Earthscan, 1997.

5. Kurzweil, *Your Bionic Future*, Scientific American Presents, 1999.

Part 2: Atlas

POPULATION AND NATURAL RESOURCES

POPULATION AND LANDUSE

POPULATION AND ATMOSPHERE

POPULATION, WASTE AND CHEMICALS

POPULATION AND ECOSYSTEMS

POPULATION AND BIODIVERSITY

Population and natural resources

WHILE many of the environmental impacts of humankind closely map demographic indicators, this leaves out one vital component: consumption. The per-capita consumption of key natural resources varies hugely around the world. Typically, but not universally, the citizens of rich industrialized nations use more of the world's resources and produce more waste. Sometimes they thereby deplete their own environments; sometimes other people's.

For many resources, the United States of America is the world's largest consumer in absolute terms. For a list of 20 major traded commodities, it takes the greatest share of 11 of them: corn, coffee, copper, lead, zinc, tin, aluminum, rubber, oil seeds, oil and natural gas. For many more it is the largest per-capita consumer.

A typical example is meat. China, with the world's largest population, is the highest overall producer and consumer of meat, but the highest per-capita consumption in the world is that of the United States. The average United States citizen consumes more than three times the global average of 37 kilos per person per year. Africans consume less than half the global average, and South Asians consume the least, at under 6 kilos per person per year[1].

Other resources are used much more variably, depending on local circumstances. Fish, for instance, has been a cheap source of protein for hundreds of millions of poor people wherever it has been available. The highest consumption levels are in some of the world's poorest states, such as the Maldives or Kiribati, where fish is plentiful. Per-capita consumption is also very high in rich nations with well-established fishing traditions – 91 and 66 kilos per capita in Iceland and Japan respectively; way above the global average of 16 kilos per capita per year[2].

Some consumption patterns reflect the rate of industrial, urban and infrastructure development rather than simply current wealth. Cement, for instance, has in recent years been used in greatest quantities in the rapidly growing Asian economies. The top three places for per-capita use in 1996 were occupied by the Republic of Korea, Taiwan and Malaysia. Each used more than twice as much cement per capita as the United States and four times as much as a typical established industrial nation with well-developed infrastructure, such as the United Kingdom[3].

Water is also heavily used in a number of developing countries. It is a key strategic resource whose location is largely fixed, like land, but for which many countries rely on their neighbors. Egypt, for instance, relies for 97 percent of its water on flows that originate outside the country, mostly upstream on the Nile. Sudan, also on the Nile, is in a similarly vulnerable position, as are the Netherlands at the mouth of the Rhine, Cambodia on the Mekong, and Syria and Iraq on the Euphrates. All rely on foreign sources for the bulk of their water[4].

Water use is often as high or higher in poor, arid countries as in rich nations. When precipitation is lowest, demand for crop irrigation is typically highest, and where water-hungry cash crops are grown as well as food, the demands are higher still. When the country is in a poor state of

TOP CONSUMERS, 1998
Primary energy*

	Metric tons oil equivalent per capita	GNP per capita US$ 1998
UA Emirates	18.95	17 870
Kuwait	9.17	id
Singapore	8.80	30 170
USA	7.83	29 240
Canada	7.18	19 170
Belgium and Luxembourg	6.21	26 340
Australia	5.56	20 640
Norway	5.48	34 310
Netherlands	5.36	24 780
Iceland	5.07	27 830
Saudi Arabia	4.98	6 910
Sweden	4.89	25 580
Finland	4.71	24 280
France	4.24	24 210
Germany	4.09	26 570

* Commercially traded fuels only

Roundwood*

	Cubic meters per capita	GNP per capita US$ 1998
Finland	12.08	24 280
Guatemala	12.03	1 640
Sweden	7.43	25 580
Canada	6.41	19 170
Gabon	3.20	4 170
New Zealand	2.90	14 600
Norway	2.50	34 310
Latvia	2.42	2 420
Austria	2.27	26 830
Chile	2.11	4 990
Eq. Guinea	1.88	1 110
USA	1.76	29 240
Estonia	1.74	3 360
Belarus	1.66	2 180
Uruguay	1.62	6 070

* Raw timber only

Passenger cars

	Cars per thousand people	GNP per capita US$ 1998
Italy	539	20 090
Germany	506	26 570
Australia	488	20 640
USA	483	29 240
Austria	481	26 830
Switzerland	477	39 980
New Zealand	470	14 600
Canada	455	19 170
France	442	24 210
Belgium	435	25 380
Sweden	428	25 580
Slovenia	403	9 780
Norway	402	34 310
Japan	394	32 350
Finland	392	24 280

Source: BP; FAO; World Bank.

PRIVATE PER-CAPITA CONSUMPTION, 1998
Expressed as US$

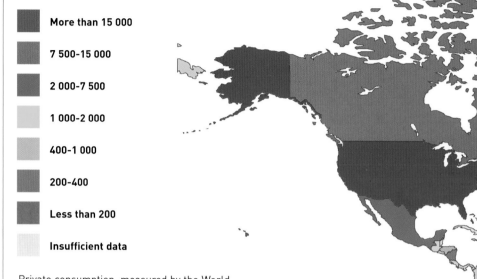

- More than 15 000
- 7 500–15 000
- 2 000–7 500
- 1 000–2 000
- 400–1 000
- 200–400
- Less than 200
- Insufficient data

Private consumption, measured by the World Bank, is the value of all goods and services, including durable products, purchased or received by households as income in kind.

CONSUMPTION GROWTH RATES AND GDP, 1990-98
The highest consumption growth rates

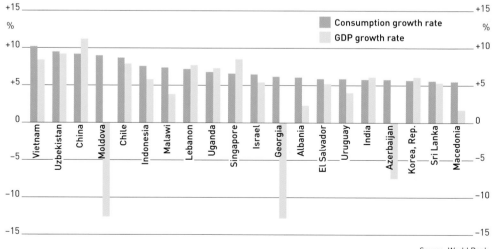

Consumption growth rate
GDP growth rate

Source: World Bank.

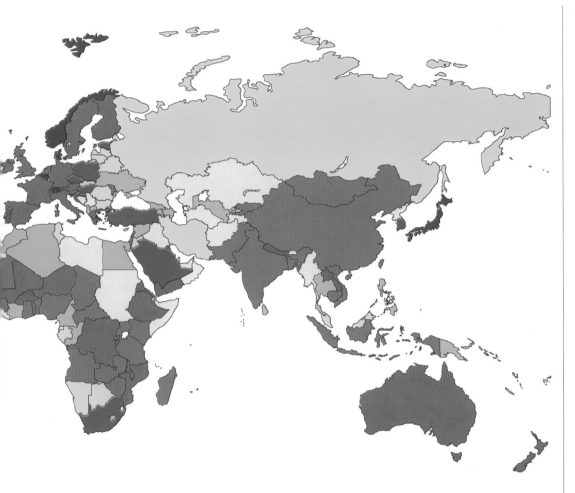

Source: World Bank; UNPD.

TOP CONSUMERS, 1998
Cereal

	Kilos cereal per capita	GNP per capita US$ 1998
Morocco	251.6	1 240
Egypt	245.2	1 290
Algeria	237.1	1 550
Syria	229.2	1 020
Turkey	224.9	3 160
Myanmar	223.6	id
Tunisia	218.6	2 060
Bosnia and Herzegovina	217.0	id
Romania	210.1	1 360
Indonesia	202.7	640
Niger	202.0	200
Albania	198.7	810
Lesotho	198.5	570
Turkmenistan	198.4	id
Lithuania	197.1	2 540

Meat

	Kilos meat per capita	GNP per capita US$ 1998
USA	122.0	29 240
Cyprus	113.6	11 920
New Zealand	110.1	14 600
Australia	108.2	20 640
Spain	107.3	14 100
Austria	104.8	26 830
Denmark	103.2	33 040
Netherlands	101.4	24 780
Bahamas	100.9	id
France	99.6	24 210
Yugoslavia	97.9	id
Mongolia	94.4	380
Canada	94.1	19 170
Slovenia	92.7	9 780
Uruguay	92.7	6 070

Fish

	Kilos fish per capita	GNP per capita US$ 1998
Maldives	160.2	1 130
Iceland	91.7	27 830
Kiribati	77.2	1 170
French Polynesia	67.3	id
Japan	66.5	32 350
Seychelles	64.8	6 420
Guyana	64.4	780
Portugal	58.9	10 670
Malaysia	52.6	3 670
Norway	50.5	34 310
Korea, Rep.	49.5	8 600
Gabon	45.5	4 170
Bermuda	44.2	id
Spain	41.1	14 100
Malta	40.7	10 100

Source FAO; World Bank.

CONSUMPTION GROWTH RATES AND GDP, 1990-98
The lowest consumption growth rates

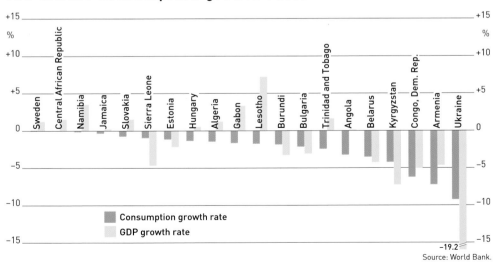

■ Consumption growth rate
□ GDP growth rate

−19.2

Source: World Bank.

development, with dilapidated infrastructure, then water use can be immensely inefficient, producing the highest water use of all, as illustrated by the rates in the arid, cotton-growing central Asian states of the former Soviet Union. During the 1990s Turkmenistan withdrew more than 5 000 cubic meters per person per year, with Uzbekistan, Kyrgyzstan, Kazakhstan, Tajikistan and Azerbaijan all withdrawing 2 000 cubic meters or more per person per year. By comparison, per-capita withdrawals in the United States were around 1 800 cubic meters, in France 650 and in the United Kingdom 200[5].

But for some resources, consumption depends upon the end use to which that resource is put, as typified by wood. While rich nations use more of it in the form of paper and packaging, poor predominantly rural nations rely on wood to a greater extent for construction and particularly for fuel. Finland, which produces large quantities of paper, is the greatest per-capita user of raw timber, but African and Asian countries are the largest users of fuelwood. Japan, though widely criticized for its harvesting of tropical timbers from Southeast Asian rainforests, lies well down the global list of timber consumers.

Two trends are causing nations, corporations and individuals to reassess their use of natural resources. Since the 1970s, there has been an increasing realization that many resources, notably metals and fossil fuels, will one day run out. And since the 1980s in particular, there has been growing concern about the environmental downside of their profligate exploitation, largely with respect to pollution and the degradation and conversion of land.

Some stories of inefficiency and extravagance have become notorious. It takes the mining of 6 tons of rock to produce a pair of typical gold rings. Only 2 to 3 percent of the energy produced by burning coal in a power station is eventually used to light a bulb or boil a kettle, because of inefficiencies at every stage of its conversion to electricity, its transmission and ultimate use. The average European uses 130 kilos of paper a year – the equivalent of two trees. The average American uses more than twice as much – a staggering 330 kilos a year. The paper and board industry is the United States' third largest source of pollution, while its products make up 38 percent of municipal waste[6].

Both governments and companies are now increasingly adopting strategies to reduce their environmental "footprint" on the world. They are doing this by reducing the amount of materials and energy used in providing their services (whether a car or a kilowatt of energy, a meal or a megabyte of information), and by reusing and recycling materials where possible. Much has been done. The gasoline consumption of the average automobile in the United States has halved since the 1970s. During the same period most European homes have been insulated to reduce heat loss by 50 percent or more. Some commercial farmers, particularly in the United States, have doubled the crops they grow with a given amount of irrigation water by using sub-surface drip irrigation.

Much more could be done at no extra cost. Modern technologies – plastic and carbon fibre, optical fibres, e-mail, drip irrigation, electronic systems controls – can all aid the process by making manufacture and communications more efficient and by substituting abundant materials for scarce ones.

Organized recycling, while not invariably energy-efficient, can also be beneficial. Growing concern at the damage to natural forests from paper production has led to a surge in paper recycling. Globally, 43 percent of paper fibre is recycled, a figure that rises to 46 percent in the United States and to 72 percent in Germany[7]. In Britain the film processing industry reuses 5 million film cassettes a year, retailers reuse 40 million clothes hangers, and the aluminum industry recycles some 2 billion cans a year. The latter saves sufficient electricity, which would otherwise go to smelting new aluminum, to power all the nation's television sets for a one-hour show every night of the year.

Energy

THE TAMING of fire was one of humankind's earliest technological achievements. It provided energy for heat and light on demand. But today the environmental impacts of the world's power plants, internal combustion engines and boilers have serious implications for the future health and well-being of the planet.

Energy is one of the most basic of human needs, not as an end in itself but as a means to numerous ends. We need energy to heat and air-condition our living spaces, to cook food and forge steel, to power engines and for transportation, and most of all to generate electricity for myriad purposes from boiling a kettle to running computer systems.

During the past 50 years, global consumption of commercial energy has risen more than fourfold, far outpacing the rise in population. One way or another, all this energy comes from natural resources – whether fossil fuels such as coal and oil, living resources such as timber and biomass, nuclear fuel such as uranium, or "renewable" resources such as flowing water and wind and the power of the sun.

A generation ago, there was concern that fossil fuels would run out, plunging the world into an energy crisis. Today the fear is that their continued use might be wrecking the global climate by emitting carbon dioxide (CO_2) as we burn carbon-containing fuels. This anxiety is substantially increased in view of the considerable unmet demand for energy in the developing world.

Energy use is closely tied to health and well-being – low energy users have high infant mortality rates, low literacy rates and low life expectancies. Worldwide, 2 billion people do not have access to electricity and use fuelwood or dung for cooking and heating – often destroying their local environments in the process. The challenge for the 21st century is to develop methods of generating and using energy that meet the needs of the poor while protecting the planet.

There are three global energy trends in relation to demographics. First and most obviously, as populations grow, energy use increases. Secondly, as wealth grows, energy use per capita also increases. In the early stages of industrialization, this is typically accompanied by a decline in the efficiency with which energy supplies are used, resulting in more pollution per dollar of output. India's emissions of CO_2 per dollar of GDP rose by 29 percent between 1980 and 1995; Malaysia's rose by 58 percent[1].

But the third stage is more optimistic[2]. Beyond a certain threshold of wealth, which may vary widely between countries, energy efficiency begins to improve. Thereafter, countries with expanding economies and growing personal wealth can, with sensible energy policies, dramatically reduce growth in energy use. They may begin to show sharp reductions in emissions of polluting gases, including greenhouse gases, particularly by shifting to cleaner sources of energy, such as natural gas and renewables.

The world is already slowly starting to wean itself from the most polluting energy source – coal. During the past 50 years, global coal use has only doubled, while oil use has risen sevenfold and

FOSSIL FUEL RESERVES, 1998
Estimated years of use at current exploitation levels

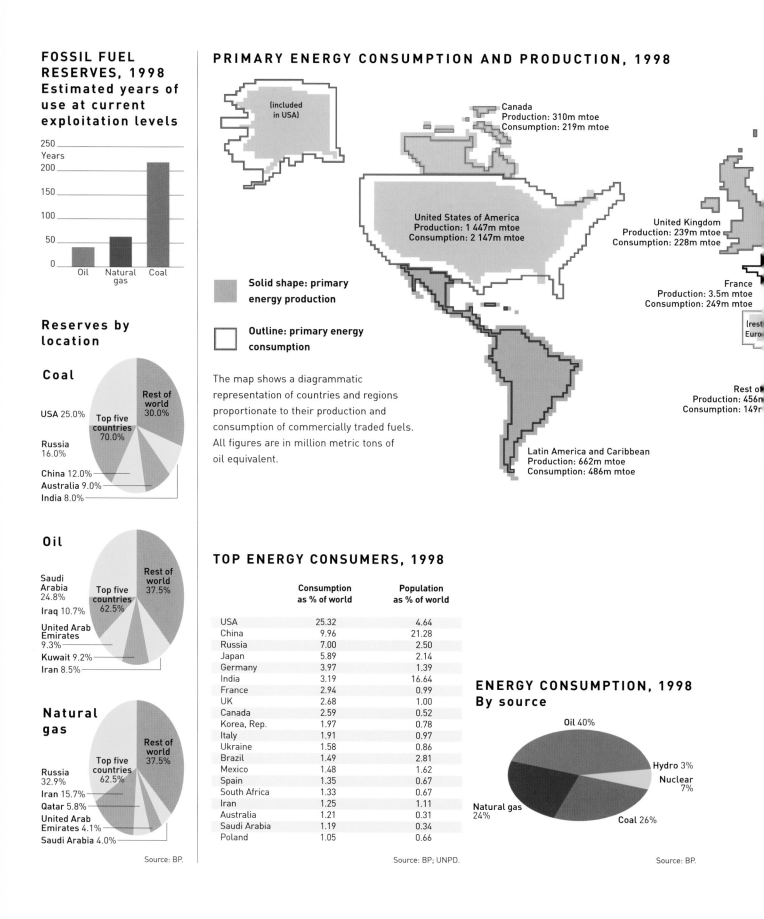

Years

(bar chart: Oil ~37, Natural gas ~60, Coal ~210)

Reserves by location

Coal
- USA 25.0%
- Russia 16.0%
- China 12.0%
- Australia 9.0%
- India 8.0%
- Top five countries 70.0%
- Rest of world 30.0%

Oil
- Saudi Arabia 24.8%
- Iraq 10.7%
- United Arab Emirates 9.3%
- Kuwait 9.2%
- Iran 8.5%
- Top five countries 62.5%
- Rest of world 37.5%

Natural gas
- Russia 32.9%
- Iran 15.7%
- Qatar 5.8%
- United Arab Emirates 4.1%
- Saudi Arabia 4.0%
- Top five countries 62.5%
- Rest of world 37.5%

Source: BP.

PRIMARY ENERGY CONSUMPTION AND PRODUCTION, 1998

(included in USA)

Canada
Production: 310m mtoe
Consumption: 219m mtoe

United States of America
Production: 1 447m mtoe
Consumption: 2 147m mtoe

United Kingdom
Production: 239m mtoe
Consumption: 228m mtoe

France
Production: 3.5m mtoe
Consumption: 249m mtoe

(rest Euro

Rest of
Production: 456m
Consumption: 149m

Latin America and Caribbean
Production: 662m mtoe
Consumption: 486m mtoe

Solid shape: primary energy production

Outline: primary energy consumption

The map shows a diagrammatic representation of countries and regions proportionate to their production and consumption of commercially traded fuels. All figures are in million metric tons of oil equivalent.

TOP ENERGY CONSUMERS, 1998

	Consumption as % of world	Population as % of world
USA	25.32	4.64
China	9.96	21.28
Russia	7.00	2.50
Japan	5.89	2.14
Germany	3.97	1.39
India	3.19	16.64
France	2.94	0.99
UK	2.68	1.00
Canada	2.59	0.52
Korea, Rep.	1.97	0.78
Italy	1.91	0.97
Ukraine	1.58	0.86
Brazil	1.49	2.81
Mexico	1.48	1.62
Spain	1.35	0.67
South Africa	1.33	0.67
Iran	1.25	1.11
Australia	1.21	0.31
Saudi Arabia	1.19	0.34
Poland	1.05	0.66

Source: BP; UNPD.

ENERGY CONSUMPTION, 1998
By source

- Oil 40%
- Hydro 3%
- Nuclear 7%
- Coal 26%
- Natural gas 24%

Source: BP.

Rest of Europe
Production: 513m mtoe
Consumption: 975m mtoe

Germany
Production: 77m mtoe
Consumption: 336m mtoe

Russia
Production: 905m mtoe
Consumption: 594m mtoe

[rest of Asia]

Japan
Production: 2.4m mtoe
Consumption: 499m mtoe

Republic of Korea
Production:
2.3m mtoe
Consumption:
167m mtoe

China
Production: 805m mtoe
Consumption: 860m mtoe

Rest of Former Soviet Union
Production: 217m mtoe
Consumption: 303m mtoe

[rest of Asia]

Middle East
Production: 1 261m mtoe
Consumption: 367m mtoe

India
Production: 205m mtoe
Consumption: 271m mtoe

Rest of Asia and Pacific
Production: 571m mtoe
Consumption: 516m mtoe

Africa
uction: 118m mtoe
umption: 113m mtoe

Source: BP.

FUELWOOD CONSUMPTION, 1988-98

	Million cubic meters 1998	Change in volume 1988-98 %	Population change %
North America	75.5	-24	10
Latin America and Caribbean	226.1	-3	19
Europe	92.8	-31	2
Africa	463.9	27	29
Asia	883.5	16	17
Oceania	8.5	-1	16
World	**1 750.3**	**9**	**16**

Source: FAO.

FUELWOOD CONSUMPTION, 1988 AND 1998 By region

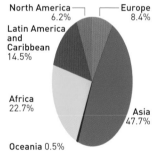

North America 6.2%
Europe 8.4%
Latin America and Caribbean 14.5%
Africa 22.7%
Asia 47.7%
Oceania 0.5%

Total consumption, 1988:
1 604 million cubic meters

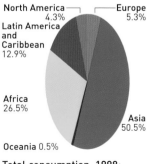

North America 4.3%
Europe 5.3%
Latin America and Caribbean 12.9%
Africa 26.5%
Asia 50.5%
Oceania 0.5%

Total consumption, 1998:
1 750 million cubic meters

Source: FAO.

OECD AND NON-OECD ENERGY CONSUMPTION

	OECD		Non-OECD	
	Consumption 1998 Million mtoe*	% change in consumption 1988-98	Consumption 1998 Million mtoe	% change in consumption 1988-98
Oil	2 131.3	14	1 257.7	8
Gas	1 101.0	31	915.4	11
Coal	1 056.2	-6	1 163.2	4
Nuclear	543.2	33	83.4	4
Hydro	116.4	13	110.0	36
Total	**4 948.1**	**14**	**3 529.7**	**8**

* Metric tons of oil equivalent
Note: During the period 1988-98, the population increased by 9% in OECD countries and by 18% in non-OECD countries.

Source: BP.

natural gas use more than tenfold[3]. China, the world's largest user of coal, has recently begun to cut its consumption despite continued fast economic growth. With similar declines in many industrialized countries, global coal use may be close to or past its peak – with positive effects on urban air pollution, acid deposition and the greenhouse effect[4].

Gains in the use of non-fossil fuels have been inconsistent. Alternative technologies that require large initial capital outlays did well until around 1990, but have since stalled. World civil nuclear reactor construction is now just a tenth of 1970s levels both because Western civil society has turned against nuclear power and because former Soviet bloc nations cannot afford the investment. Large-scale hydroelectric power has suffered from a shortage of sites and a growing awareness of its environmental downside. But smaller-scale renewable energy sources, notably wind and solar power, have seen double-digit annual growth – albeit from a lower starting point[5].

The fast-growing demand for energy in developing countries offers the opportunity for them to avoid the high-energy and pollution-intensive development paths of already industrialized countries and "leapfrog" to sustainable energy sources. There are many examples of moves around the world to more sustainable energy policies. Solar power is making inroads in many parts of rural Africa where urban electricity grids are unlikely to reach. Wind turbines are whirring on the plains of India, the steppes of Mongolia, the shores of the North Sea and among the sheep of Patagonia. Brazil fuels half its vehicles on ethanol made from fermented sugarcane juice, reducing the country's CO_2 emissions by 18 percent[6].

Many leading figures in the oil business believe that by the middle of the century the world's vehicle fleet will run on hydrogen fuel cells, probably extracted from water using electricity generated from renewable sources[7]. Iceland has plans to complete the task of creating the first "hydrogen economy" within its own shores by 2020, using its domestic geothermal and hydroelectric energy sources to convert its small self-contained vehicle fleet[8].

Most analysts still anticipate fast global rises in the use of oil and natural gas, and expect CO_2 emissions to continue to rise for many decades yet, as developing countries' economies grow. But the increases may be much less than once feared. In 1997 and 1998, the global economy grew by 6.8 percent, but CO_2 emissions held steady. The explanation appeared to lie in a combination of reduced coal use and the rise of economic growth based on new information technologies, which have lower energy requirements than traditional industries[9].

CHINA

China, the world's most populous country, mines a third of all the coal cut from the Earth, providing three quarters of the country's energy requirements. It has made Chinese cities the most polluted on Earth[10] and the country the world's second largest source of CO_2. But China is also engaged in a massive effort to clean up both its own backyard and the planet.

China is switching to natural gas, cutting coal subsidies and investing heavily in improved energy efficiency. A National Improved Stove Programme has upgraded 160 million domestic stoves. Since 1996, China has shut down 60 000 smoky and inefficient industrial boilers, while hundreds of small inefficient power stations over 25 years old are also to be closed.

Overall since the early 1980s, China has improved its energy efficiency by 47 percent, doubling economic output while raising CO_2 emissions by only 50 percent. In 1998, while increasing its economic output by more than 7.2 percent, it actually reduced its emissions of CO_2 by 3.7 percent – thanks mainly to continuing declines in coal burning[11].

Freshwater

FRESHWATER is the most fundamental of finite resources. It has no substitutes for most uses and is expensive to transport. But freshwater sources are dwindling or becoming contaminated throughout the world. Chronic or acute water shortage is increasingly common in many countries with fast-growing populations, becoming a potential source of conflict. However, existing technologies offer great potential for improving on the efficiency of its use.

The distribution of water resources around the globe is highly unequal, even at the continental level. Asia has more than 60 percent of the world population but only 36 percent of river runoff (much of it confined to the short monsoon season). South America, meanwhile, has just 6 percent of the global population but 26 percent of runoff. Canada has more than 30 times as much water available to each of its citizens as China.

Many of the world's largest river catchments run through thinly populated regions. These include the Amazon (15 percent of global runoff but 0.4 percent of global population) and the Zaire-Congo that flow into the Atlantic Ocean, and the great rivers of northern Canada and Siberia that flow into the Arctic Ocean. Meanwhile, many countries with high population density or growth rates, such as Pakistan and Egypt, are in hot, water-stressed regions where crops require irrigation[1].

Water withdrawals from rivers and underground reserves have grown by 2.5 to 3 percent annually since 1940, significantly ahead of population growth. Already, little of the water in some of the world's major rivers reaches the sea, including the Colorado in the United States, the Nile in Egypt and, for much of the year, the Yellow River in China[2].

Water tables are falling on every continent. Shortages are having an increasing effect on global grain markets, as arid countries that rely on irrigation for crop production are switching to food imports. As a result, North Africa and the Middle East were the fastest growing import markets for grain in the 1990s. The World Bank warns that freshwater is likely to become one of the major factors limiting economic development[3].

At the start of the 21st century, 49 countries with around 35 percent of the world population were believed to have less than 2 000 cubic meters of renewable freshwater available per capita per year[4], implying water scarcity or chronic shortage. Major nations in the list include India, Ethiopia, Nigeria and Kenya. Northern China also faces major shortages.

The crisis is likely to be worsened by the deteriorating quality of water, polluted by industrial wastes and sewage discharges, and spreading water-related diseases such as cholera and schistosomiasis. In addition, many regions watered by international rivers have yet to draw up agreements to share supplies. On the River Euphrates, Turkey has built several large dams without prior agreement with downstream neighbors Syria and Iraq. On the River Nile, Egypt uses 85 percent of the river's flow but has no agreement with potentially major upstream users such as Ethiopia. Unresolved disputes over riparian rights also fester within many countries.

WHERE THE WATER IS

ALL WATER
of which:

Oceans 97.5%

Freshwater
2.5%

of which:

Ice caps and glaciers
79%

Easily accessible
surface
freshwater
1%

Groundwater
20%

of which:

Lakes
52%

Soil moisture
38%

Rivers 1%
Water within living organisms 1%
Atmospheric water vapor 8%

Source: FAO.

ANNUAL FRESHWATER WITHDRAWALS
Top 15 countries

	Billion cubic meters withdrawn	% of available resources
China	525.5	18.6
India	500.0	26.2
USA	447.7	18.1
Pakistan	155.6	61.0
Japan	91.4	21.3
Mexico	77.8	17.0
Russia	77.1	1.7
Indonesia	74.3	0.7
Iran	70.0	85.8
Uzbekistan	58.1	63.4
Italy	57.5	34.4
Philippines	55.4	9.1
Egypt	55.1	94.5
Brazil	54.9	0.5
Vietnam	54.3	6.1

Note: Data on freshwater withdrawals are incomplete. These figures range from 1980 to 1998.

Source: World Bank.

FRESHWATER RESOURCES, 2000
Cubic meters available per capita per year

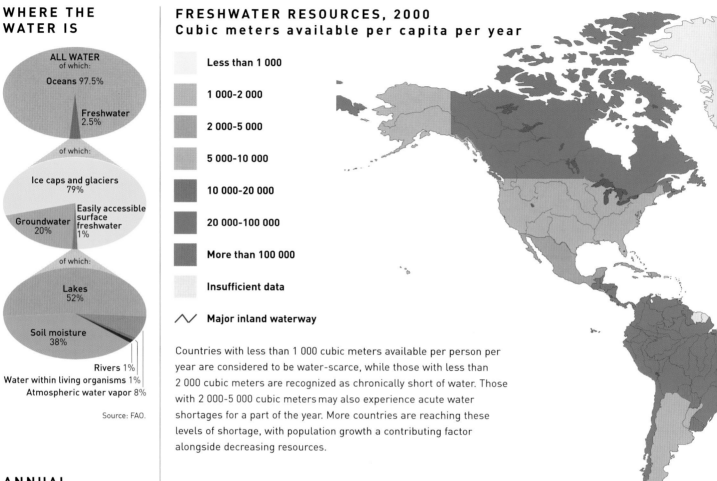

Less than 1 000

1 000–2 000

2 000–5 000

5 000–10 000

10 000–20 000

20 000–100 000

More than 100 000

Insufficient data

Major inland waterway

Countries with less than 1 000 cubic meters available per person per year are considered to be water-scarce, while those with less than 2 000 cubic meters are recognized as chronically short of water. Those with 2 000–5 000 cubic meters may also experience acute water shortages for a part of the year. More countries are reaching these levels of shortage, with population growth a contributing factor alongside decreasing resources.

TOP PER-CAPITA WATER USERS*

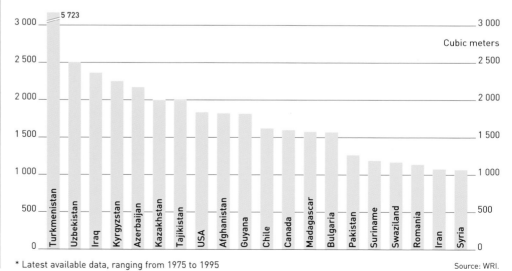

* Latest available data, ranging from 1975 to 1995

Source: WRI.

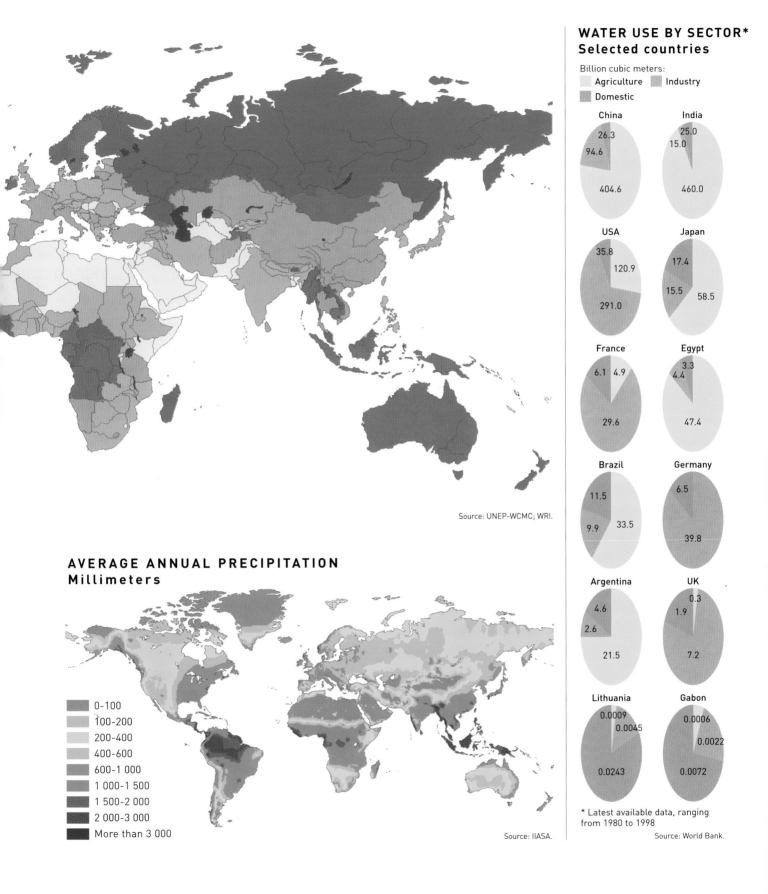

WATER USE BY SECTOR*
Selected countries

Billion cubic meters:
- Agriculture
- Industry
- Domestic

China
26.3
94.6
404.6

India
25.0
15.0
460.0

USA
35.8
120.9
291.0

Japan
17.4
15.5
58.5

France
6.1 4.9
29.6

Egypt
3.3
4.4
47.4

Brazil
11.5
9.9 33.5

Germany
6.5
39.8

Argentina
4.6
2.6
21.5

UK
0.3
1.9
7.2

Lithuania
0.0009
0.0045
0.0243

Gabon
0.0006
0.0022
0.0072

* Latest available data, ranging from 1980 to 1998

Source: World Bank.

Source: UNEP-WCMC; WRI.

AVERAGE ANNUAL PRECIPITATION
Millimeters

- 0-100
- 100-200
- 200-400
- 400-600
- 600-1 000
- 1 000-1 500
- 1 500-2 000
- 2 000-3 000
- More than 3 000

Source: IIASA.

GLOBAL LAND AREA UNDER IRRIGATION

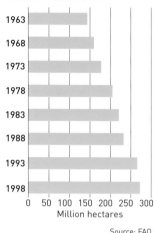

0   50 100 150 200 250 300
Million hectares

Source: FAO.

LAND DAMAGED BY IRRIGATION, 1980s
Top five irrigators

	Million hectares of land damaged	% of irrigated land damaged
India	20.0	36
China	7.0	15
USA	5.2	27
Pakistan	3.2	20
USSR	2.5	12
World	**60.2**	**24**

Source: UNEP.

WATER LOST IN IRRIGATION

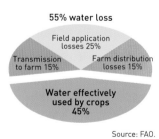

55% water loss

Field application losses 25%

Transmission to farm 15%

Farm distribution losses 15%

Water effectively used by crops 45%

Source: FAO.

More than 60 percent of the water used in the world each year is diverted for irrigating crops. Egypt, which must irrigate all its crops, uses more than five times as much water per capita as Switzerland. In Asia, which has two thirds of the world's irrigated land, 85 percent of water goes for irrigation. A worldwide doubling in the area under irrigation to more than 260 million hectares underpinned the "green revolution" that kept the world fed in the late 20th century. Almost 40 percent of the global food harvest now comes from the 17 percent of the world's croplands that are made productive in this way[5].

In some countries there is an increasing reliance on pumping underground water, often at rates that rainfall cannot replenish. Libya, for instance, by pumping "fossil" water from deep beneath the Sahara desert, uses seven times more water annually for irrigation than it receives in rainfall. India is pumping water at twice the recharge rate, causing some water tables to fall by between 1 and 3 meters a year. The country's grain production could fall by 25 percent if it gave up ground-water "mining"[6].

Most irrigation schemes around the world are extremely inefficient. Typically, less than half the water reaches crop roots. Much of it is misdirected or evaporates. Meanwhile, over-irrigation combined with inadequate drainage is causing an accumulation of salt that is reducing yields in many of the areas under irrigation. Sometimes there are major ecological impacts. Irrigation projects developed by the former Soviet Union in Central Asia to grow cotton have dramatically emptied the Aral Sea, destroying fisheries, depopulating large areas and causing epidemics of disease.

Faced with growing water shortages in many parts of the world, the main choice is between supply-side and demand-side solutions. Supply-side solutions imply more large dams and large water transfer projects. Aid agencies are increasingly reluctant to fund such projects because they have a history of heavy cost over-runs, poor financial returns, and ecological and social damage through flooded valleys and disrupted fluvial ecosystems. They have concluded that demand-side solutions offer better returns and less collateral damage. Economic analyses have demonstrated that investment in industrial and domestic water-saving devices (such as low-flush lavatories), in lining irrigation canals and in drip-feed irrigation saves more water more cheaply than can be won from dams and other supply schemes.

Many believe that as water becomes an increasingly scarce and valued resource, it will become commodified. Where it was once seen as available by right, it might be bought and sold at market prices. This offers potential benefits in its more efficient use, as water prices more closely reflect its cost, but this also holds new dangers for the poor. A thousand tons of water can produce a ton of wheat, worth US$200, but it can expand industrial output by US$14 000[7]. If the price of water were to reflect its "true" cost, there is a danger that only the wealthy industrialized sector could afford it, with serious consequences for world food availability.

Foodcrops

C AN THE WORLD go on feeding itself as populations continue to increase in the poorest, most hungry nations? Eliminating local poverty may be as important as boosting global food yields. But achieving both will ultimately depend on adopting more sustainable methods of agriculture.

Over the past four decades, worldwide food production has more than kept pace with the doubling of world population. There is currently an average of 2 790 calories of food available each day for every human on the planet – 23 percent more than in 1961 and enough to feed everyone. Moreover, there is potential slack in the system. If only a third of the cereals fed to livestock were put instead directly onto human plates, the per-capita calories available daily would rise to 3 000[1].

Gains in food availability have been greatest in the developing world, where the green revolution enabled a rise of 38 percent between 1961 and 1998 to 2 660 calories per person daily.

The increase in food production, however, has been unable to overcome inequalities of food distribution. The developed world, with a quarter of the world's population, still takes some 49 percent of the world's agricultural products, partly because it converts more grain to meat. Even so, differences in food availability within the developing world are now greater than between typical developed and developing countries.

Outright famines still occur, both because of local failures in food production, often caused by environmental degradation, and because of failures in the global trade and emergency aid systems. But there is a wider problem of persistent malnourishment. Some 790 million people do not have access to enough food to live healthy and productive lives.

Malnourishment contributes to at least a third of child deaths. In 1998, there were 78 low-income countries that neither grew enough food to feed their populations, nor had the resources to make up the deficit with imports. Of these, more than half were in Africa[2]. Here, population growth rates are highest and poverty is greatest, soils are generally most vulnerable to degradation and modern advances in agricultural technology have had the least impact[3]. The World Food Summit pledged in 1996 to halve malnutrition within 20 years. But the Food and Agriculture Organization of the United Nations (FAO) predicts that in some regions of the world chronic undernourishment is likely to persist, rising to 30 percent of the population of sub-Saharan Africa in 2010.

Poverty and hunger frequently cause a cycle of environmental decline that further undermines food security. Environmental degradation often occurs when poor nations, and poor communities within nations, cannot feed themselves without disregarding the future fertility of the land. They overcultivate or overgraze land to meet immediate needs, or annexe inappropriate land with steep slopes, and shallow, infertile, stony, toxic or poorly drained soils. In the process they are often forced to invade natural ecosystems.

The world's reserves of uncultivated land are largely in the two regions still containing substantial tropical forests: sub-Saharan Africa with 750 million hectares, and Latin America with 800 million hectares. Addressing the needs of the poorest farmers is vital to the protection of these forests.

PRODUCTION OF MAJOR FOOD CROPS, 1999
Million metric tons

North America
Cereals 389.8
Roots and tubers 26.5
Pulses 5.1

Latin America and Caribbean
Cereals 133.8
Pulses 5.8
Roots and tubers 50.5

Europe
Cereals 374.4
Pulses 8.3
Roots and tubers 135.6

Africa
Cereals 112.9
Pulses 7.9
Roots and tubers 156.6

Asia
Cereals 1 021.2
Pulses 29.8
Roots and tubers 277.3

Oceania
Cereals 32.1
Roots and tubers 3.6
Pulses 2.3

Source: FAO.

PER-CAPITA CALORIE AVAILABILITY AND LOW-INCOME FOOD-DEFICIT COUNTRIES, 1998

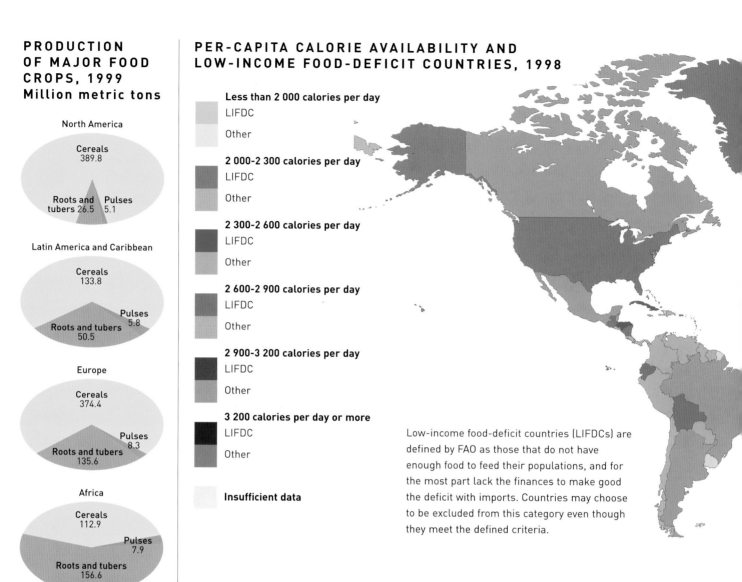

Less than 2 000 calories per day
LIFDC
Other

2 000-2 300 calories per day
LIFDC
Other

2 300-2 600 calories per day
LIFDC
Other

2 600-2 900 calories per day
LIFDC
Other

2 900-3 200 calories per day
LIFDC
Other

3 200 calories per day or more
LIFDC
Other

Insufficient data

Low-income food-deficit countries (LIFDCs) are defined by FAO as those that do not have enough food to feed their populations, and for the most part lack the finances to make good the deficit with imports. Countries may choose to be excluded from this category even though they meet the defined criteria.

WORLD AGRICULTURAL PRODUCTION

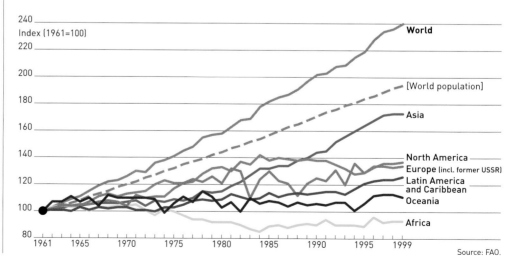

Index (1961=100)

World
[World population]
Asia
North America
Europe (incl. former USSR)
Latin America and Caribbean
Oceania
Africa

Source: FAO.

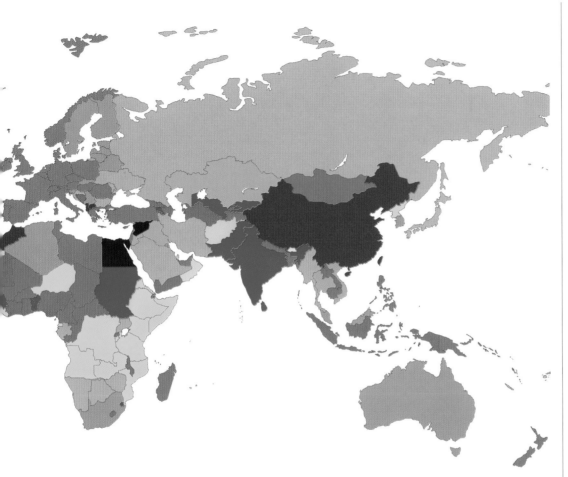

Source: FAO.

THE WORLD'S BIGGEST CEREAL PRODUCERS, 1999

	Million metric tons of cereal	% of world pro- duction	% of world popula- tion
China	457.04	22.14	21.19
USA	336.03	16.28	4.62
India	230.04	11.14	16.69
France	64.76	3.14	0.98
Indonesia	58.67	2.84	3.50
Russia	53.78	2.61	2.46
Canada	53.78	2.61	0.52
Brazil	47.64	2.31	2.81
Germany	44.33	2.15	1.37
Argentina	33.43	1.62	0.61
Vietnam	33.15	1.61	1.32
Bangladesh	31.83	1.54	0.31
Australia	31.12	1.51	1.10
Turkey	30.28	1.47	1.10
Mexico	28.65	1.39	1.63

Source: FAO; UNPD.

GROWTH IN WORLD PRODUCTION
Selected crops

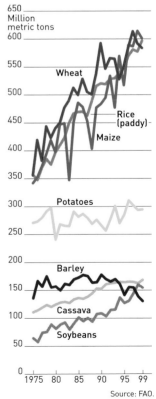

Source: FAO.

UNDERNOURISHMENT IN THE DEVELOPING WORLD, LATE 1990s
As a proportion of the total population

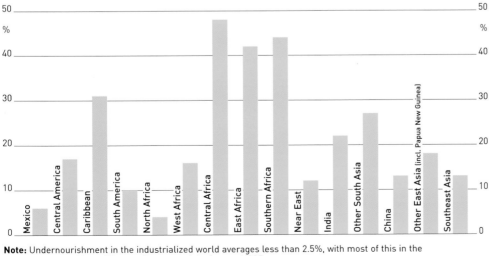

Note: Undernourishment in the industrialized world averages less than 2.5%, with most of this in the countries in transition of Eastern Europe and the former USSR.

Source: FAO.

Meeting the immediate needs of the poor is a major environmental as well as humanitarian challenge[4]. But the pursuit of sustainable agriculture also requires the world to find ways of reorganizing food trade and farming subsidies to reduce the environmental impacts of intensive agriculture in rich nations.

Overintensive agriculture to supply a fast-growing global market in food is a major cause of the degradation of natural resources. The direct environmental costs of British agriculture, for instance, have been assessed at US$3.9 billion, or US$350 per hectare per year. The costs include cleaning pesticides and nitrogen from drinking water, restoring lost habitats and eroded soils, and combating emissions of greenhouse gases[5].

While many developing countries, particularly in Asia, have seen steady increases in agricultural productivity, others have fared less well. In Africa overall, agricultural productivity has actually gone down since the 1960s, while the population has continued to rise. There is also concern that there may be a slackening of yield growth even in those areas where yields rose consistently through the 1970s and 1980s. The gains in rice productivity in Asia appeared to falter in the 1990s, with growth in rice yields down from 3 percent a year in the 1970s to less than 2 percent in the 1990s[6].

Some analysts see this as a turning point beyond which degradation of land and water resources will result in the world running increasingly short of food. China, for instance, may be forced to become a major importer of grain, disrupting world markets and reducing the supplies available for other, poorer grain-short nations, particularly in Africa[7]. Others argue that this could revive the declining agricultural sector in much of the developed world without disrupting supplies to poorer nations. A third viewpoint is that the slackening merely reflects declining population growth rates in Asia and the operation of market forces as supply catches up with demand[8].

Whatever the truth, the environmental constraints on farming will themselves change in the 21st century. Climate change will begin to have a profound effect on food production around the world, leading to famine and outward migration in some communities, but to additional wealth and inward migration in others. Recent assessments suggest that global warming will increase crop yields at high and mid-latitudes – largely comprising countries that already feed themselves and have low rates of future population growth. Increases may be most marked in North America and China, where more rainfall is predicted. Meanwhile increased heat stress and evaporation of moisture from soils is likely to reduce yields in lower latitudes – where food shortages are already greatest and predicted population growth rates highest. Studies again single out Africa as likely to suffer the greatest yield reductions, with up to 70 million more people at risk of hunger[9].

BIODIVERSITY FOR FOOD

The world currently uses only a tiny fraction of the genetic resources available for food. Of 270 000 plants known to science only around 120 are widely cultivated today and just nine of them provide 75 percent of our food[10]. For thousands of years, farmers have bred new crop varieties and tailored their farming methods to maintain both food supply and their land's fertility. The result was a huge diversity of plant varieties and farming methods. In the drive to standardize on a few high-yielding crop varieties, much of this diversity was lost, not only to farms but also to gene banks, though this trend is now reversing. A similar story can be told for livestock farming. Future advances in farming are likely to require tailoring crop varieties and farming methods more precisely to local conditions.

REDUCTION OF DIVERSITY IN FRUITS AND VEGETABLES*

Vegetable	Taxonomic name	Number held in 1903	Number held in 1983	% loss
Asparagus	*Asparagus officinalis*	46	1	97.8
Bean	*Phaseolus vulgaris*	578	32	94.5
Beet	*Beta vulgaris*	288	17	94.1
Carrot	*Daucus carota*	287	21	92.7
Leek	*Allium ampeloprasum*	39	5	87.2
Lettuce	*Lactuca sativa*	487	36	92.6
Onion	*Allium cepa*	357	21	94.1
Parsnip	*Pastinaca sativa*	75	5	93.3
Pea	*Pisum sativum*	408	25	93.9
Radish	*Raphanus sativus*	463	27	94.2
Spinach	*Spinacia oleracea*	109	7	93.6
Squash	*Cucurbita spp.*	341	40	88.3
Turnip	*Brassica rapa*	237	24	89.9

* Varieties held at the US National Seed Storage Laboratory, Colorado State University

Source: WRI.

Meat and fish

MEAT AND FISH are an increasingly important part of the world's diet. As countries and families grow richer, one of their first consumer choices is to increase their intake of these in preference to vegetables. The implications for landuse are profound, since growing biomass to feed animals takes far more energy and land than growing biomass for direct human consumption.

World meat production has more than quadrupled in the past half-century to some 220 million tons annually. The increase has more than doubled production per head of the world's population to 37 kilos a year[1]. The increase has been driven by rising incomes, population growth and urbanization[2], particularly in the emerging meat markets of East Asia, the Middle East and Latin America. Meat demand rises strongly as countries grow wealthier and urbanize[3]. Citizens in developed countries eat four times more meat than those in developing countries, a far greater difference than pertains for grain consumption.

But developing countries are catching up. Current projections suggest that developing countries' demand for meat will increase by 2.9 percent a year between 1993 and 2020 – twice the rate of population growth, with poultry demand growing fastest of all[4].

The growing demand for meat has pushed countries, particularly in densely populated regions of Europe and Asia, to switch from production of beef cattle, which traditionally feed on pasture, towards animals that eat from feedlots all year round, such as pigs (now the world's largest meat source) and poultry, which also now exceeds beef production.

It is often argued that raising animals and growing fodder crops is an inefficient use of land and resources[5]. Around 4 kilos of grain are required to produce 1 kilo of pork, and 8 kilos are needed for a kilo of beef. Certainly, the world's growing desire for meat puts new stresses on agricultural systems, and hence on two fundamental finite resources, land and water.

But there are counter-arguments. Animals provide many other resources, from hides and milk to traction power and manure. And there is little evidence that meat production causes actual food shortages, at any rate in the short term. Increasing use of feed grains does not generally appear to have damaged production of cereals for human consumption, as the market often adjusts. In times of food shortages, grain production for human consumption is maintained while production for feed is reduced[6].

In many countries wild animals, or bushmeat, remain a significant source of protein – from rabbits through kangaroos to elephants. This informal, and often illegal, trade is rarely enumerated. But the spread of guns, coupled with the opening up of forest regions along logging roads, is thought to have dramatically increased the market in bushmeat in many countries. In equatorial Africa, where elephant meat can turn up on supermarket shelves and apes are another delicacy, recent estimates put this at more than 1 million tons a year[7].

Not all animal protein comes from the land, however. The oceans have always been a major

ANIMAL PRODUCTS IN THE HUMAN DIET, 1998
Calories per capita per day

North America

1 018 calories

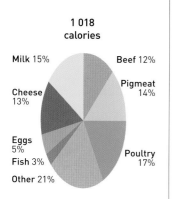

Milk 15%
Beef 12%
Cheese 13%
Pigmeat 14%
Eggs 5%
Fish 3%
Poultry 17%
Other 21%

Latin America and Caribbean

541 calories

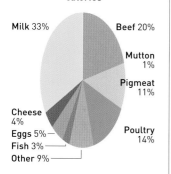

Milk 33%
Beef 20%
Mutton 1%
Pigmeat 11%
Cheese 4%
Eggs 5%
Fish 3%
Poultry 14%
Other 9%

Europe

915 calories

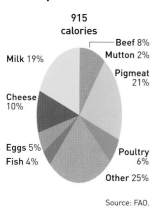

Milk 19%
Beef 8%
Mutton 2%
Pigmeat 21%
Cheese 10%
Eggs 5%
Fish 4%
Poultry 6%
Other 25%

Source: FAO.

PROPORTION OF DAILY CALORIE INTAKE MADE UP OF ANIMAL PRODUCTS, 1998

- Less than 5%
- 5-10%
- 10-15%
- 15-20%
- 20-25%
- 25-30%
- 30-35%
- 35-40%
- 40-45%
- Insufficient data

While the diet of the world's wealthier nations generally contains a higher proportion of animal products than that of the developing world, there are some notable exceptions amongst those countries with a long-standing tradition of livestock husbandry or fishing.

TOP FISH PRODUCERS

	Metric tons of fish	% of world production 1997	% of world population 1997
China	36 333 545	29.75	21.37
Peru	7 877 252	6.45	0.42
Japan	6 690 716	5.48	2.16
Chile	6 083 913	4.98	0.25
USA	5 448 385	4.46	4.67
India	5 378 004	4.40	16.59
Russia	4 715 024	3.86	2.54
Indonesia	4 403 810	3.61	3.49
Thailand	3 488 104	2.86	1.03
Norway	3 222 970	2.64	0.08
Korea, Rep.	2 596 474	2.13	0.79
Iceland	2 209 607	1.81	0.005
Philippines	2 136 249	1.75	1.23
Denmark	1 865 760	1.53	0.09
Vietnam	1 546 000	1.27	1.31
Mexico	1 528 520	1.25	1.62
Argentina	1 352 400	1.11	0.61
Bangladesh	1 342 730	1.10	2.11
Spain	1 341 311	1.10	0.68
Malaysia	1 276 282	1.04	0.36

TOP MEAT PRODUCERS

	Metric tons of meat	% of world production 1999	% of world population 1999
China	59 356 512	26.27	21.19
USA	37 179 800	16.46	4.62
Brazil	13 123 030	5.81	2.81
France	6 462 480	2.86	0.98
Germany	6 340 270	2.81	1.37
Spain	4 875 330	2.16	0.66
India	4 677 070	2.07	16.69
Russia	4 344 000	1.92	2.46
Mexico	4 289 282	1.90	1.63
Italy	4 043 075	1.79	0.96
Canada	3 779 300	1.67	0.52
Argentina	3 702 561	1.64	0.61
Australia	3 606 100	1.60	0.31
UK	3 591 848	1.59	0.99
Japan	2 998 288	1.33	2.12
Poland	2 971 500	1.32	0.65
Netherlands	2 935 900	1.30	0.26
Pakistan	2 270 180	1.00	2.55
Denmark	2 006 853	0.89	0.09
Philippines	1 996 683	0.88	1.25

Source: FAO; UNPD.

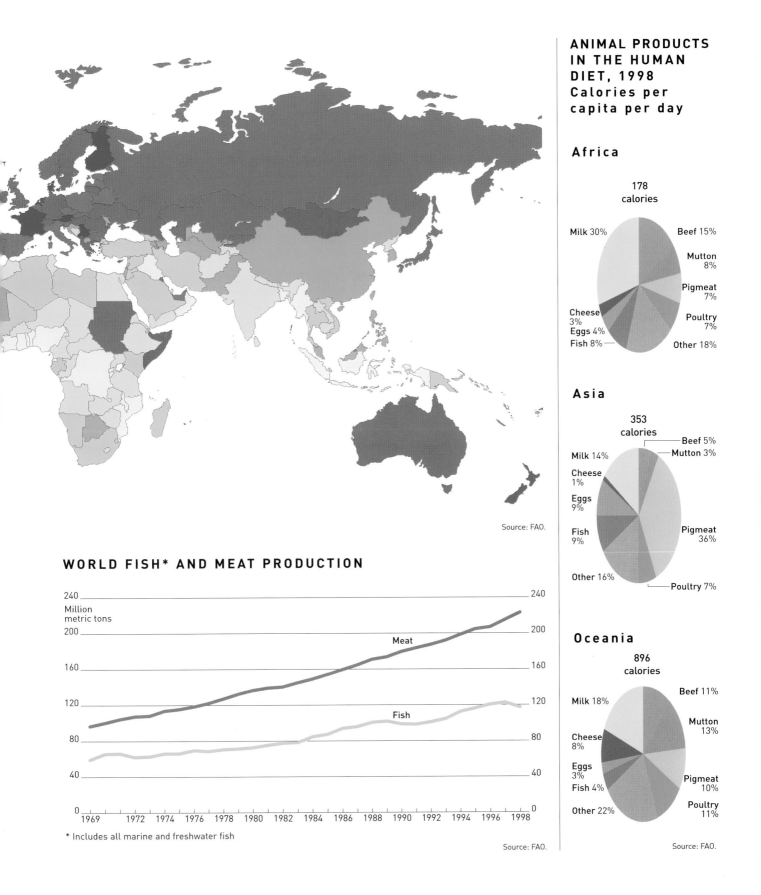

ANIMAL PRODUCTS IN THE HUMAN DIET, 1998
Calories per capita per day

Africa

178 calories

Milk 30%
Beef 15%
Mutton 8%
Pigmeat 7%
Poultry 7%
Other 18%
Cheese 3%
Eggs 4%
Fish 8%

Asia

353 calories

Beef 5%
Mutton 3%
Milk 14%
Cheese 1%
Eggs 9%
Fish 9%
Pigmeat 36%
Other 16%
Poultry 7%

Oceania

896 calories

Milk 18%
Beef 11%
Mutton 13%
Cheese 8%
Eggs 3%
Fish 4%
Pigmeat 10%
Poultry 11%
Other 22%

Source: FAO.

Source: FAO.

WORLD FISH* AND MEAT PRODUCTION

Million metric tons

Meat

Fish

1969 1972 1974 1976 1978 1980 1982 1984 1986 1988 1990 1992 1994 1996 1998

* Includes all marine and freshwater fish

Source: FAO.

THE GROWTH OF WORLD AQUACULTURE
Freshwater and marine fisheries

30
Million metric tons
25
20
15
10
5
0

1984 86 88 90 92 94 96 98

Source: FAO.

source of sustenance – and never more so than today. Though for how much longer this "wild" food source will fulfill a dominant role in meeting human dietary needs is far from clear.

Worldwide, humanity gets 16 percent of its animal protein from marine sources. Around half a billion people gain their livelihoods from harvesting the oceans. Over the past 50 years, the world's fishing industry has changed from a largely local and coastal trade – which depleted fish stocks near heavily populated areas but left the rest of the ocean alone – into a global activity with global impacts.

Of some 3 million fishing vessels known to be at sea worldwide, more than a million are large "industrial" vessels that can and do travel the globe. South American ships fish off New Zealand, Japanese trawlers work the South Atlantic and so on.

The world's marine fish catch increased fivefold between 1950 and 1990, reaching around 90 million tons a year. But these global fisheries are now themselves facing a crisis of diminishing returns – a classic global "tragedy of the commons" in which a shared resource is depleted by short-term greed because there is no common policy to maintain it for the long term. Despite increasing investment in ships, nets and tracking equipment, the catch has stagnated since 1990. Current estimates are that it costs between US$90 billion and US$130 billion annually to land a global fish catch worth US$70 billion, the difference being met by government subsidies[8].

According to the Food and Agriculture Organization of the United Nations (FAO), nine of the world's 17 major international fish stocks are at or beyond the point at which yields will decline. One extreme case is the North Atlantic, where cod stocks are at half their former levels. The Grand Banks cod fishery off Newfoundland, tapped for more than 500 years since the Basques first found it, was shut in 1993 after a collapse in stocks, putting thousands out of work. The North Sea's cod fishery could soon go the same way[9]. Asian fleets fished out the North Atlantic squid stocks in the 1980s. Atlantic mackerel, redfish and herring catches are all less than half their size of 30 years ago.

Increasingly, the world is turning to aquaculture to maintain fish supplies. It is the fastest-growing food production system in the world, with global production increasing by 11 percent annually through most of the 1990s until around a quarter of the fish brought to table came from aquaculture. Most of this relates to just a few species: carp in China, easily the world's largest fish farmers; catfish in the United States; and salmon in Europe[10].

But there has been an ecological price to pay. Fish farms are an increasingly important market for feed, including grain and fishmeal. The growing demand for fishmeal means that production from aquaculture is not simply an addition to wild catches, but consumes a significant fraction of that catch.

Aquaculture has become a major threat to coastal ecosystems, particularly mangroves. From Ecuador to the Philippines, mangroves are being converted on a huge scale into brackish shrimp ponds in what has been characterized as the aquatic equivalent of "slash-and-burn" farming[11]. In the past four decades Indonesians have converted 269 000 hectares of mangroves to shrimp ponds to supply the international market. Most are productive for less than a decade before loss of nutrients and a build-up of toxins force them to be abandoned and replaced[12].

Forest products

ORESTS ARE A PRINCIPAL global economic as well as ecological resource. This creates major challenges for the world as it tries to find ways of using them sustainably – to benefit their inhabitants and the wider community while maintaining their many ecological functions.

Forests have arguably played a bigger role in the development of human societies than any other resource, bar water and cultivable land[1]. The prime direct or marketable product of most forests today is wood for use as timber, fuelwood, pulp and paper, providing some 3.4 billion cubic meters of timber-equivalent a year globally. After a 60 percent increase between 1960 and 1990, global wood consumption fluctuated but rose no further during the 1990s, largely due to the more efficient use of timber and paper recycling.

There is no sharp divide in total wood consumption between poor and rich nations, largely because poor nations have a large demand for wood as fuel. The world's leading per-capita consumers of timber (all using more than three times the global average) include nations at all levels of economic development: Liberia and Zambia; Malaysia and Costa Rica; Sweden and the United States of America. By continent, Africa is the second largest per-capita consumer of wood, after North America[2].

But the way wood is used varies dramatically with levels of economic development. Worldwide, half of consumption is for fuel, but in developing countries this figure rises to 80 percent. For almost 3 billion people, wood is the main energy source for heating and cooking. While the collection of wood for fuel is generally a less important cause of deforestation than forest clearance for farming, it is a prime cause of the loss of African tropical forests, particularly in the hinterland of cities, which still rely on wood for their energy requirements. Many countries, particularly in Asia, face a growing domestic shortage of wood for this basic purpose, notably Bangladesh, Nepal and Pakistan[3].

Among industrialized nations, the predominant use of wood is as "industrial roundwood", a category that encompasses building material, paper and packaging. Each citizen of the United States uses 15 times as much wood for this purpose as an average citizen of a developing country. Over half the timber harvested for industrial use goes to North America, Europe and Japan, a figure that rises to 70 percent for paper. Global paper use has grown sixfold since 1950, using a fifth of all the wood harvested[4].

With the exception of China and Brazil – two very large wood-producing nations – most industrial roundwood production takes place in the developed world. Industrialized nations both produce and consume more than twice as much industrial roundwood as developing countries[5].

The focus of industrial roundwood production is moving towards harvesting from plantations. Between 1980 and 1995, the extent of plantations doubled to 180 million hectares, an area the size of Mexico[6]. They offer the potential for high yields of fast-growing species on small areas of land, offsetting the cost of planting, and offering a viable source of timber where accessible natural forests

WORLD FUELWOOD
Regional production

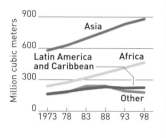

Top producers, 1998

	Cubic meters
India	274 334 000
China	190 947 000
Indonesia	157 023 008
Brazil	114 052 000
Nigeria	89 096 000
USA	70 160 000
Ethiopia	47 665 000
Congo, Dem. Rep.	45 910 000
Russia	39 910 000
Philippines	39 046 000

Source: FAO.

WORLD TIMBER PRODUCTION, 1998
Cubic meters

■	More than 400 million
■	100-400 million
■	25-100 million
■	10-25 million
■	5-10 million
■	1-5 million
■	100 000-1 million
■	Less than 100 000
■	Insufficient data

While developing and developed countries produce similar amounts of raw timber, wealthier industrialized countries use a much higher proportion for manufacturing purposes, for example paper and furniture production. Developing countries use much of their timber as fuelwood.

WORLD CHARCOAL
Regional production

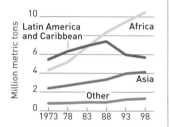

Top producers, 1998

	Metric tons
Brazil	3 600 000
India	2 259 000
Kenya	2 233 000
Nigeria	1 468 000
Sudan	1 159 000
Zambia	1 041 000
USA	853 000
Ghana	752 000
Thailand	669 000
Colombia	661 000

Source: FAO.

WORLD TIMBER PRODUCTION

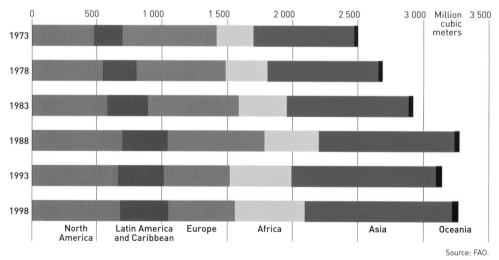

Source: FAO.

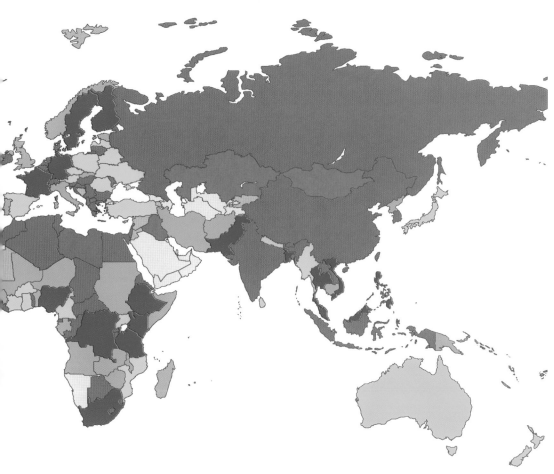

Source: FAO.

TOP PLYWOOD PRODUCERS, 1998

	Cubic meters
USA	15 732 000
Indonesia	7 015 000
China	4 978 000
Malaysia	3 904 000
Japan	3 267 000
Canada	1 750 000
Brazil	1 500 000
Russia	1 094 000
Finland	992 000
Korea, Rep.	641 000

88% of plywood is produced in these countries

Source: FAO.

TOP PAPER AND PAPERBOARD PRODUCERS, 1998

	Metric tons
USA	75 812 000
China	32 333 000
Japan	29 886 000
Canada	21 207 000
Germany	16 311 000
Finland	12 703 000
Sweden	9 879 000
France	9 143 000
Italy	8 246 000
Korea, Rep.	7 749 000

76% of paper and paperboard is produced in these countries

Source: FAO.

WORLD PAPER AND PAPERBOARD PRODUCTION

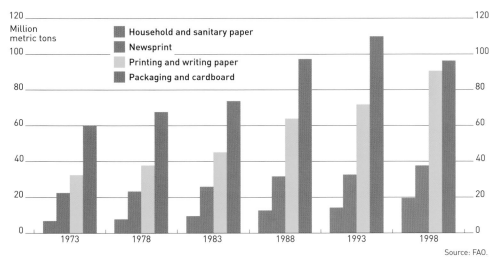

Million metric tons

- Household and sanitary paper
- Newsprint
- Printing and writing paper
- Packaging and cardboard

1973 1978 1983 1988 1993 1998

Source: FAO.

TOP PAPER AND PAPERBOARD CONSUMERS*, 1998

	Metric tons
USA	80 175 300
China	39 358 600
Japan	30 126 000
Germany	16 856 000
UK	11 785 900
France	10 613 000
Canada	9 678 300
Italy	9 584 000
Brazil	6 598 600
Spain	6 189 000

75% of paper and paperboard produced worldwide is consumed in these countries

* Production plus imports minus exports

Source: FAO.

TOP PRODUCERS OF SELECTED FOREST PRODUCTS, 1998

Natural rubber

	Metric tons
Thailand	2 162 411
Indonesia	1 564 324
Malaysia	885 700
India	550 000
China	440 000
Vietnam	225 700
Côte d'Ivoire	115 668
Sri Lanka	95 710
Nigeria	90 000
Philippines	64 000

95% of world production

Coconuts

	Metric tons
Indonesia	13 000 000
India	11 100 000
Philippines	10 905 300
Sri Lanka	1 850 000
Thailand	1 372 000
Mexico	1 302 500
Vietnam	1 271 380
Papua New Guinea	734 000
Malaysia	711 000
Brazil	652 213

91% of world production

Coir

	Metric tons
India	450 000
Sri Lanka	130 000
Malaysia	32 200
Bangladesh	11 420
Thailand	8 000

100% of world production

Brazil nuts

	Metric tons
Bolivia	30 000
Brazil	23 000
Côte d'Ivoire	5 200
Peru	431
Ghana	5

100% of world production

Source: FAO.

are in increasingly short supply[7]. Previously a feature largely of industrialized countries, plantations are now being cultivated in developing countries, with most of them planning to double their plantations by 2010[8].

Plantations take some of the stress off natural forests, but only for as long as natural forests are not logged to make way for them. There is increasing evidence that they do not confer the same ecological benefits. For example, they do not provide the same protection against soil erosion and flooding[9] and they are more vulnerable to fires. They are normally monocultures with a seriously impoverished biological diversity, and offer virtually none of the non-timber forest products of the kind that sustain many local economies and cultures.

Non-timber forest products include fruits and nuts, rattan, medicinal plants and bushmeat. Many people living in or near tropical rainforests rely for half or more of their protein on wild animals caught in the forest. The subsistence meat harvest in the Brazilian Amazon is put at up to 160 000 tons a year, or up to 20 million animals. A study in the rainforests of southern Cameroon found more than 500 plant species and 280 animal species in use and often on sale in local markets[10].

Because many non-timber forest products are used within the forests or traded informally, their value to national and community economies is frequently underestimated by governments when considering the economic potential of natural forests relative to other land uses. One exception was the formation of "extractive reserves" in the Brazilian Amazon in the late 1980s, dedicated to Brazil nut harvesting, rubber tapping and other non-destructive uses of the forest.

But just as timber can be overharvested, so can these non-timber resources, especially when local products gain access to large urban markets. The African bushmeat industry, which has become an international business, may exceed a million tons a year. Such levels of exploitation are unsustainable and can damage the forest ecology, since the same animals often disperse seeds[11].

In an effort to promote more sustainable management of natural forests, environmental groups and foresters around the world have banded together to certify and label for customers timber and other products that come from well-managed forests. The largest of these consortiums is the Forest Stewardship Council, which by 1999 had issued certificates approving over 15 million hectares of forest worldwide. Many major retail groups in Europe and North America have pledged to purchase timber products only from such supplies.

Governments are also increasingly attempting to realize value from their forests by charging access fees to ecotourists, hunters, or scientists seeking plant-based pharmaceuticals.

International trade

Reconciling open trade with environmental protection is a central dilemma for the world in the 21st century. Trade issues go to the heart of whether increased wealth is good or bad for the environment. Will global markets provide the means to take ecological concerns into account, or merely encourage the excessive consumption, pollution and waste that stoke the engines of environmental destruction?

Trade has been one of the driving forces of civilization since antiquity, when maritime trade through the Indian and Pacific Oceans sustained Chinese imperial dynasties. The search for spices, gold and other luxuries first brought Europe into regular contact with both Asia and Africa, while trade sustained the early colonies of the Americas.

Trade, by expanding export markets and boosting timber demand for ships, has always had the potential to trigger environmental destruction. Plantations of crops bound for Europe displaced most of the coastal rainforests of West Africa in the 19th century[1]. More recently, Japanese demand for timber fuelled the plundering of the rainforests of Southeast Asia. But trade has allowed other countries to conserve natural resources through substituting local products with imports.

World trade at the start of the 21st century is running at unprecedented levels and for the first time is being regulated by a single body. The World Trade Organization (WTO) was set up in 1996 and has more than 130 member nations. But its rules, which aim to maximize global trading, present a dilemma for environmental protection. On the one hand they encourage economic efficiency which, by ensuring the careful use of materials, should also promote environmental efficiency. On the other, they may undermine livelihoods and invalidate national and international laws framed to address specific environmental threats.

Most economic activities create ecological "externalities", such as pollution or loss of finite natural resources, that are not reflected in the price of the product. Some governments attempt to fill this gap by taxes on pollution, regulations on the environmental behavior of manufacturers, or subsidies for environmentally preferable methods. But such interventions can be seen as "protectionist" if they skew trade against foreign competitors.

A parallel debate concerns the role of wealth in environmental protection. Some argue that poverty is the real enemy of the environment, and that increasing trade opens up markets for the products of the poor, diminishing poverty and providing the means, incentives and technical know-how to use resources efficiently and invest in cleaner production, thereby encouraging sustainable economic growth[2].

Others believe that a growth in international trade is already undermining poor economies by increasing penetration by foreign companies. They say that this process has hastened the pauperization of Africa, whose share of world exports fell from 4.2 percent in 1985 to 2.3 percent in 1996, of which South Africa made up almost a quarter[3].

Proponents of lowering barriers to trade argue that bans on subsidies for farming and the

MERCHANDISE, 1998
Top exporters

	Value Billion US$	% of world exports
USA	682.5	12.6
Germany	539.7	10.0
Japan	387.9	7.2
France	304.8	5.6
UK	272.9	5.0
Italy	242.3	4.5
Canada	214.3	4.0
Netherlands	198.7	3.7
China	183.8	3.4
Benelux	178.5	3.3

Top importers

	Value Billion US$	% of world imports
USA	944.4	16.8
Germany	466.6	8.3
UK	315.2	5.6
France	286.3	5.1
Japan	280.5	5.0
Italy	215.6	3.8
Canada	206.2	3.7
Hong Kong* (China)	186.8	3.3
Netherlands	184.2	3.3
Benelux	166.5	3.0

* Imports less re-exports = 36.5; share = 0.6

COMMERCIAL SERVICES, 1998
Top exporters

	Value Billion US$	% of world exports
USA	240.0	18.2
UK	100.5	7.6
France	84.6	6.4
Germany	78.9	6.0
Italy	66.6	5.1
Japan	61.8	4.7
Netherlands	51.6	3.9
Spain	48.7	3.7
Benelux	35.4	2.7
Hong Kong (China)	34.2	2.6

Top importers

	Value Billion US$	% of world imports
USA	165.8	12.7
Germany	125.0	9.6
Japan	110.7	8.5
UK	78.8	6.0
France	65.4	5.0
Italy	62.9	4.8
Netherlands	46.6	3.6
Canada	35.2	2.7
Benelux	33.9	2.6
Austria	30.1	2.3

Source: WTO.

MAJOR TRADE FLOWS IN OIL, 1999
Million metric tons

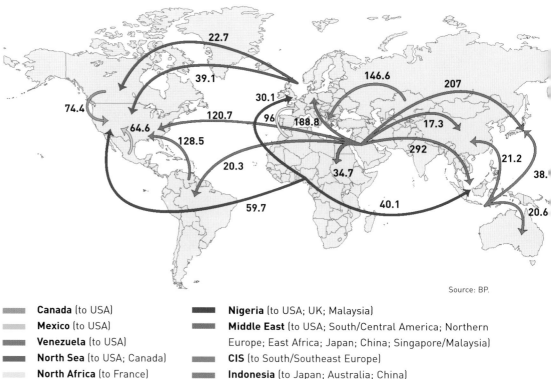

Source: BP.

Canada (to USA)
Mexico (to USA)
Venezuela (to USA)
North Sea (to USA; Canada)
North Africa (to France)
Nigeria (to USA; UK; Malaysia)
Middle East (to USA; South/Central America; Northern Europe; East Africa; Japan; China; Singapore/Malaysia)
CIS (to South/Southeast Europe)
Indonesia (to Japan; Australia; China)

GROWTH OF WORLD TRADE

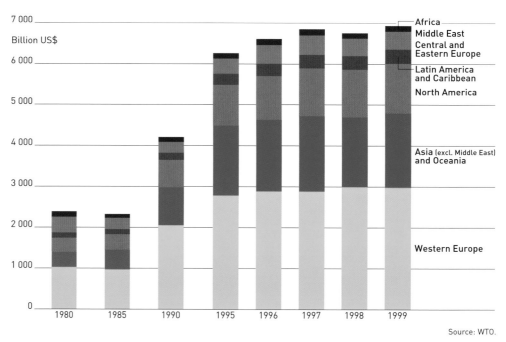

Source: WTO.

MAJOR TRADE FLOWS IN WHEAT AND WHEAT FLOUR, 1997
Million metric tons

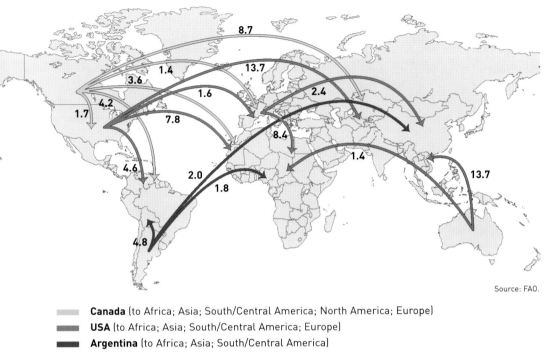

Source: FAO.

▬▬▬	**Canada** (to Africa; Asia; South/Central America; North America; Europe)
▬▬▬	**USA** (to Africa; Asia; South/Central America; Europe)
▬▬▬	**Argentina** (to Africa; Asia; South/Central America)
▬▬▬	**European Union** (to Africa; Asia)
▬▬▬	**Australia** (to Africa; Asia)

TRADE FLOWS IN WOOD AND WOOD PRODUCTS, 1997
Between selected producers and importers (US$ thousands)

From	Canada	China	France	To Germany	Italy	Japan	UK	USA
Brazil	15 202	92 259	136 785	102 717	91 478	210 854	208 198	616 707
Canada	–	632 571	221 999	624 768	436 431	2 633 646	459 665	17 744 929
China	1 444		249	1 649	1 421	279 775	5 170	20 037
Finland	47 493	213 473	753 657	1 956 913	341 561	346 636	1 467 817	574 507
France	37 488	147 947	–	767 392	524 446	18 710	449 700	142 688
Germany	45 299	263 845	1 158 327	–	810 763	62 978	1 481 371	575 841
Indonesia	11 620	1 336 311	36 139	62 357	71 835	1 471 700	110 066	385 175
Malaysia	8 961	878 757	33 176	58 840	25 300	1 816 419	85 293	143 418
Russia	3 297	210 620	43 022	110 755	100 462	617 660	113 967	60 704
Sweden	12 717	159 006	650 023	2 037 475	556 635	184 999	1 789 568	134 542
USA	3 146 159	1 319 397	325 170	722 209	671 410	2 513 838	672 982	–

The flows between these countries represent 41% of world trade in roundwood, wood panels, sawnwood, pulp and paper.

Source: FAO.

COMMODITY PRICES

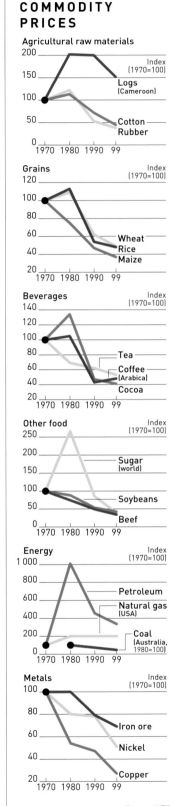

Source: WTO.

Trade dependency

The extent to which countries are dependent on international trade depends on many factors, including population and natural resources. Small, rich countries with few natural resources but high populations are generally the most dependent on trade. Thus the top ten countries for whom trade represents the highest proportion of GDP include Singapore (top at 93 percent), Panama, Bahrain and the Netherlands Antilles. The ten least trade-dependent nations are mostly those that are politically isolated (Iraq, Myanmar, Democratic People's Republic of Korea), poorest and most politically dislocated (Democratic Republic of Congo, Liberia, Haiti) or the richest with large internal markets (United States, Japan). The last two, though not trade-dependent, nevertheless occupy top places in volumes of trade by virtue of their economic size.

energy industries will benefit the environment. One test case concerns Western agriculture, where subsidies designed to maintain rural populations have encouraged more intensive farming, including heavy use of pesticides and fertilizers. The hidden environmental and human health costs of modern farming methods in Britain have been put at US$350 per hectare each year, approaching the value of European Union subsidies[4]. If future trade rules outlawed the subsidies, economists and environmentalists agree that these environmental costs would also fall as farming became less intensive.

Another test case is Chinese energy. State subsidies are a major cause of the overuse of fossil fuels, causing smogs and acid deposition and adding to climate change. During the late 1990s, while negotiating to join the WTO, China cut subsidies on coal by more than 50 percent. This resulted in real cuts in the use of coal at a time when its economy was growing by an average of 8 percent a year[5].

One important impact of international trade, particularly on fast-growing countries, is to increase the impetus for their economies to be based on specialization for export markets. In developing countries still heavily dependent on agriculture, this typically means a commodity crop such as coffee, cocoa or bananas. This can both encourage deforestation and the drainage of wetlands, and push once biodiverse farming areas into species-poor monocultures of varieties frequently alien to local ecosystems – with high inputs of toxic chemicals such as pesticides.

The WTO's charter, however, does require it to promote environmentally responsible trade and allows it to exempt conservation laws from its rules banning protectionism. The Organization formally recognizes some international environmental legislation as a legitimate constraint on trade, including the Montreal Protocol on Substances that Destroy the Ozone Layer. But a series of rulings in its first years appeared to back trade against the environment.

In 1998, for example, it ruled against the United States, which had banned imports of shrimps worth US$2.5 billion a year from four Asian countries – Thailand, Pakistan, Malaysia and the Philippines – because fishermen in these countries used nets that captured up to 20 000 endangered Olive Ridley turtles. Such nets were illegal under United States law. The WTO invoked the rule that it is generally illegal to discriminate, either through labelling or outright bans, between identical products on the basis of how they are produced.

The shadow of the WTO has also hung over negotiations for future environmental laws. These include proposed controls on persistent organic pollutants (POPs) such as pesticides, and on genetically modified (GM) products. Talks on a Biosafety Protocol under the Convention on Biological Diversity broke down in early 1999 because of fears that it could become a protectionist device, but agreement was nevertheless reached early in 2000, setting rules for controlling trade in GM products. The Protocol explicitly allows countries to respond to fears about health or environmental dangers from GM by preventing trade, but also leaves them open to WTO sanctions.

Despite such concerns, the governments of industrialized countries have generally argued that the environment should play a bigger role in trade law. But some developing countries say this will undermine their economic development by imposing "Western" environmental laws more appropriate to richer economies.

Behind all this are cultural as well as economic and environmental concerns about the impact of globalization. The globalization of trade in agricultural goods is likely to intensify standardization of farming methods and crops, ensuring a further loss of species and genetic diversity on the farm. Moreover, current concepts of free trade are hard to reconcile with successful communal styles of ownership of land and resources that often underpin indigenous communities that live in greater harmony with their environment. A global standardization on Western lifestyles, it is argued, will promote polluting and resource-depleting activities such as high levels of car ownership and meat-rich diets.

Population and landuse

O ver thousands of years, humans have occupied most of the land surface of the planet, affecting its ecosystems in ways that have ranged from the subtle management of forests to the total transformation involved in creating the urban environment. Too often humankind has tamed nature by destroying it. However, new land management strategies that seek to answer human needs while respecting natural ecosystems offer some solutions.

For much of human existence, the land available for human use has appeared limitless. Wherever population densities rose too high for comfort, or the natural resource base declined, people moved on to occupy new lands, whether a neighboring woodland or a new country.

Extensification – the expansion of arable land – has overwhelmingly been a response to fast-rising populations, with subsistence in food the main driving force. The 60 years from 1860 to 1920 saw 440 million hectares of land brought under cultivation (an area larger than India)[1]. More than half of this took place in the temperate lands of North America and in the region that became the Soviet Union. A similar scale of transformation took place in the subsequent 60 years, from 1920 to 1980. By then, most of the potentially productive temperate lands of the northern hemisphere, including Europe and East Asia, were occupied and the rate of population growth was slackening. The new "frontier lands", where population growth rates remained high, were in Africa, South Asia and South America.

New land for arable farming has generally been obtained through the annexation of grazing pastures, deforestation and the drainage of wetlands. The largest areas of pasture "lost" to cropland were in the United States Great Plains, the South African veldt, the Russian steppe and the campos and pampas of Brazil and Argentina. This type of conversion destroys many herds of wild animals, whether bison, gazelles or elephants, while the compression of flocks into ever smaller and more arid regions contributes to soil degradation and desertification.

Drainage has been under way in Europe for many centuries, but only became a worldwide phenomenon in the late 19th century, as the global market for commodities grew and new drainage technologies emerged. These used cheap clay-tile pipes and steam-powered machines for digging ditches and other heavy work. Passage of the Swamp Lands Acts in the United States accelerated drainage of much of the Midwest, encouraging the conversion of land to agriculture at a time of rising grain prices.

Arid lands, meanwhile, have been made agriculturally productive through irrigation. Again, the western states of the United States led the way, but equivalent areas elsewhere, including modern India, Pakistan and Egypt, also came under irrigation, largely carried out by British colonial engineers.

As the global economy has grown, ever more land has been cleared, drained or irrigated to plant cash crops for export, such as sugar and palm oil, coffee and rubber, or to grow food crops for livestock. With the potential for new colonization reduced in much of the world, farming has

WORLD LANDUSE, 1998⁺

Arable land
1 380 m hectares

Permanent crops*
132 m hectares

Permanent pasture
3 427 m hectares

Forest and woodland
3 454 m hectares

Other
4 656 m hectares
including 200 m hectares
of built up land

**Total world land area:
13 049 million hectares**

North America
1 872 m hectares

14% 0.1% 12%
24% 49%

Latin America and Caribbean
2 018 m hectares

1% 7%
30% 15%
47%

Europe
2 260 m hectares

8% 1% 13%
40% 38%

Africa
2 964 m hectares

1% 6%
30% 46%
17%

Asia
3 085 m hectares

2% 16%
34% 33%
15%

Oceania
849 m hectares

0.3% 7%
51% 31%
11%

⁺ Figures for forests and woodland
are 1995 data and are approximate
* Crops that do not have to be re-
sown each year
** Including Russia, where most of
Europe's forest is found

Source: FAO; WRI.

HUMAN TRANSFORMATION OF THE LAND, LATE 1990s

Almost pristine

Partially transformed

Almost fully transformed

While the map shows a considerable proportion of the world's land mass as "almost pristine", in reality little of it has escaped the hand of humankind. The relatively recently discovered and still only partially understood phenomena of global distillation (see page 98) and climate change are expected to have profound effects on those parts of the planet that have escaped deliberate transformation.

ROAD NETWORK DENSITY, LATE 1990s
Kilometers of route per 100 square kilometers of land area

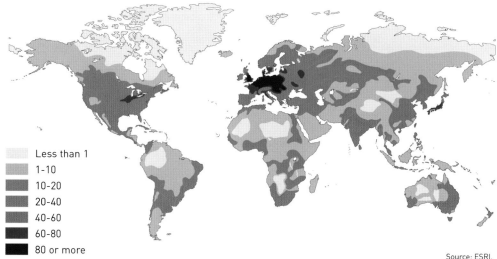

Less than 1
1-10
10-20
20-40
40-60
60-80
80 or more

Source: ESRI.

Source: ESRI.

POPULATION ENGAGED IN AGRICULTURE
Actual numbers

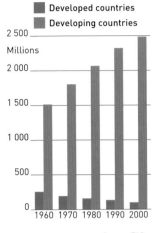

- ■ Developed countries
- ▨ Developing countries

Source: FAO.

PROPORTION OF POPULATION ENGAGED IN AGRICULTURE

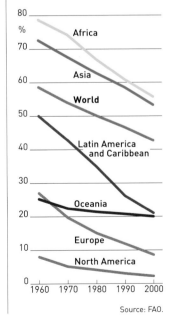

Source: FAO.

HUMAN DISTURBANCE, BY REGION, 1990s

	Undisturbed %	Partially disturbed %	Human dominated %
Europe	15.6	19.6	64.9
Asia	42.2	29.1	28.7
Africa	48.9	35.8	15.4
North America	56.3	18.8	24.9
Latin America and Caribbean	62.5	22.5	15.1
Australasia	62.3	25.8	12.0
Antarctica	100.0	0.0	0.0
World	**51.9**	**24.2**	**23.9**
World reduced by area of rock, ice and barren land	*27.0*	*36.7*	*36.3*

Source: UNEP.

increasingly invested in intensification, through purchases of fertilizers, high-yield seeds and machinery. Most of this investment has not been by subsistence farmers, however, but by commercial farmers, both large and small, responding to market conditions[2]. Intensification – and extensification where it is still possible – became dependent on markets, with demand driven by increased consumption per person as well as population growth.

While less important in terms of area, mining, industrial development and urbanization have also contributed to the transformation of natural ecosystems into human landscapes. For instance, Brazilian deforestation began in the 16th century and intensified with the discovery of gold. It has been estimated that 95 000 square kilometers of Brazilian rainforest were lost to gold mining in the 18th century[3].

The second half of the 20th century saw an unprecedented covering of the landscape with urban concrete and tarmac, destroying or displacing wildlife and causing major disruption to drainage and rivers by preventing natural seepage. Drains replaced rivers in great urban areas such as Metropolitan Tokyo, the largest concreted area on Earth. Concrete has also been used in an effort (sometimes misguided) to manage other aspects of the environment – to prevent flooding, coastal erosion and landslides, for instance. It has been estimated that the banks and beds of a fifth of Japan's rivers are concreted[4].

But urbanization and high population density need not mean the loss of all wildlife habitats. Though far from "natural", suburban residential areas and abandoned industrial landscapes are increasingly recognized as important reservoirs of wildlife – often more so than neighboring agricultural landscapes[5]. In England and elsewhere in Europe, a high proportion of the rare and endangered species of invertebrates and flowering plants such as orchids live in former urban industrial sites[6,7]. Green strips of land either side of highways and railroads often act as migration corridors for wildlife through urban areas.

But even densely populated agricultural landscapes can be managed to maximize their ecological value. "Agroecology" looks to maximize biological output while lowering chemical inputs[8]. Some of the best examples have been researched by anthropologists looking at traditional farming systems, such as the "home gardens" of Java (one of the world's most densely populated islands). These gardens may grow up to 90 species of plants, including crops of coffee, mango, guava, tomatoes and so on, beneath a forest-like canopy.

Conversely, thinly populated landscapes can suffer appalling ecological degradation. Where land is not in short supply it may be wasted and degraded as if it were an essentially infinite resource. The oilfields of western Siberia are a spectacular example of a wetland landscape that, while almost uninhabited, is highly degraded – fragmented and polluted by roads, powerlines, pipelines, survey tracks, well flares and waste sumps[9]. Similarly, relatively thinly spread populations of settlers in the Brazilian Amazon have cleared huge areas of forest for pasture.

Human occupation of the land does not necessarily destroy ecosystems. It may simply transform them, creating new habitats. The growing organic farming movement in developed countries is combining quality food production with low or no chemical inputs, benefiting biodiversity as well, it is argued, as human health. Equally, sustainable forest harvesting, encouraged by the Forest Stewardship Council and others, can command premium prices for production systems geared to both ecological and human needs. Despite many failures, humankind is increasingly learning to manage ecosystems for sustainable use rather than to sacrifice them to human development.

Croplands

THE WORLD has doubled food production in the past 35 years, more than keeping pace with population growth. This has largely been made possible by new crop varieties, increased chemical inputs to fields and the extension of land under irrigation. But it is questionable whether we can continue to increase output as populations rise.

Of the world's agricultural land, only around a third is used to grow crops, with the remaining two thirds dedicated to livestock pasture. In recent decades, for the first time in history, increased yields have been achieved largely through intensified farming, rather than by extending the tilled land. Sustained by chemical fertilizers, pesticides, irrigation and mechanization, the use of a few high-yield crop varieties has developed and spread, contributing to an enterprise known generically as the "green revolution". This has also, of course, been driven by demographics – the demand of more mouths to feed and, in the developing world, more people working in the fields.

The green revolution has modified natural ecosystems into a highly simplified and nutrient-rich state. A handful of plants, bred into entirely new strains, have become the dominant plants on the planet. The four main grain crops – wheat, rice, maize and barley – occupy a total of some 500 million hectares[1], mostly in those countries with the highest populations. The green revolution was not all good, however. It spread a farming method that relies heavily on chemical fertilizers, mono-cultural cropping practices and decreased fallow times, coupled with more intensive plowing. Local water supplies became degraded and crop diversity decreased, leading to land degradation and erosion. Concern has increased over the implications of pests that thrive on now dominant strains of grain and maize.

Chemical applications to fields have soared. The doubling of agricultural production during the past 35 years has required a 600 percent increase in nitrogen fertilizer and a 250 percent increase in phosphate fertilizer. This has been accompanied, over the same period, by a 70 percent increase in irrigated cropland, but only a 10 percent increase in the area of cultivated land[2]. One immediate effect of such high fertilizer use is that human activity has taken over from nature as the dominant source of fixed nitrogen in the environment. Natural sources from soil bacteria, algae and lightning release 140 million tons of fixed nitrogen a year; human sources now total 210 million tons per year, of which 86 percent comes from agricultural activity, with fertilizer responsible for most of it[3].

More than half of all the commercial fertilizer ever produced has been applied to fields since 1984. However, largely because of widespread overuse, a half of that application never reached plant tissue, but evaporated or washed into rivers. The result has been a nitrogen overload of natural ecosystems, particularly in Western Europe and East Asia, where average annual applications on arable land are highest[4]. Application rates generally reflect wealth or the pressure in densely popu-lated countries to raise food production.

Changes caused by nitrogen overload range from the seemingly harmless, such as the spread of nettles in English hedgerows, to toxic algal blooms in lakes, rivers and coastal waters, resulting

WORLD ARABLE AND CROPLAND
By region

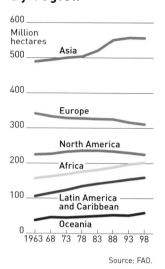

Source: FAO.

CROPLANDS AT RISK OF DEGRADATION, 1999

Very high risk

High risk

Moderate risk

Low risk

The map shows cropland areas at risk of degradation on the basis of susceptibility owing to climate and soil type, set against population densities. Areas with susceptible soils and high population densities are considered most at risk. However the risk is reduced wherever countries are taking active measures to preserve their soils.

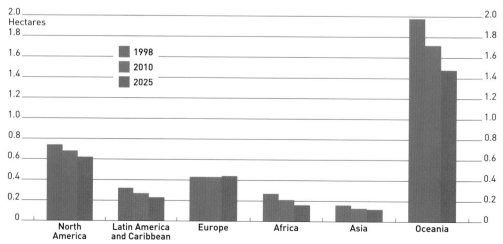

GLOBAL SOIL LIMITATIONS TO AGRICULTURE

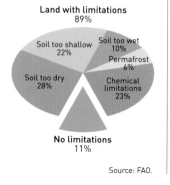

Land with limitations 89%

Soil too shallow 22%

Soil too wet 10%

Permafrost 6%

Soil too dry 28%

Chemical limitations 23%

No limitations 11%

Source: FAO.

ARABLE LAND PER CAPITA, BY REGION
Current and projected

1998
2010
2025

North America
Latin America and Caribbean
Europe
Africa
Asia
Oceania

Source: FAO; UNPD.

WORLD CROP YIELDS

Cereals, by region

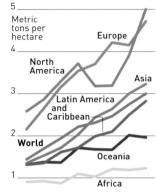

Source: WSP-USDA.

World average for selected crops

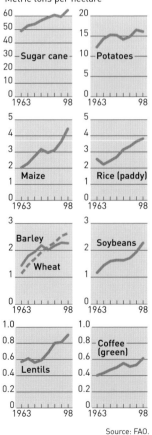

Source: FAO.

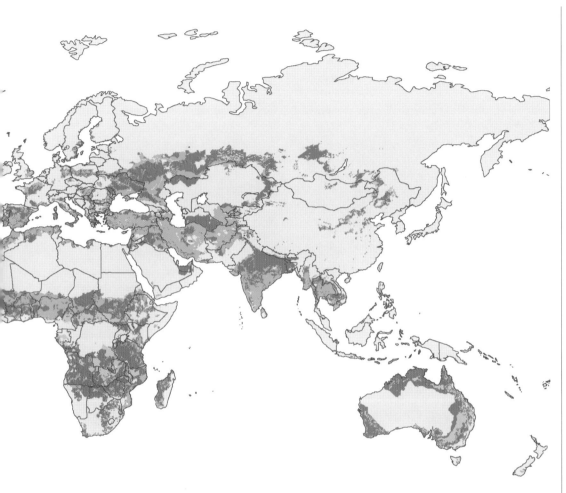

TRACTORS: AN INDICATOR OF MECHANIZATION

Tractors in use, 1998, selected countries

Tractors per thousand agricultural workers	
USA	777
France	641
Japan	436
Spain	282
Libya	102
Argentina	69
Russia	56
Korea, Rep.	38
Chile	23
Iran	12
Botswana	8
Pakistan	4
Zimbabwe	3
Vietnam	2
Kenya	Less than 1

Increases in tractor use

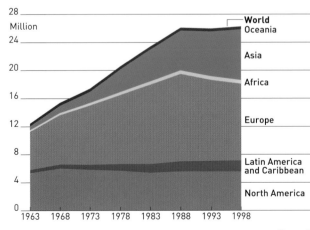

Source: FAO.

SHARE OF AREA PLANTED TO MODERN CROP VARIETIES IN DEVELOPING COUNTRIES (%)

Rice[+]	1970	1983	1991
Developing countries	30	59	74
Sub-Saharan Africa	4	15	id
West Asia and North Africa	0	11	id
Asia*	12	48	67
China	77	95	100
Latin America	4	28	58

Wheat[+]	1970	1983	1990
Developing countries	20*	59*	70
Sub-Saharan Africa	5	32	52
West Asia and North Africa	5	31	42
Asia*	42	79	88
China	id	id	70
Latin America	11	68	82

Maize	1990
Developing countries	57
Sub-Saharan Africa	43
West Asia and North Africa	53
Asia*	45
China	90
Latin America	46

+ Excluding tall varieties released since 1965. If these varieties are included, the area under modern varieties increases, especially for rice in Latin America
* Excluding China

Source: FAO.

from a process called eutrophication, and the leaching of key nutrients such as calcium and magnesium from soils[5]. In addition, nitrogen evaporation from soils (along with methane emissions from rice paddies) is contributing to global emissions of greenhouse gases.

Worldwide pesticide use has also soared, reaching 5 million tons annually[6]. Three quarters of pesticides, predominantly herbicides, are applied in Europe, North America and Japan, where farmers can most easily afford them. In tropical developing countries the greatest need is for the more toxic broad-spectrum insecticides, largely applied to export crops such as cotton, bananas and coffee. In such export crop plantations, acute pesticide poisoning can affect 10 percent of the workforce[7]. But the pesticide poison cycle reaches further. Pesticides evaporate into the atmosphere at the point of use and circulate the planet, eventually distilling out in the chill air of the Arctic where they poison polar bears, whales and even humans.

Hectare for hectare, most irrigated land is more productive than rainfed land, and in some regions, such as the Nile delta and the Sind in Pakistan, it is essential to crop production. The amount of irrigated land worldwide has tripled since 1950 to cover 270 million hectares, accounting for more than a third of the global harvest[8]. Most of this is in densely populated regions of Asia, where it allows two or three crops a year, and in the Middle East, where without it there would be virtually no agriculture. In many parts of the world, countries are reaching absolute limits of the availability of water (much as they did with farmable land 40 years ago) and must improve the efficiency of its use if they are to raise production.

Increases in large stands of monoculture crops have had important ecological consequences. With this type of cultivation the range of plant pests becomes less diverse, but more abundant, reflecting the plants themselves. Organic matter in the soil is lost, altering the soil biota and generally involving a loss of soil fertility. These changes increase the need for pesticides and fertilizers and, combined with the physical impacts of erosion, cause soil degradation.

Croplands tilled and then left without the protective cover of vegetation are particularly vulnerable to soil loss through wind and water erosion. Worldwide an estimated 12 million hectares of croplands fall out of use for this reason each year. Economists have estimated the value of this lost soil, in terms of nutrients and water-holding capacity, at about US$400 billion a year[9]. Erosion rates are highest in Asia, Africa and South America, estimated at typically 30 or 40 tons per hectare annually, while about half that amount is being lost in Europe and North America[10]. The high rates reflect poor land management, poverty and the cultivation of marginal and sloping land, as well as population density and the resulting pressure to cut fallow periods and grow several crops a year. Land is also degraded by salinization – generally as a result of the waterlogging of irrigated land, which can bring salts to the surface, forming a white crust toxic to most plants.

The rate of soil degradation raises questions about the long-term sustainability of yield increases without a rising tide of inputs[11], while concern for sustainability has increased interest in new methods of farming, based on lower inputs and greater attention to ecological principles using local knowledge and natural biological means of pest control[12].

Typical methods include using organic fertilizer from farm animals and planting leguminous crops to fix nitrogen in the soil, growing plants that repel pests, protecting soils by terracing and reducing tillage, and harvesting rainwater in arid regions.

Pastures

P ASTURES, which cover more than a quarter of the Earth's land surface, are facing pressures from the rapidly increasing demand for meat and from cultivators trying to convert them to croplands. Can these seemingly fragile lands be sustainably managed, or must they fall prey to human consumption?

The world's expanse of pastures – grazing lands ranging from the Argentinian pampas and the arid scrublands of the Sahel, to the Mongolian grassland steppes and the rainfed grasslands of New Zealand – remained almost stationary during the past three centuries. Increases in the less densely populated regions of tropical Africa and Latin America, often at the expense of forests, were matched by declines, each of around 20 percent, in Europe, Southeast Asia and North America, where increasing population densities forced a switch from grazing to more intensive cultivation and the feeding of animals using grains such as maize[1]. More recently however, parts of Asia, particularly China and Saudi Arabia, have seen substantial increases, accounting for much of the 9 percent rise in global pasture land over the last 25 years[2].

It is estimated that 73 percent of the world's grazing land has so deteriorated that it has lost at least 25 percent of its animal carrying capacity[3]. Traditional livestock herders are often demonized as the cause, but some researchers have defended the traditional techniques of pastoralists, saying that they have frequently been forced to occupy already degraded land – unsuitable for cultivation because of its low and unreliable rains, poor drainage, extreme temperatures and rough terrain. Moreover, the policies of many developing world governments towards pastures can often be inappropriate, geared towards Western-style cattle grazing based on intensification, standardization and individual land ownership. This is very different from the indigenous and ecologically more viable methods of tropical rangeland management, based on diversity and migration across unfenced areas[4]. It has also been argued that rangeland vegetation and soils are far more resilient than once assumed, able to recover when the animals move on or the rains return[5].

Livestock provide meat, dairy products, hides, tallow and other products. They are also the main source of motive power on more than 300 million hectares of cropland[6] and represent a form of capital for many rural families, realizable in hard times or as a dowry for a bride. Around the world grazing systems vary greatly. Even in rich developed countries large areas of land unsuitable for cultivation are grazed with little or no chemical inputs – notably the hills and mountains of much of Europe, and the sheep pastures of southern South America, Central Asia, Australia and New Zealand. In such conditions, as well as in the tropics, livestock can improve biodiversity, soil and vegetation cover – notably by removing and controlling the growth of "bush" that can trigger fires, and by dispersing seeds on their hooves and in their dung[7].

Manure from livestock is vital to land fertility in both natural and agricultural ecosystems, particularly where national and personal incomes are too low to allow the purchase of chemical fertilizers. While grazing and eating, ruminants in particular collect and concentrate nutrients and convert them into manure, which fertilizes the soil and maintains soil structure. In effect their

Rainforest clearance

In Latin America in particular, rainforests are being cleared to make way for cattle pastures. In Brazil, for example, an estimated 70 percent of deforestation has been attributed to clearance for livestock. This often destroys soil fertility within a few years, forcing the abandonment of some areas and the clearance of more forest[8].

WORLD PASTURE
By region

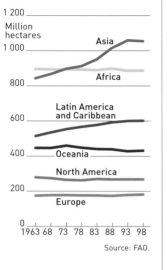

Source: FAO.

WORLD PASTURE, 1998
Proportion of land area

Less than 5%

5-10%

10-20%

20-30%

30-40%

40-50%

50-70%

More than 70%

Insufficient data

The map shows the percentage of a country's land area used permanently (five years or more) for herbaceous forage crops, either cultivated or growing wild (wild prairie or grazing land). Owing to varying definitions, shrubland and savannah may also be included for some countries.

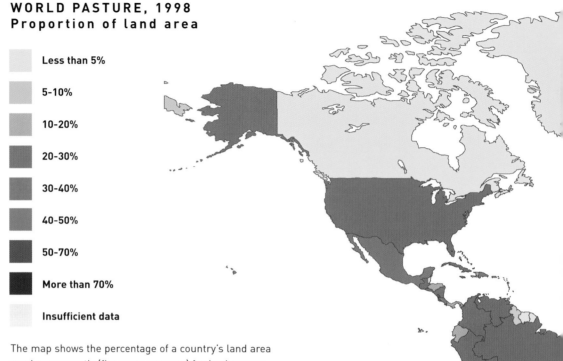

POPULATION OF GRASSLAND ECOSYSTEMS, LATE 1990s

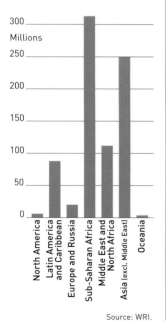

Source: WRI.

STOCKS OF FARM ANIMALS
Numbers in 1999 and % change since 1964

| | Cattle | | Sheep | | Goats | | Pigs | | Chickens | |
	Millions 1999	% change	Millions 1999	% change	Millions 1999	% change	Millions 1999	% change	Millions 1999	% change
North America	111.50	-7	7.92	-71	1.43	-64	74.61	11	1 865.1	116
Latin America and Caribbean	351.55	88	87.83	-29	37.57	22	72.25	32	2 172.0	412
Europe	103.55	-10	138.27	6	14.98	14	172.81	50	1 252.7	32
Africa	223.34	72	240.34	76	205.64	109	27.02	336	1 142.1	274
Former USSR	62.28	-27	49.91	-63	5.81	3	35.37	-13	585.7	37
Asia	449.64	39	378.68	55	443.78	106	525.38	207	7 014.4	462
Oceania	363.40	1 293	165.72	-23	0.72	119	5.26	68	107.4	284
World	**1 665.26**	**69**	**1 068.67**	**5**	**709.93**	**93**	**912.70**	**99**	**14 139.4**	**233**

Source: FAO.

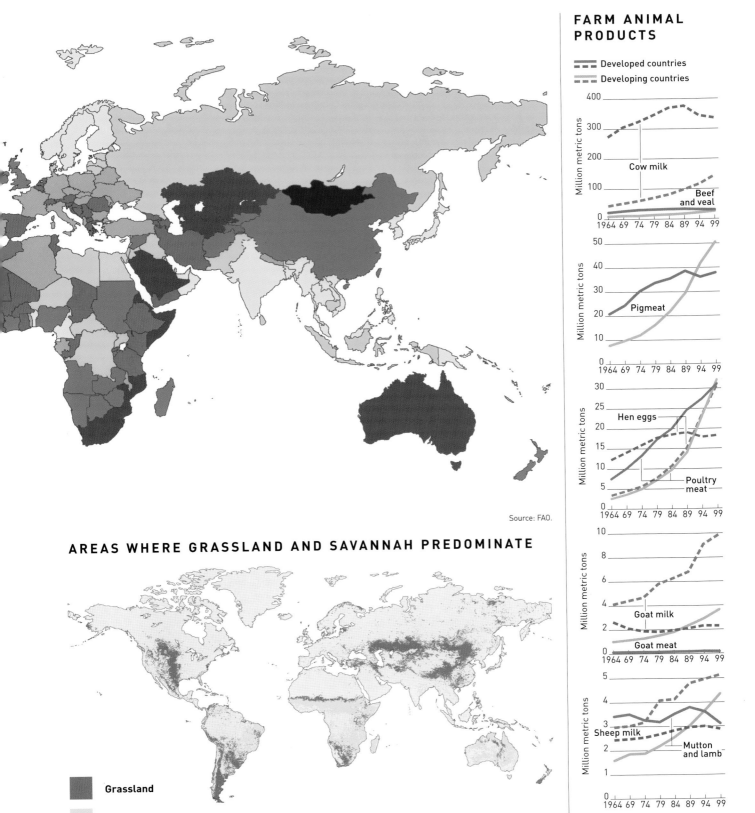

FARM ANIMAL PRODUCTS

- - - Developed countries
- - - Developing countries

Cow milk

Beef and veal

Pigmeat

Hen eggs

Poultry meat

Goat milk

Goat meat

Sheep milk

Mutton and lamb

Source: FAO.

AREAS WHERE GRASSLAND AND SAVANNAH PREDOMINATE

Grassland

Savannah/shrub

Source: USGS.

Source: FAO.

FARM BREEDS AND NUMBER AT RISK OF EXTINCTION, 1990s

	Number of breeds	Number of breeds at risk
Cattle	787	135
Sheep	920	119
Goat	351	44
Pig	353	69
Buffalo	72	2
Horse	384	120
Ass	77	9
Total	**2 944**	**498**

Source: FAO.

digestive systems are speeding up the recycling of nutrients. In traditional farming systems, animals are often tethered on croplands, so helping sustain crop production.

Studies in Africa have shown livestock-mediated nutrient recycling to be essential to maintaining croplands without large inputs of chemical fertilizer, and the value of livestock in fertilizing crops rises with increased population density. In the East African highlands, such as the Kiambu district of Kenya, where population density can exceed 500 people per square kilometer, livestock are vital parts of the cropping system[9]. In contrast, more intensively managed pastures, where artificial fertilizer is added to accelerate the growth of grass, may have an overall negative effect on the long-term health of the environment[10]. The nitrogen suppresses biodiversity and causes the glut that leads to eutrophication of rivers.

Demand for meat, however, has outstripped available pastures, with the result that more and more livestock are fed on fodder crops. This is a global trend but applies particularly in the most densely populated countries. Between 1990 and 1995, four fifths of China's increase in grain consumption went to feed livestock. Worldwide, 40 percent of grain is grown to feed livestock. The main fodder is maize, the production of which, for the first time in history, edged ahead of wheat globally in the late 1990s.

The shortage of pastures has also helped change the kind of livestock being raised. The global population of cattle, which traditionally feed on pastures, is rising much less quickly than animals that eat from feedlots, such as pigs (now the world's largest meat source) and poultry, which also now exceeds beef production. But intensive livestock systems tend to reduce "barnyard biodiversity" in the same way that the green revolution in crops has reduced it amongst plants. Many traditional livestock breeds have disappeared. Of the 3 800 breeds of cattle, water buffalo, goats, pigs, sheep, horses and donkeys catalogued by the Food and Agriculture Organization, 16 percent have become extinct and a further 15 percent are rare[11].

In Western countries, where population densities are often high and most land and livestock owners are dependent upon the major corporations that control food distribution networks, the intensification of livestock production is most marked. In developing countries, livestock owners are often the poor and politically marginalized[12], and grazing stocks of cattle, sheep and goats still occupy traditional pastures with no chemical inputs. But these pastoralists, too, are dependent on markets for a part of their income, and attempts to rear ever larger herds in fragile arid regions and on hillsides can lead to soil degradation and the specter of desertification.

Reviving traditional methods, most of which rely on a series of finely balanced factors including the ability to migrate across large areas of rangeland, herd sizes and the mix of animals being reared, will prove hard when demands on pastures from cultivators are growing and two thirds of the world's agricultural land is already given over to livestock pastures[13].

LIVESTOCK AND POLLUTION
Livestock herds are large-scale producers of gas emissions. All animals emit carbon dioxide, while ruminants also produce another greenhouse gas, methane. A third gas responsible for global warming, nitrous oxide, is released from manure. Intensive "factory farming" has created an increasing waste problem. The Netherlands is being forced to reduce its pig production because of problems with disposing of slurry safely without polluting rivers or intensifying acid deposition problems through the evaporation of ammonia.

Mineral extraction

MINING is the world's fifth largest industry. It has provided the raw materials for the construction and commodities of the modern world: tower blocks and airplanes, televisions and toothpaste. Much of it is dominated by transnational corporations serving global markets through the intense exploitation of mineral-rich land.

Humans have always used materials dug from the ground, whether stone and clay to make shelter, precious metals for adornment and ceremonial purposes, or more workaday minerals for tools. Their use became a marker for our technological progress through the iron and bronze ages, and throughout history the search for minerals helped drive the expansion of civilizations into new territory. The Romans first went to Britain to extract tin, while gold and silver drew Europeans to the New World and the British, French and Belgians to Africa. The desire to extract minerals also drove railroad construction across the United States, Canada and Siberia.

While bulky and more widely available materials tend to be extracted locally, largely reflecting local population levels, rarer materials have always had an international market. Two thirds of European investment in Africa before the 1930s went into mining, until the sector made up half of the continent's exports. Gold and diamonds underpin the (ill-distributed) wealth of South Africa.

Rising demand for materials has created increasingly global industries, in which local demand and demographics are largely irrelevant to levels of exploitation. Today, one of the front lines of exploration for minerals is in the Asian islands of Borneo and New Guinea, which contain the world's largest copper and gold mines, but few of the world's people.

Traded globally but produced in intense local mining areas, mineral extraction often reflects the negative social and ecological impact of global economic forces. Rising demand has driven technologists to find ways of extracting the more valuable materials from low-grade ores, with a resulting dramatic increase in the disturbance of the land. The copper industry increased production 22-fold in the 20th century, partly by extracting metal from a 0.5 percent ore, compared with a 3 percent limit at the century's start. The industry's 99.5 percent discard of mined ore is matched by wastes of upwards of 60 percent in the mining of iron, 70 percent for manganese, and 99.75, 99.95 and 99.99 percent respectively for tungsten, zinc and gold. Canada produces 60 times more mining waste than urban refuse[1]. The 20th century also saw the rapid growth of new extraction industries – bauxite for aluminum, uranium for nuclear weapons and power, and petrochemicals for plastics.

In consequence, over the past century mining has removed an estimated 100 million people from their land and destroyed forests and farmland, either directly for extraction or to accommodate the waste. The extraction and refining of ores requires the use of toxic substances such as cyanide and mercury, which are often allowed to pollute land and river systems. It is estimated that a ton of mercury is released into the Amazon environment for every ton of gold extracted[2], poisoning local wildlife including fish eaten by humans.

Minerals making history

The industrial revolution was characterized more than anything else by changes in the use made of minerals such as iron. Between 1870 and 1913, iron ore production in Britain, Germany and France rose 83-fold. Today iron and its harder, more durable alloy, steel, make up 85 percent of world metals and a tenth of total world materials production.

WORLD MINERAL PRODUCTION

Bauxite

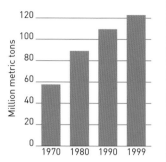

Copper

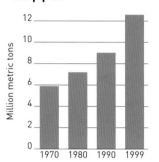

Tin

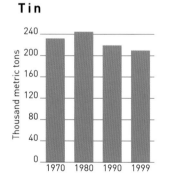

Iron ore

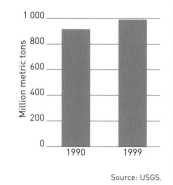

Source: USGS.

WORLD MINERAL EXTRACTION SITES AND COAL AND LIGNITE DEPOSITS, LATE 1990s

Metallic minerals
- ● Large
- • Medium

Non-metallic minerals
- ▲ Large
- ▲ Medium

Diamonds
- ◆ Large
- ◆ Medium

Large: more than 5% of world production
Medium: 1-5% of world production

■ **Major coal and lignite deposits**

Mining has provided the raw materials for the construction and commodities of the modern world, yet it has removed an estimated 100 million people from their land and destroyed forests and farmland, either directly for extraction or to accomodate the waste.

TOP BAUXITE PRODUCERS, 1999

	Million metric tons
Australia	46.5
Guinea	15.0
Brazil	11.8
Jamaica	11.6
China	8.5
India	7.0
Venezuela	4.5
Suriname	3.7
Russia	3.5
Guyana	1.8

93% of world production

TOP COPPER PRODUCERS, 1999

	Thousand metric tons
Chile	4 360
USA	1 660
Indonesia	765
Australia	730
Canada	630
Peru	540
Russia	520
China	450
Poland	450
Mexico	375

83% of world production

TOP TIN PRODUCERS, 1999

	Thousand metric tons
China	80
Indonesia	42
Peru	27
Brazil	17
Bolivia	12
Australia	9
Malaysia	7
Russia	5
Portugal	4
Thailand	1

97% of world production

Source: USGS.

Source: Times.

TOP DIAMOND PRODUCERS, 1998

Gemstones

	Million carats
Australia	18.4
Botswana	13.5
Russia	10.5
South Africa	4.1
Angola	2.4

89% of world production

Industrial diamonds

	Million carats
Australia	22.5
Congo, Dem. Rep.	13.0
Russia	10.5
South Africa	6.2
Botswana	5.0

95% of world production

Source: USGS.

GOLD PRODUCTION
Total for time period specified

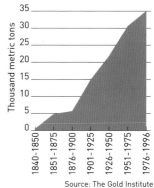

Source: The Gold Institute.

TOP IRON ORE PRODUCERS, 1999

	Million metric tons
China	205
Brazil	190
Australia	150
India	75
Russia	70
USA	57
Ukraine	50
Canada	35
South Africa	33
Sweden	21

89% of world production

TOP CEMENT PRODUCERS, 1999

	Million metric tons
China	520.0
USA (incl. Puerto Rico)	87.3
India	87.0
Japan	80.0
Korea, Rep.	55.0
Brazil	43.0
Germany	37.0
Turkey	37.0
Italy	35.0
Thailand	34.0

65% of world production

TOP GOLD PRODUCERS, 1999

	Metric tons
South Africa	474
USA	360
Australia	312
China	178
Canada	166
Indonesia	105
Russia	104
Peru	89
Uzbekistan	80
Ghana	73

79% of world production

Source: USGS.

It is estimated that only some 128 000 tons of gold have ever been mined. About 15 percent of this has been lost, is unrecoverable or unaccounted for. Of the existing 108 000 tons, just over two thirds are privately owned as jewelry, coins or bullion, with the remaining 31.5 percent held as official stocks by central banks.

Source: USGS.

COAL PRODUCTION

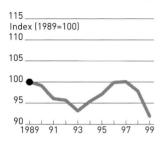

Index (1989=100)

Top producers, 1998

Hard and brown coal
Million metric tons

China	1 236
USA	1 014
India	326
Australia	285
Russia	233
South Africa	223
Poland	180
Ukraine	77
Kazakhstan	70
Indonesia	60

81% of world production

Source: World Energy Council.

OIL PRODUCTION

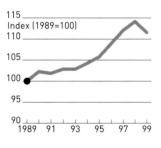

Index (1989=100)

Top producers, 1999

Million metric tons

Saudi Arabia	411.8
USA	354.7
Russia	304.8
Iran	175.2
Mexico	166.1
Venezuela	160.5
China	159.3
Norway	149.1
UK	137.1
Iraq	125.5

62% of world production

Source: BP.

Acid emissions from Russia's metal smelting have destroyed vegetation over hundreds of square kilometers of the Arctic Kola peninsula. The Sudbury nickel smelter in Ontario did similar damage in Canada in the 1970s and 1980s. The South African mining industry, which employs some 800 000 people and generates half the country's foreign exchange, is also responsible for around a million tons of sulfur emissions a year. It is one of Africa's largest sources of acid pollution[3].

While lending itself to large-scale industrial enterprise, mining for minerals also employs millions of artisan miners across the world. In Latin America an estimated 1 million artisan miners are at work, exploiting gold in particular. Mining "rushes", whether involving artisans or corporations, frequently cause social conflict, often over pollution. Amazon gold miners have clashed with the Yanomami in the Amazon. Mines at Bougainville and Grasberg in New Guinea have caused civil insurrection. Such disputes are often exacerbated when governments appear to side with mining companies against the interests of the local communities.

Some refining and smelting processes require large amounts of energy. Many of the world's major hydroelectric dams have been constructed to supply cheap electricity for smelting aluminum. The Hoover dam on the River Colorado in the United States is one such example. Another is the Akosombo dam in Ghana. Built in the 1960s to provide hydropower to smelt bauxite for a United States company, Akosombo flooded more than 5 percent of the country and displaced 80 000 people to create the largest artificial lake on Earth.

Since the 1960s, growing environmental awareness coupled with real shortage of some strategic metals has encouraged a new trend towards recycling. Glass, aluminum, gold and iron are all recycled on a large scale. New materials have also reduced the pressure on some mineral resources – glass fibers are replacing copper in cable systems, for instance. Resource managers dream of "closing the loop", with 100-percent recycling. Even industries making complex products are moving towards a recycling strategy – for instance the European automobile manufacturing industry, which is dedicated to making the majority of car parts recyclable.

But there may be practical limits to this approach. Recycling is not an absolute virtue. Some analysts argue that the environmental cost is sometimes greater than the cost of starting from scratch with new raw materials. In most instances, efforts to reduce the use of raw materials and energy, and to avoid the unnecessary purchase of new items such as automobiles and office equipment, should be the preferred strategy.

The impact of recycling on overall mineral exploitation has so far been small. Production of metals and minerals has more than doubled since the early 1960s, while petrochemicals production has risen more than fivefold[4].

PETROCHEMICALS

The petrochemicals industry is, apart from the growing of food, the largest and most lucrative on Earth. Its biggest product, oil, is the greatest single source of commercial energy – and hence of greenhouse gas emissions – with its dominance near-total in the transport sector. Its price is one of the most significant determinants of global economic growth; its extraction from the Earth the leading economic activity in many countries, particularly in the Middle East; and its processing is a major activity in many others. Oil spills – from maritime production platforms, tankers and waste discharges from land – are the leading source of marine pollution. But reserves, particularly of the cleaner-lighter fractions, are diminishing and many analysts say production is unlikely to rise further. This will increase pressure to tap known existing reserves in hostile and ecologically sensitive environments, such as the Arctic, and within protected rainforests.

Migration and tourism

MIGRATION takes many forms: temporary and permanent; between and within countries; legal and illegal; forced or voluntary; to cities or suburbs; for tourism or to escape persecution; for economic gain or at the point of a gun; daily commuting or in search of food. One thing in common is that all are on the increase. The world is on the move, and the environmental causes and consequences are profound.

The history of humankind's subjugation of the planet is in many respects a history of migration. In the past 500 years, the colonization by Europeans of the Americas and Australasia, in particular, has transformed the ecology of three continents. And the forced movement of some 15 million African slaves to America and a similar number of Russian political prisoners to Siberian gulags fundamentally changed the social ecology of those regions.

International migration at the end of the 20th century was at unprecedented rates, with an estimated 120 million people living or working outside their country of origin in the 1990s, compared to 75 million in 1965. A common perception is that most of these migrants are moving from poor to rich nations, but in reality half of all cross-border migration takes place within the developing world[1].

People move for many reasons: political, ethnic, economic, military or environmental – often a combination of several such factors. Migration is a natural safety valve for local problems and a source of labor and capital for fast-growing economies. But high rates of migration may denote a serious environmental crisis in the source region – and can trigger environmental degradation in the receiving area.

Up to 10 million people fled drought and famine in the Sahel region of Africa in the 1970s and 1980s, settling in wetter coastal regions, including neighboring countries. At least half of them never returned home[2]. In Mauritania, environmental degradation has helped to force the proportion of the total population living in the coastal zone from 9 to 41 percent since 1968.

In the 1980s, land scarcity caused by a fast-rising population in Bangladesh led to conflicts that drove 12 to 17 million Bangladeshis into neighboring Indian states of West Bengal and Assam[3]. Millions fled Rwanda in the 1990s during ethnic conflicts triggered in part at least by the country's poverty, water scarcity and declining soil fertility, all stemming from its very high population density of 400 people per square kilometer[4].

Defining "environmental refugees" is hard. The numbers could be much higher than those with refugee status under the United Nations High Commissioner for Refugees (UNHCR) definition. A study for the Washington-based Climate Institute includes among environmental refugees people displaced by land shortages, deforestation, soil erosion, desertification, water deficits, extreme weather events and disease. It put the current annual total of such people at 25 million, which the author[5] called "cautious and conservative". The same study suggests that factors such as climate change and rising sea levels could put the figure at 200 million by the year 2050.

The distinction between environmental refugees and economic migrants is also sometimes

INTERNATIONAL MIGRANTS, 1990s
Excluding refugees

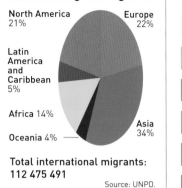

North America 21%

Europe 22%

Latin America and Caribbean 5%

Africa 14%

Oceania 4%

Asia 34%

Total international migrants:
112 475 491

Source: UNPD.

INTERNATIONAL MIGRANTS
Including refugees

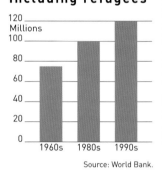

120 Millions
100
80
60
40
20
0
1960s 1980s 1990s

Source: World Bank.

COUNTRIES WITH HIGHEST NUMBERS OF REFUGEES, 1999

	Population of concern*	As % of host population
Iran	1 835 700	2.7
Yugoslavia	1 660 030	15.6
Russia	1 489 580	1.0
Germany	1 239 500	1.5
Pakistan	1 202 460	0.8
Bosnia and Herzegovina	1 109 120	28.9
USA	1 093 900	0.4
Azerbaijan	791 550	10.3
Rwanda	711 470	9.8
Sierra Leone	704 730	14.9
Tanzania	634 530	1.9
Afghanistan	628 410	2.9
Sri Lanka	612 730	3.3

* Includes refugees, asylum seekers, returned refugees and internally displaced people

Source: UNHCR; UNPD.

INTERNATIONAL MIGRANT POPULATIONS, 1990s
Proportion of each country's total population, excluding refugees

- Less than 1%
- 1-3%
- 3-5%
- 5-10%
- 10-20%
- 20-50%
- More than 50%
- Insufficient data

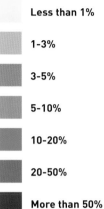

The study of migrant populations is relatively young and the underlying causes of migration poorly defined, particularly with regard to the linkages between economic and environmental factors.

Note: The term refugees on this page refers to those with refugee status under the UNHCR definition: Persons recognized under the 1951 Convention; the OAU Convention; in accordance with the UNHCR statute; persons granted a humanitarian or comparable status and those granted temporary protection.

REFUGEES AND OTHERS OF CONCERN TO UNHCR, 1999

Region of residence	Refugees	Asylum-seekers	Returned refugees	Internally displaced people	Returned internally displaced	Various	Total population of concern
North America	636 300	605 630	id	id	id	id	1 241 930
Latin America and Caribbean	61 200	1 510	6 260	id	id	21 200	90 170
Europe	2 608 380	473 060	952 060	1 603 300	370 000	1 279 000	7 285 800
Africa	3 523 250	61 110	933 890	640 600	1 054 700	36 990	6 250 540
Asia	4 781 750	24 750	617 620	1 724 800	10 590	149 350	7 308 860
Oceania	64 500	15 540	id	id	id	id	80 040
World	**11 675 380**	**1 181 600**	**2 509 830**	**3 968 700**	**1 435 290**	**1 486 540**	**22 257 340**

Change since 1998 (%)

Region	Refugees	Asylum-seekers	Returned refugees	Internally displaced people	Returned internally displaced	Various	Total population of concern
North America	-3.6	-6.2	id	id	id	id	-4.9
Latin America and Caribbean	-17.5	319.4	-20.4	id	id	6.0	-11.9
Europe	-2.2	-18.0	233.5	22.7	38.8	15.3	17.3
Africa	7.7	-3.5	-28.0	-59.8	95 781.8	-39.0	-0.5
Asia	0.8	-10.4	94.7	-15.3	-94.1	-11.0	-2.2
Oceania	-13.2	198.8	id	id	id	id	0.7
World	**1.6**	**-10.4**	**31.6**	**-19.6**	**220.3**	**9.5**	**3.7**

Source: UNHCR.

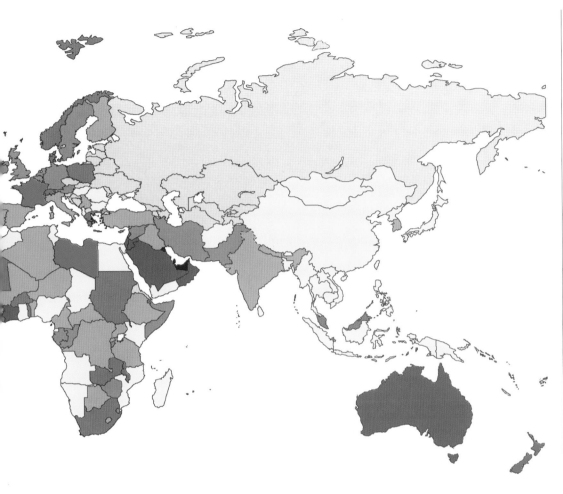

Source: UNPD.

INTERNATIONAL TOURIST ARRIVALS

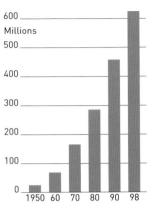

Source: World Tourism Organization.

INTERNATIONAL TOURISM RECEIPTS

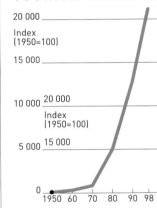

Source: World Tourism Organization.

TOP TOURIST DESTINATIONS, 1997

	Tourist arrivals Thousands	As % of world arrivals	As % of local population	Tourism earnings as % of GNP	Earnings per tourist US$
France	66 864	10.95	114	1.84	419
USA	47 754	7.82	18	0.95	1 534
Spain	43 403	7.11	110	4.67	614
Italy	34 087	5.58	59	2.57	872
UK	25 515	4.18	43	1.64	785
China	23 770	3.89	2	1.14	508
Poland	19 520	3.20	50	6.25	445
Mexico	19 351	3.17	21	2.18	392
Canada	17 285	2.83	57	1.50	507
Hungary	17 248	2.82	170	5.74	150
Czech Rep.	16 830	2.76	163	6.82	217
Austria	16 647	2.73	206	5.49	744
Germany	15 837	2.59	19	0.71	1 042
Russia	15 350	2.51	10	1.71	450
Switzerland	10 600	1.74	146	2.52	745

Source: World Tourism Organization; UNPD; World Bank.

TOP SPENDERS ON TOURISM, 1997

	Expenditure Million US$	% of world expenditure
USA	51 220	13.56
Germany	46 200	12.23
Japan	33 041	8.75
UK	27 710	7.34
Italy	16 631	4.40
France	16 576	4.39
Canada	11 304	2.99
Austria	10 992	2.91
Netherlands	10 232	2.71
China	10 166	2.69
Russia	10 113	2.68
Belgium	8 275	2.19
Switzerland	6 904	1.83
Poland	6 900	1.83
Brazil	6 583	1.74

Source: World Tourism Organization.

SELECTED TOURIST FLOWS, 1998
Thousands

From	Mediter-ranean	To Carib-bean	South-east Asia
Africa	3 367	8	174
Americas	12 406	9 726	1 973
Europe	151 981	3 549	4 501
East Asia and Pacific	5 959	70	22 372
Middle East	2 886	2	183
Total*	187 399	15 286	30 538

From	USA	To China	Europe+
Africa	234	38	608
Americas	28 143	809	6 984
Europe	10 735	2 039	87 790
East Asia and Pacific	8 201	20 733	3 823
Middle East	206	21	511
Total*	47 754	23 770	119 832

* Includes numbers not specified here
+ North, East and Central

Source: World Tourism Organization.

far from clear. Though nominally economic migrants, many of the estimated 1 million people who flood illegally into the United States annually from Mexico are in part driven by declining ecological conditions in a country where 60 percent of the land is classified as severely degraded[6]. Likewise, an estimated 1.3 million Haitians have fled their deforested and degraded island in the past two decades.

Mass migration frequently causes environmental damage on a similar scale. The desperate hand-to-mouth existence of many migrants, coupled with the likelihood that their settlement will be temporary, encourages a short-term attitude to their new surroundings. Rwandan refugees destroyed large areas of forest in neighboring Zaire (now the Democratic Republic of Congo) in the mid-1990s. Even state-sponsored migrants often find that the land set aside for them is insufficient to make a living. Surrounding natural resources, such as forests, are plundered in the immediate interests of survival. Examples include migrants from large Brazilian cities to the Amazon and Indonesia's transmigrants, who are a major cause of illegal deforestation in Kalimantan, Irian Jaya and other receiving regions.

Another major form of migration is business and leisure travel, by some measures the world's largest industry, accounting for 11 percent of global GDP[7] and a similar proportion of world employment. Tourism and business travel are temporary migrations with a growing global environmental impact. Civil aircraft alone are responsible for 5 percent of anthropogenic sources of greenhouse gases.

International tourism displaces the environmental impacts of rich nations to the often poorer destinations favored by holiday-makers. Those impacts can sometimes be beneficial. In many parts of the world, tourism sustains natural ecosystems and populations of wildlife by providing a strong financial incentive for their preservation. Examples include the elephant and gorilla parks of Africa and the coral reefs of the Caribbean.

But equally the pressures of mass tourism may destroy what the tourists come to see. In Nepal, trekkers burn about 6 kilos of wood each per day in a country desperately short of fuel. A big hotel in Cairo uses as much electricity as 3 600 middle-income households. In the Caribbean, tourist demand for seafood is a prime cause of the decline of lobster and conch populations, while cruise ships are calculated to produce 70 000 tons of waste a year[8].

The natural ecosystems of the Mediterranean, already under stress from local populations, are further damaged by the region's status as the destination of almost a third of all cross-border tourism. Typical is Malta, which receives a million tourists a year – three times its permanent population – turning the whole island into a peri-urban area and exhausting local water supplies.

Concern about such damage has fostered a growing interest in "ecotourism". The fastest growing sector of the business in the 1990s, it is intended to maximize the local social benefits from tourism, provide incentives for conservation and minimize environmental damage[9]. Well designed programs can encourage tour operators and hoteliers to invest in renewable energy and waste reduction measures, as well as involve the tourists themselves in local conservation initiatives. But badly designed ecotourism can have the reverse effect – for example expelling inhabitants from their land to provide parkland for animals and using scarce "natural" construction materials to provide authentic tourist experiences.

Urbanization

FOR THE FIRST time in history humans are predominantly urban. Cities occupy less than 2 percent of the Earth's land surface, but house almost half of the human population and use 75 percent of the resources we take from the Earth[1].

The statistics of urban growth in the late 20th century surpass any other demographic indicators. The proportion of the world's population that lives in cities rose from 29 percent in 1950 to 47 percent in 1998, and 55 percent is anticipated by 2015. Although two thirds of urban residents live in cities of less than a million people, megacities with a population of more than 10 million are on the increase. In 1975 there were five, by 1995 there were 15 and by 2015 there are expected to be 26.

Some modern megacities have an ancient history. Cairo, Istanbul (Constantinople) and Baghdad began the second millennium as they ended it – among the world's top 20 cities. But as industrialization has moved around the globe the roll call amongst the top ten has changed. At the start of the 20th century, these were all in the wealthy and rapidly industrializing North. By 2015 Tokyo and New York alone will remain, to be joined by cities from the developing world, which has seen a sixfold increase in urban populations in just 50 years.

Cities grow around activities best carried out centrally, such as government, manufacturing, wholesaling and ports. They are encouraged by the development of new services such as banking and the accumulation of skilled labor, by the opportunities to socialize and enjoy recreation and cultural activities, and by the value of cities as centers for national and international communication.

Large numbers of people are flocking to cities in search of work as the mechanization of farming is reducing the demand for labor in the countryside. China has a "floating population" of 80 million rural people who have moved to the cities in recent years[2]. Between a third and a fifth of the residents of its two largest cities, Shanghai and Beijing, are migrants[3].

The globalization of industry and trade is further stimulating urbanization, and cities are undoubted economic powerhouses. The World Bank estimates that urban areas in the developing world account for between 65 and 80 percent of national GDP (roughly double what might be expected from their populations). Sao Paulo alone contributes 40 percent of Brazil's GDP.

Cities represent, for many, the good life. On average, urban dwellers have higher incomes and live healthier, easier lives than their rural counterparts[4]. Surveys in 17 countries show that urban children under two have a 25 percent better chance of survival to adulthood than rural children[5].

But the benefits are not universal. While on the whole urban populations have greater access to clean water and sanitation than their rural counterparts, between a quarter and a half of urban inhabitants in developing countries live in slums and squatter settlements with extremely limited services. Such overcrowding encourages epidemics of tuberculosis, diarrhea and other communicable diseases[6]. In Karachi, a city of 10 million people and growing by half a million a year, 40 percent of the population lives in squatter colonies and one in five babies do not reach their first birthday. Worldwide, more than a billion people live in urban areas where air pollution exceeds

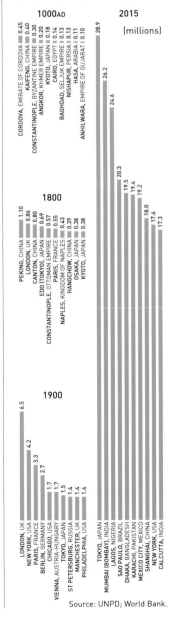

CITIES IN TIME

1000AD

CORDOVA, EMIRATE OF CORDOVA 0.45
KAIFENG, CHINA 0.40
CONSTANTINOPLE, BYZANTINE EMPIRE 0.30
ANGKOR, KHMER EMPIRE 0.20
KYOTO, JAPAN 0.18
CAIRO, EGYPT 0.14
BAGHDAD, SELJUK EMPIRE 0.13
NISHAPUR, PERSIA 0.13
HASA, ARABIA 0.11
ANHILWARA, EMPIRE OF GUJARAT 0.10

1800

PEKING, CHINA 1.10
LONDON, UK 0.86
CANTON, CHINA 0.80
EDO (TOKYO), JAPAN 0.69
CONSTANTINOPLE, OTTOMAN EMPIRE 0.57
PARIS, FRANCE 0.55
NAPLES, KINGDOM OF NAPLES 0.43
HANGCHOW, CHINA 0.39
OSAKA, JAPAN 0.38
KYOTO, JAPAN 0.38

1900

LONDON, UK 6.5
NEW YORK, USA 4.2
PARIS, FRANCE 3.3
BERLIN, GERMANY 2.7
CHICAGO, USA 1.7
VIENNA, AUSTRIA-HUNGARY 1.7
TOKYO, JAPAN 1.5
ST PETERSBURG, RUSSIA 1.4
MANCHESTER, UK 1.4
PHILADELPHIA, USA 1.4

2015 (millions)

TOKYO, JAPAN 28.9
MUMBAI (BOMBAY), INDIA 26.2
LAGOS, NIGERIA 24.6
SAO PAULO, BRAZIL 20.3
DHAKA, BANGLADESH 19.5
KARACHI, PAKISTAN 19.4
MEXICO CITY, MEXICO 19.2
SHANGHAI, CHINA 18.0
NEW YORK, USA 17.6
CALCUTTA, INDIA 17.3

Source: UNPD; World Bank.

THE WORLD'S LARGEST CITIES

	Population Millions		Rank in
	2015	1996	1996
Tokyo	28.9	27.2	1
Mumbai*	26.2	15.7	5
Lagos*	24.6	10.9	12
Sao Paulo	20.3	16.8	3
Dhaka*	19.5	9.0	22
Karachi*	19.4	10.1	16
Mexico City	19.2	16.9	2
Shanghai	18.0	13.7	6
New York	17.6	16.4	4
Calcutta	17.3	12.1	8
Delhi*	16.9	10.3	14
Beijing	15.6	11.4	11
Metro Manila*	14.7	9.6	18
Cairo	14.4	9.9	17
Los Angeles	14.2	12.6	7
Buenos Aires	13.9	11.9	9
Jakarta*	13.9	8.8	23
Tianjin	13.5	9.6	19
Seoul	13.0	11.8	10
Istanbul*	12.3	8.2	24
Rio de Janeiro	11.9	10.3	15
Hangzhou*	11.4	4.6	42
Osaka	10.6	10.6	13
Hyderabad*	10.5	5.7	34
Tehran	10.3	6.9	26
Lahore*	10.0	5.2	36
Bangkok	9.8	6.7	29
Paris	9.7	9.6	20
Lima	9.4	6.8	28
Kinshasa*	9.4	4.4	47
Moscow	9.3	9.3	21
Madras*	9.2	6.1	32
Changchun*	8.9	4.4	44
Bogota	8.4	6.2	31
Harbin*	8.1	4.7	40
Bangalore*	8.0	5.0	39

* Cities which will have increased their populations by more than 50% between 1996 and 2015

Source: UNPD.

URBAN GROWTH RATES

Even though urban populations are rising rapidly, urban growth rates are slowing down

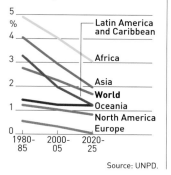

Source: UNPD.

WORLD CITIES, LATE 1990s

■ **1-2 million inhabitants**

■ **2-3 million inhabitants**

■ **3-5 million inhabitants**

■ **5-10 million inhabitants**

□ **More than 10 million**

The proportion of the world's population that lives in cities rose from 29 percent in 1950 to 47 percent in 1998, and 55 percent is anticipated by 2015.

URBAN POPULATIONS BY REGION, 2000

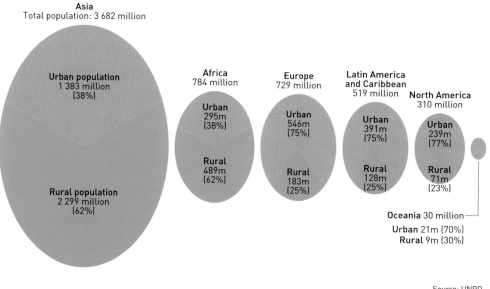

Asia
Total population: 3 682 million

Urban population 1 383 million (38%)

Rural population 2 299 million (62%)

Africa 784 million

Urban 295m (38%)

Rural 489m (62%)

Europe 729 million

Urban 546m (75%)

Rural 183m (25%)

Latin America and Caribbean 519 million

Urban 391m (75%)

Rural 128m (25%)

North America 310 million

Urban 239m (77%)

Rural 71m (23%)

Oceania 30 million
Urban 21m (70%)
Rural 9m (30%)

Source: UNPD.

RURAL AND URBAN POPULATION TRENDS

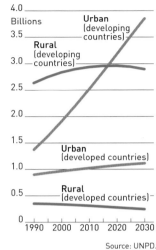

Source: UNPD.

Source: UNPD.

POPULATIONS WITH ACCESS TO WATER AND SANITATION, 1990s

Safe drinking water

	% urban access	% rural access
Middle East and North Africa	97	72
Sub-Saharan Africa	77	39
South Asia	86	78
East Asia and Pacific	95	58
Latin America and Caribbean	88	42
World	**90**	**62**

Sanitation

	% urban access	% rural access
Middle East and North Africa	92	53
Sub-Saharan Africa	70	35
South Asia	73	20
East Asia and Pacific	77	20
Latin America and Caribbean	82	44
World	**79**	**25**

Source: UNICEF.

EDUCATIONAL LEVELS, FERTILITY AND UNDER-FIVE MORTALITY RATES, 1992-98
Selected countries

	% with secondary education*		Total fertility rate+		Under-five mortality++	
	Urban	Rural	Urban	Rural	Urban	Rural
Bolivia	72.2	20.8	3.3	6.3	71.9	134.3
Brazil	68.6	31.3	2.3	3.5	49.1	79.4
Dominican Rep.	54.3	22.2	2.8	4.0	54.7	70.0
Nicaragua	58.1	18.0	2.9	4.9	48.8	64.3
Kenya	49.4	23.1	3.1	5.1	88.3	108.6
Madagascar	52.6	16.8	4.2	6.5	127.1	173.8
Mozambique	13.9	1.4	4.6	5.2	150.4	236.9
Togo	32.4	7.7	3.2	6.1	101.3	157.4
Bangladesh	42.2	15.0	2.1	3.4	96.2	130.9
Philippines	82.0	59.6	3.0	4.6	45.8	62.5
Uzbekistan	99.7	99.6	2.7	3.7	51.8	56.8
Vietnam	81.3	62.3	1.6	2.5	30.4	48.3

* Or beyond + Number of children a woman would be expected to have at current trends
++ Deaths per thousand live births

Source: World Bank.

acceptable levels[7]. The death toll from lung disease associated with urban air pollution could be half a million a year in China alone. The notorious traffic congestion in Bangkok costs an estimated 2 percent of Thailand's GDP. Cities can also be violent. The greatest causes of death among young people in Sao Paulo are traffic accidents and homicide.

Cities also have a large ecological "footprint". They call on resources over a wide area to provide food and raw materials. Vancouver's half a million people consume resources from an estimated 2 million hectares – 200 times the area of the city itself[8]. London's footprint is 120 times the size of the city, drawing on resources from the wheat prairies of Kansas, the tea gardens of Assam and the copper mines of Zambia among other places[9]. Locally, cities put huge strains on natural ecosystems, polluting rivers and coastal waters, consuming forests and water, degrading soils, disrupting drainage and stunting crops. Urban smog and acid deposition in China are estimated to be reducing crop yields by up to a third[10].

Cities stop growing if and when the problems of congestion and pollution overwhelm the benefits, making the cities inefficient as well as unpleasant. Smoggy and congested Mexico City was once expected to grow to more than 30 million people by the year 2000, but was at around half that in 1996 and is not expected to be above 20 million in 2015[11]. And even while cities are still growing rapidly in the developing world, the growth rates themselves are on a downward trend.

In the developed world, many cities are losing population as fertility rates fall below replacement levels and inhabitants leave for more attractive suburbs or rural areas. Good transportation systems and electronic communications encourage this. One result has been the formation of large low-density peri-urban zones, sometimes embracing several cities to create polycentric urban areas, such as the Japanese urban heartland between Tokyo and Osaka, the Rhine-Ruhr region of Europe and the east coast of the United States from Boston via New York to Washington DC.

The critical question for cities is whether the wealth they generate can justify their large ecological footprint, and whether development policies can reduce that footprint. A well-run urban sector can ensure national prosperity; a badly run sector can become a drag on the whole country. And cities do have potential advantages. Well-planned cities can utilize high population densities to minimize resource use and energy consumption – by developing mass transit systems to supplement car use, for instance[12]. In developed and developing country alike, many cities include large areas of productive agricultural land amid the highways and high-rise. It is estimated that up to a fifth of the world's food is grown in "urban" areas. Other cities, particularly in Western Europe, are investing large sums in recycling and composting as part of ambitious waste-management programs.

Moreover, while city dwellers do tend to use more resources, they have fewer children and thus help drive down national rates of population growth. Children that may have been a boon in villages helping work the land become a burden in cities, where they need to be educated if they are to find gainful employment[13].

THE AUTOMOBILE

With urbanization, and especially with urban sprawl, comes the automobile. Motorized transport becomes essential for commuting, shopping and many other activities, and as public transport is often poor, most people aspire to own a vehicle. In 1998 the world automobile fleet exceeded 500 million for the first time – one for every 12 of the world's people and ten times the figure of half a century ago. Two thirds are in Western Europe and North America. One countervailing trend is that some rich, developed nations can afford such good urban mass transit systems that people prefer them to driving cars in congested city streets, while poorer services in more thinly populated rural areas lead to greater car ownership and heavier use than in cities.

Population and atmosphere

P EOPLE have been altering the atmosphere on a small scale ever since they learnt to make fire. But today's fires and industrial processes create so much smoke, gas and particulate matter that they can degrade ecosystems hundreds of kilometers away and threaten to transform climate worldwide.

Wherever humans have lived in dense settlements, pollution from smoke and gases has been a problem. The first attempt to ban coal burning to reduce smoke in London was in 1273[1]. But during the industrial age the amount of fossil-fuel burning – in the form of coal, oil and gas – has risen steeply. All these fuels generate smoke and gaseous compounds when burnt, producing a series of chemical reactions with oxygen in the air to create sulfur dioxide (SO_2), oxides of nitrogen (NO_x) and carbon dioxide (CO_2). Between 1800 and the mid-1990s, the world population increased sixfold, while global CO_2 emissions rose 800-fold over the same period, notably from burning fossil fuels[2]. Growing wealth and new fuel-burning technologies, particularly for generating electricity and powering the internal combustion engine, drove this.

Industrialization has also added to the range of pollutants in the air. A variety of synthetic compounds, invented mostly in the 20th century, are now widely dispersed in the atmosphere. These include certain pesticides and compounds containing chlorine and bromine used as inert gases in refrigerators and sprays and as solvents. The volume of all these emissions to the air, and the persistence of some of them, has caused their build-up and transformation in the atmosphere to levels that cause ecological damage on a wide, and sometimes global, scale.

SO_2 and NO_x both acidify water droplets in the air. The resulting acid deposition (through rain, fog or snow) may fall locally or travel long distances in clouds. Below a pH of 4, it can acidify soils and leach metals from them, poisoning trees. And it can make lakes and streams too acidic for some fish, such as the brown trout. In the 19th century, European acidification of ecosystems was confined to regions close to industrial centers such as the German Hartz mountains and the English Pennines, where tree growth became patchy. But in the mid-20th century increased fossil-fuel burning caused the first internationally recognized case of transboundary air pollution – with German, British and Polish pollution causing acid deposition and fish deaths, particularly in Scandinavia[3].

In other atmospheric chemical transformations, NO_x reacts with hydrocarbons in sunlight to create a new range of photochemical pollutants, notably low-level ozone, the component of smog most dangerous to human health and crops[4]. Atmospheric emissions of nitrogen compounds also add to those from intensive agriculture, sewage discharges and the cultivation of leguminous crops to disrupt the global nitrogen cycle, causing overfertilization of both marine and terrestrial ecosystems[5].

In the latter half of the 20th century, it became clear that other pollutants were accumulating globally. Pesticides such as DDT and toxaphene, and industrial synthetic compounds such as polychlorinated biphenyls (PCBs), collectively known as persistent organic pollutants (POPs),

THE TEN BIGGEST PER-CAPITA CO$_2$ EMITTERS, 1995

	Emissions* Metric tons	GDP per capita US$ 1995
United Arab Emirates	30.9	17 696
Kuwait	28.8	15 760
USA	20.5	26 026
Singapore	19.1	25 156
Norway	16.7	33 692
Australia	16.2	19 522
Canada	14.8	19 350
Saudi Arabia	13.9	6 875
Trinidad and Tobago	13.3	4 139
Kazakhstan	13.2	1 273

* From fossil-fuel burning and cement manufacture

Source: WRI.

CO$_2$ EMISSIONS
Kilos of carbon per square kilometer

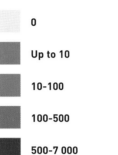

0

Up to 10

10-100

100-500

500-7 000

The map shows the varying levels of CO$_2$ emissions around the world in 1995 as a result of fossil-fuel burning, cement production and gas flaring.

ATMOSPHERIC CONCENTRATIONS OF GREENHOUSE AND OZONE-DEPLETING GASES

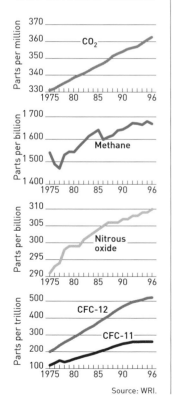

Source: WRI.

THE RISE OF CO$_2$, 1850-1995
Global emissions from fossil-fuel burning and cement manufacture

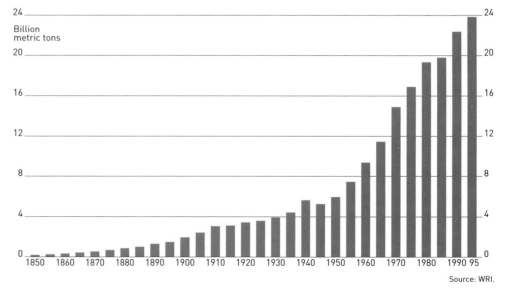

Source: WRI.

Source: CDIAC.

PER-CAPITA CO$_2$ EMISSIONS, 1995
By region

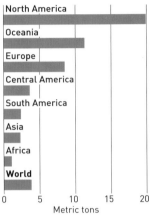

Metric tons

Source: WRI.

THE OZONE HOLE
South polar minimum ozone, September 10, 2000

On September 10, 2000, NASA recorded the biggest ever area of minimum Dobson units of ozone, measuring around 28.4 million square kilometers. Later that month, an all-time low of only 98 Dobson units was recorded, though over a smaller area.

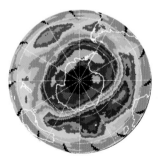

Dobson units of ozone

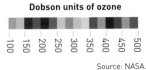

Source: NASA.

OZONE DEPLETION AND SKIN CANCER
Levels of risk under the Montreal Protocol

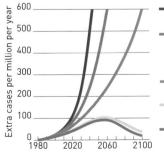

Extra cases per million per year

— No restriction on ozone-depleting substances

— Montreal Protocol on Substances that Deplete the Ozone Layer 1987

— London Amendments 1990

— Copenhagen Amendments 1992

— Montreal Amendments 1997

Source: EEA.

OZONE LOSSES AND UV-B INCREASES, 1998

	% ozone loss	% UV-B increase
Northern hemisphere, mid-latitudes		
winter/spring	6	7
summer/fall	3	4
Southern hemisphere, mid-latitudes		
year-round	5	6
Antarctic spring	50	130
Arctic spring	15	22

Note: Figures are approximate and assume that other factors, such as cloud cover, are constant.

Source: UNEP.

GLOBAL DISTILLATION: THE MIGRATION PROCESS OF POPs

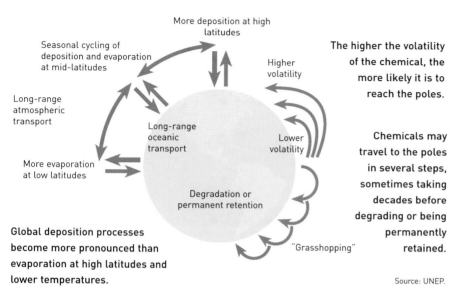

More deposition at high latitudes

Seasonal cycling of deposition and evaporation at mid-latitudes

Higher volatility

Long-range atmospheric transport

Long-range oceanic transport

Lower volatility

More evaporation at low latitudes

Degradation or permanent retention

"Grasshopping"

The higher the volatility of the chemical, the more likely it is to reach the poles.

Chemicals may travel to the poles in several steps, sometimes taking decades before degrading or being permanently retained.

Global deposition processes become more pronounced than evaporation at high latitudes and lower temperatures.

Source: UNEP.

have been recognized as dangerous since the early 1960s – they are toxic, soluble in fat, and accumulate in body tissue[6]. But in the 1990s two further concerns emerged: first that they are "endocrine disrupters", disrupting hormone systems and threatening the health of both wildlife and humans[7]; and, secondly, that many are now accumulating in ecosystems globally – sometimes at higher concentrations than are present where they are first released. In a process known as "global distillation", many of these substances evaporate into the air where they are released and then preferentially settle out in the colder air of the polar regions. Though global emissions of most POPs are falling, their presence in Arctic ecosystems continues to rise and concentrations in the diets of some Arctic inhabitants exceed tolerable daily intakes[8]. POPs are currently the subject of negotiations intended to bring them under a global agreement, with some being phased out and others tightly controlled.

Chlorofluorocarbons (CFCs), halons and other chlorine and bromine compounds were identified as a potential threat to stratospheric ozone in the 1970s. By the late 1980s, they had thinned the ozone layer at all latitudes by around 5 percent, and, in the freezing air over the Arctic and Antarctic, created ozone "holes" in which 50 to 80 percent of the ozone was destroyed for several weeks each spring[9].

The current use of ozone-depleting chemicals is strongly regulated by international political agreement – notably the Montreal Protocol of 1987 – which called for production phase-out in the developed world by 1996, with a more gradual phase-out in developing countries. Though production phase-out in developed nations has been partly counterbalanced by growing production in developing nations, particularly China, production in these countries has been frozen at 1999 levels and must be phased out for most uses by 2009[10]. The ozone layer itself will take another half century to recover.

The most fundamental effect of atmospheric pollution has been on the global carbon cycle. Carbon is a key element for life. It makes up half the mass of plants and animals[11] and, as CO_2, it is a major "greenhouse gas" responsible for maintaining the atmospheric temperature at levels fit for those organisms.

In the past 150 years, human activity has released more than 350 billion tons of carbon into the air in the form of CO_2. Though up to a half is currently absorbed by oceans or terrestrial ecosystems, this has been sufficient to raise CO_2 concentrations in the air by 30 percent since pre-industrial times[12]. Carbon is also present in the second most important anthropogenic greenhouse gas, methane, produced in agricultural activities such as rice paddies, the domestication of ruminants and the clearance of natural vegetation. The industrial age has seen a 145 percent rise in methane concentrations in the atmosphere[13].

The cumulative effect of different air pollution is reducing the atmosphere's ability to cleanse itself. Most pollutants are removed from the atmosphere through oxidation by the hydroxyl radical. Some research suggests that hydroxyl levels in the atmosphere, particularly temperate northern latitudes, are falling[14]. As a result, some compounds are lasting longer in the air than before, causing ever more pollution.

Climate change

T HE WORLD is warming up. Average temperatures are half a degree centigrade higher than a century ago. The nine warmest years this century have all occurred since 1980, and the 1990s were probably the warmest decade of the second millennium[1]. Pollution from "greenhouse gases" such as carbon dioxide (CO_2) and methane is at least partly to blame.

The UN's Intergovernmental Panel on Climate Change (IPCC) concluded in 1995 that "the balance of evidence suggests a discernible human influence on global climate"; and that the accumulations of greenhouse gases are behind the marked global warming trend of the past 20 years. Its case was based on two pillars: the known physical heat-capturing properties of the greenhouse gases that are accumulating in the atmosphere, and the detailed patterns of average temperature change in the atmosphere, which mirrored that predicted by global climate models.

Emission rates for the most important anthropogenic greenhouse gas, CO_2, have risen 120-fold in the past 150 years[2]. Whereas in the 19th century emissions were overwhelmingly from deforestation and other landuse changes, they are now predominantly from burning fossil fuels. A direct product of industrialization, emissions now amount to 6 billion tons of carbon a year, or around 1 ton of carbon per head of the world's population. But emissions are very uneven. Per-capita North American emissions are 18 times those of Africa, nine times those of Asia and 2.3 times those of Europe[3]. Low gasoline prices and the pervasive automobile culture in the United States ensure that its CO_2 output, already the highest in the world, is continuing to rise, while levels in much of Europe are stable or falling.

Total emissions of greenhouse gases, including CO_2 from deforestation and agricultural emissions of methane, are more evenly distributed. For instance, Germany emits three times more CO_2 than Brazil from burning fossil fuels. But Brazil's total emissions of greenhouse gases now probably exceed Germany's, thanks largely to emissions from deforestation[4].

Unless the world curbs growing CO_2 output, concentrations in the air are likely to double from pre-industrial levels by 2080, and may warm the world by 3°C. Climate models predict that land areas will warm twice as much as the oceans; high latitudes will warm more quickly in winter; and there will be substantial changes in precipitation, especially in the tropics[5].

There is a high risk of extreme weather, including intense El Niño events in the Pacific Ocean, hurricanes in coastal areas and droughts in continental interiors. Rising sea levels as glaciers and ice sheets melt, and thermal expansion of the oceans, may inundate heavily populated coastal regions, such as large parts of Bangladesh and eastern China and some island nations, such as the Maldives[6]. Sea levels are already committed to a substantial rise, probably of 1 or 2 meters over the next 500 years, as a result of warming to date, which will slowly penetrate to the ocean depths, causing thermal expansion as it goes[7].

Possible ecological impacts include the destruction of most of the Amazon rainforest (from

CONTRIBUTION OF DIFFERENT GASES TO GLOBAL WARMING, 1997

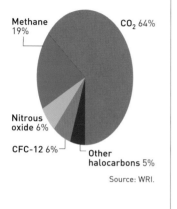

Methane 19%

CO₂ 64%

Nitrous oxide 6%

CFC-12 6%

Other halocarbons 5%

Source: WRI.

CONTRIBUTION OF HUMAN ACTIVITIES TO CO₂ EMISSIONS, 1995

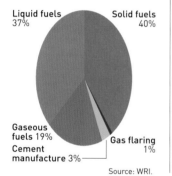

Liquid fuels 37%

Solid fuels 40%

Gaseous fuels 19%

Gas flaring 1%

Cement manufacture 3%

Source: WRI.

CHANGES IN TEMPERATURE AND SOIL HUMIDITY ESTIMATED FOR 2025 Northern hemisphere winter

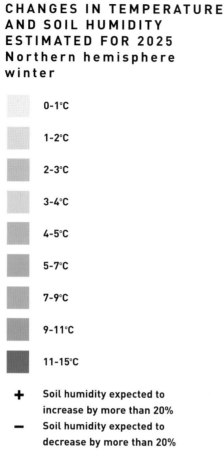

0-1°C

1-2°C

2-3°C

3-4°C

4-5°C

5-7°C

7-9°C

9-11°C

11-15°C

+ Soil humidity expected to increase by more than 20%

− Soil humidity expected to decrease by more than 20%

Note: Temperature increases in the Antarctic region are predicted to fall into the 0-4°C range.

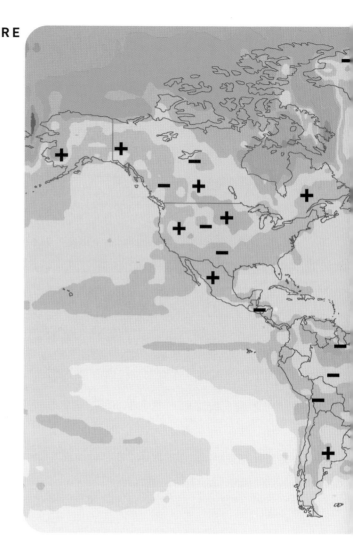

Unusually wet

Unusually dry

Associated disease outbreaks

■ Rift valley fever

■ Malaria

■ Hantavirus

■ Encephalitis

■ Dengue

■ Cholera

Respiratory illness resulting from:

■ Heatwave

■ Fire and smoke

PRECIPITATION ANOMALIES AND DISEASE OUTBREAKS 1997-98

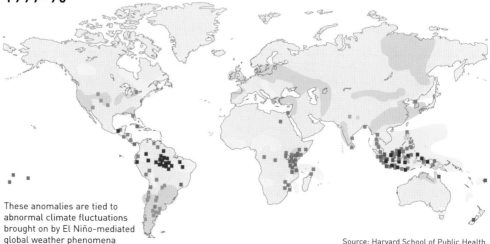

These anomalies are tied to abnormal climate fluctuations brought on by El Niño-mediated global weather phenomena

Source: Harvard School of Public Health.

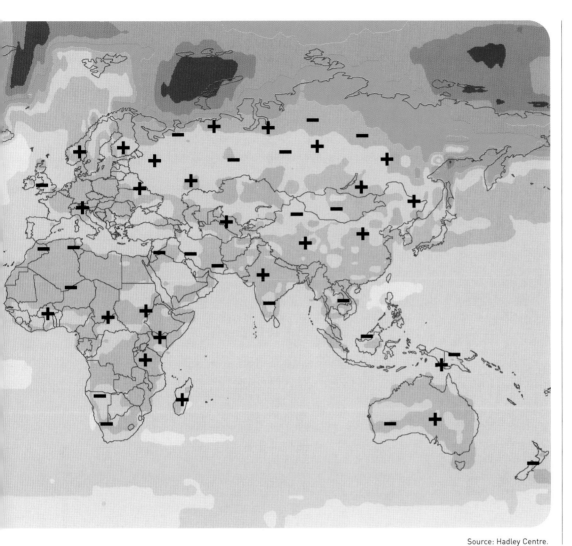

Source: Hadley Centre.

KYOTO PROTOCOL
Target reductions in greenhouse-gas emissions, by 2012

	Target change from 1990 emissions (%)
Australia	+8
Bulgaria	-8
Canada	-6
Croatia	-5
Estonia	-8
European Union	-8
Hungary	-6
Iceland	+10
Japan	-6
Latvia	-8
Liechtenstein	-8
Lithuania	-8
Monaco	-8
New Zealand	0
Norway	+1
Poland	-6
Romania	-8
Russia	0
Slovakia	-8
Slovenia	-8
Switzerland	-8
Ukraine	0
USA	-7

The Protocol aims to cut the combined emissions of greenhouse gases from developed countries by roughly 5 percent from their 1990 levels by 2008-12, and it specifies the amount each industrialized nation must contribute toward meeting that reduction goal. Nations with the highest CO_2 emissions are expected to reduce emissions the most.

Source: UN.

GLOBAL TEMPERATURE ANOMALIES

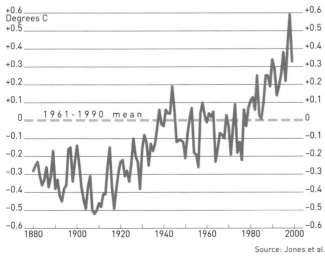

Source: Jones et al.

GLOBAL SEA-LEVEL RISE
Estimated and predicted

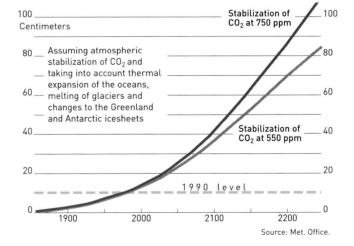

Stabilization of CO_2 at 750 ppm

Assuming atmospheric stabilization of CO_2 and taking into account thermal expansion of the oceans, melting of glaciers and changes to the Greenland and Antarctic icesheets

Stabilization of CO_2 at 550 ppm

1990 level

Source: Met. Office.

Long-term effects

Because CO_2 has a lifetime in the atmosphere of more than a century, historic emissions are important to current concentrations of the gas in the atmosphere. Over the past 200 years, North America, Europe and the former Soviet Union, currently with 20 percent of the world's population, have contributed 80 percent of CO_2 emissions[15].

warming and drying) by the end of the 21st century. The loss of forests globally will further accelerate the emissions of CO_2 into the air, exacerbating climate change. Recent modelling studies suggest that changes in rainfall and evaporation rates are likely to cause a decline in runoff of 25 percent or more in much of Southern Africa, South and Central America, India, Australia and the Mediterranean basin. But runoff could increase by similar amounts in the United States, China and the catchment of the Aral Sea in Central Asia[8].

Warming is also likely to spread pests and diseases to new regions. Nearly two thirds of the world's population could be living in malaria transmission zones within a century[9]. Declining rainfall and a low technical capacity to adapt are likely to cause falling crop yields in much of Africa and India.

There is also increasing concern about the risk of major climatic "surprises". Warming might reduce the strength of the North Atlantic ocean circulation through the 21st century, with possible collapse of the Gulf Stream and cooling of Western Europe in the 22nd century[10].

In general, fossil-fuel emissions of greenhouse gases and consumption by consumers go hand-in-hand: the richest nations have the highest emissions. But there is growing evidence that fossil-fuel emissions can be "delinked" from population size and economic activity. One route is a change in energy-generating technology. France generates most of its electricity from nuclear power and has per-capita emissions of CO_2 less than two thirds those of its neighbor, the United Kingdom. Another is more efficient use of energy. China has halved its energy consumption per unit of economic output since 1980 by cutting subsidies to coal, the most polluting fuel[11].

The first serious effort to curb emissions of CO_2 and other greenhouse gases was behind the Kyoto Protocol of 1997, with most industrialized nations agreeing to cut emissions of six greenhouse gases by around 5 percent by 2012. Flexibility mechanisms will allow them to meet the targets by investing in emissions reduction or carbon-sink enhancing projects (such as planting forests) in other countries. Recent research has suggested that the inclusion of projects to cut the atmospheric build-up of greenhouse gases other than CO_2, notably methane, could cut the cost of meeting the Kyoto Protocol by 60 percent[12].

The European Union has proposed that, in the longer run, the world should aim to prevent greenhouse gas emissions rising above twice pre-industrial levels. There is no single route to achieve this. Scenarios suggested by the IPCC involve a rise in global emissions of about 25 percent in the next half-century (compared to a doubling likely if conditions at the time of the Kyoto Protocol persisted unaltered) before falling back to less than half current emissions.

Signs that this may be possible without dramatic damage to economic development emerged during the late 1990s, when global CO_2 emissions did not rise in line with growing economic activity. This was due largely to increased fuel efficiency and a declining use of coal[13]. A new IPCC assessment on future emission scenarios foresees a long-term "delinking" of CO_2 emissions from wealth and population: "Technology is at least as important a driving force of future greenhouse gas emissions as population and economic development." Some scenarios with a world population of 15 billion had lower emissions than others with a population of 7 billion[14].

Air pollution

D URING the 20th century air pollution, once a localized problem, became a global one. Nowhere is immune from toxic fallout or changes to the planet's atmospheric chemistry. Even so, the most intense effects on both ecosystems and human health are local.

Approximately half of the world's population now lives in urban areas, and half of all the world's urban residents are exposed to potentially harmful amounts of sulfur dioxide (SO_2), ozone and particulate matter in "smogs"[1]. The chemistry of smogs takes different forms. Winter smogs largely arise from burning coal to warm buildings during cold weather. When the smoke and SO_2 combine with fog in windless weather they create a pollution cap that the sun is not strong enough to clear.

Some 4 000 people died from lung and heart conditions during a London "peasouper" smog in December 1952. Similar smogs now occur regularly in northern Chinese and Indian cities, including Delhi and Beijing. China's smogs cause more than 50 000 premature deaths and 400 000 new cases of chronic bronchitis a year in 11 of its largest cities alone[2].

Summer smogs, first reported in Los Angeles, involve pollutants – mainly from vehicle exhausts – that undergo photochemical changes in bright sunlight, creating substances such as ozone, a gas that can trigger asthma attacks. Conditions are worst in thin air at higher altitudes and if the air is trapped inside a valley. Both situations apply in Mexico City, the world's second largest urban agglomeration, where smog alerts close factories and force cars off city streets several times a year. Globally, some 50 percent of cases of chronic respiratory illness are now thought to be associated with air pollution[3].

A particularly toxic component in some urban air is lead, the heavy metal which has for many years been added to gasoline to raise octane levels and help engines run more smoothly. It is emitted as tiny particles in exhausts, contaminating both air and food. Elevated lead levels are widespread among children in cities where leaded petrol is sold. Lead damages the neurological development of children, lowering IQ and causing attention and behavioral problems. Many nations have reduced or banned lead additives. Elsewhere, urban areas can have high lead con-tamination even with relatively low vehicle numbers. Lead levels in the air of large African cities such as Cairo, Cape Town and Lagos are up to ten times those typical of European cities[4].

Analysts at the World Bank argue that exposure to lead is due less to urban demographics, vehicle numbers or national wealth and more to direct political choice. The Bank says that removing lead from gasoline is one of the most cost-effective ways of improving both the urban environment and human health[5].

Smogs are generally very acidic. Some of the pollutants they contain travel long distances on the winds, causing acid deposition in surrounding countryside and even in neighboring countries. In the 1980s, "acid rain" was identified as a major international environmental problem, spilling over from densely populated and heavily industrialized areas of both Europe and North America

Atmospheric chemistry

Humankind has been manipulating atmospheric chemistry on a small scale, usually accidentally, for many centuries. Urban areas contain enough heat-absorbing construction material to keep cities warmer than surrounding areas. Sulfate particles in urban smog, on the other hand, reduce solar heating. Deforestation has upset the hydrological cycle, often reducing rainfall downwind. For half a century scientists have attempted, generally unsuccessfully, to "seed" clouds with tiny particles to encourage the formation of raindrops. In recent decades evidence has grown that humans are altering climate on the global scale by adding greenhouse gases to the atmosphere.

TOP VEHICLE-OWNING COUNTRIES, 1998

	Vehicles per thousand people	GNP per capita US$ 1998
USA	767	29 240
Australia	605	20 640
Italy	591	20 090
New Zealand	579	14 600
Canada	560	19 170
Japan	560	32 350
France	530	24 210
Germany	522	26 570
Austria	521	26 830
Switzerland	516	39 980
World	**116**	**4 890**
China	*8*	*750*
India	*7*	*440*

Source: World Bank.

GLOBAL DENSITY OF INDUSTRIAL FACILITIES, 1990s

Source: ESRI.

The maps show the most significant centers of manufacturing, taking into account the size of the labor force and the value of output.

COUNTRIES WITH THE GREATEST INCREASE IN OWNERSHIP OF VEHICLES, 1980-98

	Vehicles per thousand people 1980	1998	% increase 1980-98
Korea, Rep.	14	226	1 514
Thailand	13	103	692
Nigeria	4	26	550
China	2	8	300
Pakistan	2	8	300
Uganda	1	4	300
Turkey	23	81	252
India	2	7	250
Poland	86	273	217
Indonesia	8	22	175
Bolivia	19	52	174
Hungary	108	268	148
Greece	134	328	145
Portugal	145	347	139
Israel	123	264	115
Mauritius	44	92	109
Finland	228	448	96
Spain	239	467	95
Chile	61	110	80
Italy	334	591	77

Source: World Bank.

CITIES WITH REPORTED LEVELS OF ATMOSPHERIC POLLUTANTS ABOVE WHO GUIDELINES, 1990-95

Country	City	TSP	NO$_2$	SO$_2$	Country	City	TSP	NO$_2$	SO$_2$
		Micrograms per cubic meter					Micrograms per cubic meter		
Argentina	Cordoba City	97	97			Shenyang	374	73	99
Brazil	Rio de Janeiro	139		129		Taiyuan	568	55	211
	Sao Paulo		83			Tianjin	306	50	82
Bulgaria	Sofia	195	122			Urumqi	515	70	60
Chile	Santiago		81			Wuhan	211		
China	Anshan	305	88	115		Zhengzhou	474	95	63
	Beijing	377	122	90		Zibo	453		198
	Changchun	381	64		Colombia	Bogota	120		
	Chengdu	366	74	77	Denmark	Copenhagen		54	
	Chongquing	320	70	340	Ecuador	Guayaquil	127		
	Dalian	185	100	61		Quito	175		
	Guangzhu	295	136	57	Egypt	Cairo			69
	Guiyang	330	53	424	France	Paris		57	
	Harbin	359			Germany	Munich		53	
	Jinan	472		132	Ghana	Accra	137		
	Kunming	253			Greece	Athens	178	64	
	Lanzhou	732	104	102	Hungary	Budapest		51	
	Liupanshui	408		102	India	Ahmedabad	299		
	Nanchang	279		69		Bangalore	123		
	Pinxiang	276		75		Calcutta	375		
	Quingdao		64	190		Chennai	130		
	Shanghai	246	73	53		Delhi	415		

INDUSTRIAL FACILITIES IN EUROPE, 1990s

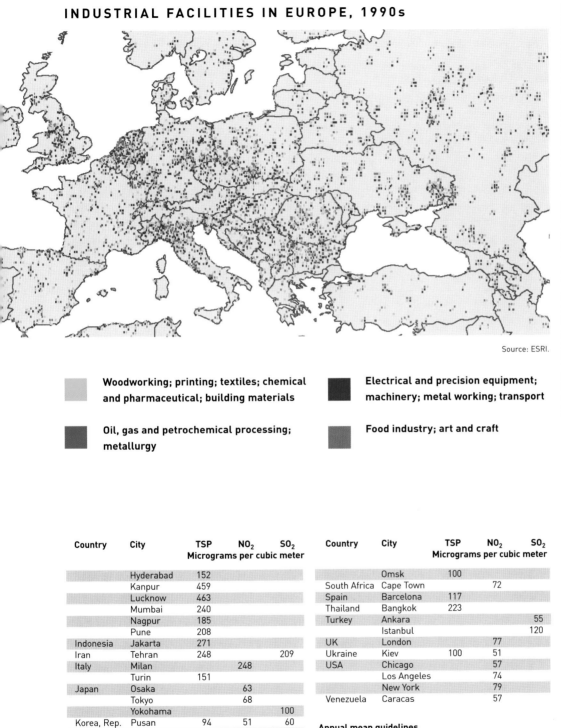

Source: ESRI.

Woodworking; printing; textiles; chemical and pharmaceutical; building materials

Electrical and precision equipment; machinery; metal working; transport

Oil, gas and petrochemical processing; metallurgy

Food industry; art and craft

SULFUR DEPOSITION IN THE EASTERN USA, 2000

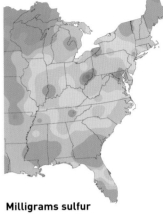

Milligrams sulfur per square meter

Less than 200
200-300
300-400
400-500
500-600
600-700
700-800
800-900
More than 900

Source: NADP/NTN.

Country	City	TSP	NO₂	SO₂
		Micrograms per cubic meter		
	Hyderabad	152		
	Kanpur	459		
	Lucknow	463		
	Mumbai	240		
	Nagpur	185		
	Pune	208		
Indonesia	Jakarta	271		
Iran	Tehran	248		209
Italy	Milan		248	
	Turin	151		
Japan	Osaka		63	
	Tokyo		68	
	Yokohama			100
Korea, Rep.	Pusan	94	51	60
	Seoul		60	
	Taegu		62	81
Mexico	Mexico City	279	130	74
Netherlands	Amsterdam		58	
Philippines	Manila	200		
Portugal	Lisbon		52	
Romania	Bucharest		71	
Russia	Moscow	100		109

Country	City	TSP	NO₂	SO₂
		Micrograms per cubic meter		
	Omsk	100		
South Africa	Cape Town		72	
Spain	Barcelona	117		
Thailand	Bangkok	223		
Turkey	Ankara			55
	Istanbul			120
UK	London		77	
Ukraine	Kiev	100	51	
USA	Chicago		57	
	Los Angeles		74	
	New York		79	
Venezuela	Caracas		57	

Annual mean guidelines
TSP: Total suspended particulates, 90 micrograms per cubic meter
NO₂: Nitrogen dioxide, 50 micrograms per cubic meter
SO₂: Sulfur dioxide, 50 micrograms per cubic meter
Where no figure is shown for the above, its concentrations are within WHO guidelines or are unavailable

Source: World Bank.

SO₂ EMISSIONS FROM FOSSIL-FUEL BURNING

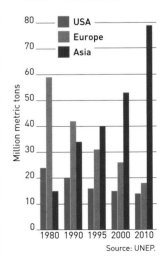

■ USA
■ Europe
■ Asia

Source: UNEP.

BIOMASS BURNING AND CO_2 EMISSIONS, 1990s

	Biomass burned* Million metric tons per year	Carbon released
Savannahs	3 690	1 660
Agricultural waste	2 020	910
Tropical forests	1 260	570
Fuelwood	1 430	640
Temperate and boreal forests	280	130
Charcoal	20	30
World	8 700	3 940

* Dry matter

Source: UNEP.

Researchers have only quite recently realized the importance of biomass burning in overall emissions of greenhouse gases. More than half of the carbon released into the atmosphere comes from biomass burning, the remainder being produced by fossil-fuel burning, cement manufacture and gas flaring.

into prime agricultural areas. Mountain regions suffered worst because their higher rainfall increased the volume of acid deposition, and their often thin soils could not neutralize the acid. Lakes and streams in "pristine" parts of Scandinavia and Scotland became acidified, losing fish over large areas. The most intense fallout occurred in the "black triangle" bordering Germany, the Czech Republic and Poland.

Since 1985, international treaties and heavy investment by power station operators in "desulfurization" equipment have cut sulfur pollution in Europe and North America by as much as 80 percent. Meanwhile nitrogen emissions from vehicles have stabilized, with the impact of cleaner cars counterbalanced by increased car use. Critical loads for acidification are still being exceeded in 10 percent of the land area of Western and Central Europe[6]. In some places, acidified soils and surface water are recovering. But in others the large amounts of acid accumulated in soils mean recovery could take decades[7]. The 1998 *Forest Condition Survey of Europe* by the UN Economic Commission for Europe found a quarter of the continent's trees were missing more than a quarter of their leaves. Air pollution was the main cause[8].

As more countries industrialize, acidification of the environment is becoming a global problem. Asian emissions of SO_2 were expected to exceed those of Europe and North America combined in the year 2000. The largest source is China, which emits 18 million tons of SO_2 a year. China's losses to crops and forests from acid deposition stand at US$5 billion a year[9]. Japan, which invested heavily to clean up its own emissions, is now suffering cross-border pollution from its neighbors[10]. Modelling studies suggest that without a clean-up, acid fallout over large areas of China will by 2020 exceed the levels reached in Central Europe in the 1970s[11].

Under certain meteorological conditions, smogs can spread very large distances to remote, unpopulated areas. In winter, weather systems take smog from Russian industrial centres north into the Arctic, where it lingers for many months – a phenomenon known as Arctic haze[12]. Similarly, Asian smogs sometimes travel on westerly winds across the Pacific to North America in spring[13].

The smoke from some forest fires can also be categorized as human-induced pollution, and can spread thousands of kilometers. In late 1997, Indonesian forest fires polluted neighboring countries, causing plane and shipping crashes as well as thousands of hospital admissions for lung and eye complaints. Health costs from the fires were later put at US$940 million[14].

Population, waste and chemicals

Waste is an inevitable by-product of most human activities. People have been generating and discarding materials since hunter-gatherers threw bones and vegetable remains outside their caves. For many hundreds of years those wastes consisted exclusively of matter which biodegraded easily (such as vegetable and human wastes), or were inert (such as bones and wood ash). Given the relatively small population, the quantities of waste were minor and could be readily absorbed by the environment; indeed they had value in fertilizing the soil.

As the global population grew, and urban and industrial development accelerated, the opportunities to dispose of materials, including biodegradable ones, diminished while the quantities and nuisance value of wastes increased. Society now has large volumes of waste to deal with: in the United Kingdom, for example, more than 500 million tons of waste are generated each year, of which some 30 percent are mineral wastes, 20 percent industrial, 40 percent agricultural and 5 percent municipal. A sometimes inordinate focus on household waste has often disguised the much larger volumes generated by up-stream activities such as extraction, manufacture and distribution: it is often claimed that for every ton of finished product, ten tons of wastes are created.

Laws to raise waste management standards were first introduced at the beginning of the 20th century, and today there is a plethora of such regulation. As well as protecting public health and reducing local nuisance, these laws are increasingly aimed at protecting the wider global environment. Waste is no longer a local issue. There are global concerns about the consumption of finite resources and the impacts of their acquisition, as well as the effects of waste management and the transboundary nature of pollution.

Certain wastes – such as polychlorinated biphenyls (PCBs), now phased out, and those from the nuclear industry – take many years to reach a state where they pose no further threat. Concern about long-term harm has influenced disposal methods. We have learned, in theory, how to manage landfill sites to contain leakage, and how to seal radioactive waste in concrete tanks for safe, long-term storage. We have developed combustion technologies to minimize emissions, and found ways to clean those emissions. Yet despite the many advances, disposing of waste is still problematic. Some potential disposal sites are ruled out by geological factors and some by their distance from the point of arising, but almost all are opposed by nearby residents. Proposals to site a recycling collection point attract as much opposition as those to construct a high-tech incinerator. We all want the goods and services which industrialized society provides – from power supplies to computers, fast food to vitamin pills – yet we do not want the resulting waste to affect us as individuals. This is exacerbated by mistrust of waste management systems and the risk of accident.

Industrial waste reflects not only the type of industry, but also how efficiently it is operated, and whether "clean technologies" are adopted. It is estimated that 26 percent of Europe's waste comes from manufacturing. In 1996, the United Kingdom generated 56 million tons of manufacturing

Landfill and methane emissions

The primary disposal route for all wastes is landfill, with more than 80 percent being disposed of that way. The anaerobic decomposition of waste in landfill sites is a major source of methane emissions: of the total global emissions of methane, estimated in 1999 at 535 million tons annually, 375 million tons are the result of human activities, and 18 percent of those come from waste disposal[1].

MUNICIPAL WASTE IN OECD COUNTRIES, MID-1990s

	Municipal waste	Of which household
	Kilos per capita	
Australia	690	400
Austria	480	310
Belgium	470	id
Canada	630	310
Czech Rep.	230	150
Denmark	530	500
Finland	410	180
France	560	410
Germany	400	380
Greece	310	id
Hungary	420	270
Iceland	560	240
Ireland	430	290
Italy	470	400
Japan	400	id
Korea, Rep.	390	id
Luxembourg	530	250
Mexico	330	260
Netherlands	580	470
New Zealand	id	390
Norway	620	300
Poland	290	210
Portugal	350	id
Spain	370	id
Sweden	440	360
Switzerland	610	430
Turkey	590	id
UK	490	460
USA	720	id

	% re-cycled	% incin-erated	% land-filled
Australia	id	id	id
Austria	38	14	48
Belgium	14	31	55
Canada	19	6	75
Czech Rep.	id	id	99
Denmark	23	54	22
Finland	33	2	65
France	9	32	59
Germany	29	17	51
Greece	7	–	93
Hungary	–	7	93
Iceland	14	17	69
Ireland	8	–	92
Italy	–	6	94
Japan	4	69	27
Korea, Rep.	24	4	72
Luxembourg	28	43	28
Mexico	1	–	99
Netherlands	38	27	35
New Zealand	id	id	id
Norway	15	16	69
Poland	2	–	98
Portugal	12	–	88
Spain	12	4	83
Sweden	19	42	39
Switzerland	40	46	14
Turkey	2	2	81
UK	7	9	83
USA	27	16	57

Source: OECD.

WORLD WASTE MANAGEMENT, 1990s
Selected cities

■ Proportion of inhabitants with connection to sewerage systems

▌ Proportion of inhabitants with regular refuse collection services

id **Insufficient data**

Data on waste management and pollution are extremely sparse, particularly at the global level. However, data on rates of urban refuse collection and drainage, even when few and far between, are a reasonable indicator of the overall ability of a nation or region to regulate waste and pollution.

USA: MATERIALS IN THE MUNICIPAL WASTE STREAM, 1960-90

	Paper and paperboard		Glass		Metal		Aluminum		Plastics	
	Million tons	% recycled	Million tons	% recycled	Million tons	% recycled	Million tons	% recycled	Million tons	% recycled
1960	29.9	18	6.7	1	10.1	1	0.4	n	0.4	n
1970	44.2	17	12.7	2	13.3	3	0.8	n	3.1	n
1980	54.7	22	15.0	5	12.7	7	1.8	17	6.8	n
1990	73.3	29	13.2	20	13.5	20	2.7	37	16.2	2

	Rubber and leather		Textiles		Wood		Food waste		Garden waste	
	Million tons	% recycled	Million tons	% recycled	Million tons	% recycled	Million tons	% recycled	Million tons	% recycled
1960	2.0	15	1.7	n	3.0	n	12.2	n	20.0	n
1970	3.2	9	2.0	n	4.0	n	12.8	n	23.2	n
1980	4.3	2	2.6	n	6.7	n	13.2	n	27.5	n
1990	4.6	4	5.6	4	12.3	3	13.2	n	35.0	12

n = negligible: less than 50 000 tons or 0.05 percent

Source: EPA.

Source: World Bank.

NUCLEAR WASTE FROM SPENT FUEL IN NUCLEAR POWER PLANTS
Selected OECD countries*

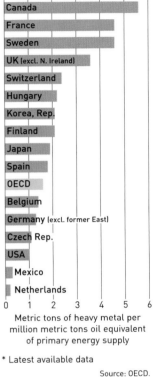

Canada
France
Sweden
UK (excl. N. Ireland)
Switzerland
Hungary
Korea, Rep.
Finland
Japan
Spain
OECD
Belgium
Germany (excl. former East)
Czech Rep.
USA
Mexico
Netherlands

0   1   2   3   4   5   6

Metric tons of heavy metal per million metric tons oil equivalent of primary energy supply

* Latest available data

Source: OECD.

RECYCLED PAPER PRODUCTION
Relative to total paper production

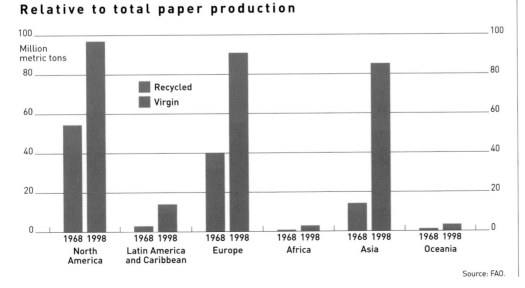

100

Million metric tons

80

60

■ Recycled
■ Virgin

40

20

0

| 1968 1998 | 1968 1998 | 1968 1998 | 1968 1998 | 1968 1998 | 1968 1998 |
| North America | Latin America and Caribbean | Europe | Africa | Asia | Oceania |

Source: FAO.

GLASS WASTE RECYCLING, 1992-95
As a proportion of total consumption, selected countries

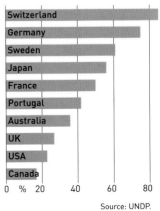

Switzerland
Germany
Sweden
Japan
France
Portugal
Australia
UK
USA
Canada

0   %   20   40   60   80

Source: UNDP.

Trends in recycling

Poor communities recover every valuable item from waste: Asian recyclers use rubber from scrap tyres to make shoes, make their own recycled paper and flatten cans to make metal sheets for roofing. Annually 200 million tons of waste cross OECD borders en route to reprocessing facilities, a business worth over US$20 billion. Waste paper travels from North America to the Far East; Europe's surplus glass is sent to South America; some of the West's waste plastics are shipped to China. A shortage of reprocessing capacity limits recycling, and industries established to process consistently clean virgin materials cannot readily adapt to the vagaries of secondary materials. Cost is another issue: collecting small quantities of materials from many locations is logistically and economically more difficult than obtaining large quantities from a single source. Indeed recycling may not always be resource-efficient when collection and reprocessing involve long-haul transport. Recycling is not keeping pace with waste increases in most countries.

waste[2]. These quantities are diminishing, but not fast enough to counteract the rises caused by increased consumption. Pressure for industry to reduce wastage comes from both internal and external economic drivers. Producer responsibility initiatives – already in place or proposed for a range of goods from batteries and packaging to vehicles and electronic equipment – make industry responsible for its products after use, and should result in fewer harmful components, as well as design decisions which will make disassembly and recycling easier.

Industrialization and level of affluence influence both the composition and quantity of waste generated by society. Research shows that in lower income regions of the world (such as Jakarta, Indonesia or Lucknow, India) 73 to 96 percent of the typical family's waste comprises food and biodegradable material, while in the higher income area of Brooklyn, New York, that figure is 26 percent[3]. Waste densities vary too: in high income countries, waste density is lower because it contains more lighter materials and manufactured goods, more paper and less food waste.

The link between affluence and municipal waste generation is surprisingly close: a 40 percent increase in the GDP of countries belonging to the Organisation for Economic Co-operation and Development (OECD) since 1980 has been accompanied by the same percentage growth in municipal waste. The OECD predicts that there will be a further 70 to 100 percent increase in GDP in its region by 2020. Unless the link between waste generation and GDP is severed, there could be a commensurate increase in waste. This is likely to be further exacerbated by certain social trends, such as the increase in single-person households due to higher divorce rates and the ageing population, particularly in the developed world. As the developing world industrializes and grows more affluent, it too can be expected to increase waste generation.

How can the links be broken? Technological developments in materials have already helped to reduce waste: food cans and glass milk bottles are each half the weight they were 50 years ago. This, alongside new materials, is reflected in the composition of household waste. In the United States, for example, the combined percentage of glass and metals in the waste stream diminished from 22 percent in 1970 to around 16 percent in 1990. Plastics rose from 2 percent to 9 percent, while paper and card remained fairly constant at around 38 percent[4]. By contrast, paper makes up just 5 percent of the waste in Ghana[5].

Trial schemes which charge householders for the waste they produce have raised awareness, although they have also thrown up a few new problems, such as wastes being dumped by roadsides to avoid the charges. The Swiss Environment Ministry reports that another method of avoiding waste charges – the burning of domestic refuse in gardens or fireplaces – is now the country's biggest cause of dioxin pollution. While the national emissions of dioxin from municipal incineration facilities are just 16 grams per year, uncontrolled burning of waste by householders emits between 27 and 30 grams of dioxin each year, despite the fact that only 1 to 2 percent of Switzerland's municipal waste is burned illegally, while 46 percent is burned in properly managed plants.

Sustainable development policies require us to take a more holistic view of waste and resources. We need to change attitudes, and to husband resources more carefully, particularly those which are finite. Observing the proximity principle and providing waste treatment and disposal facilities within a region's boundaries can do a great deal to reduce the environmental impact of managing waste.

TOXIC WASTE

The international community is working to strengthen legislation on the use, movement and disposal of toxic and hazardous waste, and to rid the developing world and countries in transition of dumps of dangerous and obsolete pesticides, which frequently expose local communities to poisons in their air, food and water. To date just 3 500 tons have been removed from Africa and the Near East at a cost of US$24 million. But estimates suggest that a further 20 000 tons remain in Africa, 80 000 tons in Asia and Latin America, and up to 200 000 tons in Central and Eastern Europe[6].

Industrial chemicals

Humans have found chemicals essential for modifying and controlling their environment from the earliest times. Ancient civilizations smelted metals for tools, weapons and ornaments and these operations produced chemical wastes. The Romans conducted metal mining and smelting operations in many parts of their empire and the resulting environmental impacts are still measurable today; lead levels in some soils in several parts of England still reflect metal processing carried out 2 000 years ago[1].

The industrial revolution saw a massive rise in population accompanied by an increase in industries of all kinds. Textiles, steel, glass and soap manufacture were all dependent on the ready availability of basic chemicals like sulfuric acid and the alkali sodium carbonate. The chemical industry was born as the technology to mass produce these commodities developed.

Our current standard of living would be impossible without industries such as steel, non-ferrous metals, power generation and chemicals manufacture. However, they have also had a profound effect on our environment. Our bodies and our surroundings are contaminated by their wastes. Soil, atmosphere and water contain reservoirs of waste metals and organic chemicals which reach us through our food, drinking water and the air we breathe.

One chemical that has had a particularly strong environmental impact is chlorine. Chlorine was originally a waste product of alkali manufacture, but as the 20th century progressed it found many new uses. The chlorine industry grew rapidly following the Second World War, producing products such as pesticides, solvents, dry cleaning fluids and PVC plastic. These goods brought many advantages, and it was not until the 1960s and 1970s that it was recognized that many chlorine compounds were toxic and environmentally persistent.

Polychlorinated biphenyls (PCBs) are an example of the early products of the chlorine industry which were to prove highly damaging to the environment. PCBs are non-flammable oily liquids or waxes which found uses as hydraulic fluids, as additives to oils, in sealants, in electrical applications and in paints. First manufactured in 1929 in the United States, evidence that they were persistent, accumulated in plants and animals, and toxic became overwhelming in the 1960s. Because of the large number of different PCBs it has proved difficult to untangle all of their toxic impacts, but many are suspected of promoting cancers, damaging the immune and reproductive systems and interfering with hormone systems through endocrine disruption. Particularly disturbing is evidence that children born to mothers contaminated with high levels of PCBs suffer impaired nervous system development[2]. The products were phased-out or banned in Western countries in the 1970s, though their manufacture continued in Eastern countries for many years more.

Not all chemical pollutants are deliberately manufactured. The by-products and compounds of chemical processes can be transformed in the environment into different, sometimes more hazardous, breakdown products. Dioxins, for example, are by-products of combustion and waste incineration processes. The rapid increase in the use of coal as a fuel during the 19th century

PCBs and bioaccumulation

PCBs accumulate in the fat of plants and animals, and low levels in plants are concentrated at each subsequent step in the food chain. This process of biomagnification exposes top predators such as birds of prey, marine mammals and humans to the highest levels and puts them at the greatest risk of toxic effects. The bodies of humans and animals in even the most remote locations carry a burden of these wastes which will remain for generations to come. The process of global distillation (see page 98) means that people and animals in the Arctic contain particularly high levels[3,4].

INDUSTRIAL OUTPUT
Selected countries

	Industry value added, 1998	
	Million US$	as % of GDP
USA	2 139 903	26
Japan	1 399 697	37
China	469 925	49
UK	420 731	31
Brazil	225 681	29
India	107 506	25
Mexico	106 247	27
Gabon	3 311	60
Panama	1 646	18
Congo	981	50
Georgia	821	16
Haiti	774	20
Madagascar	525	14
Moldova	501	31

Note: Data on waste production are very sparse; industrial output serves as a crude indicator of industrial waste output.

Source: World Bank.

INDUSTRIAL WASTE IN OECD COUNTRIES, LATE 1990s

Czech Rep. — 353

Luxembourg
Finland
Australia
Sweden
Poland
Turkey
France
Hungary
OECD
Austria
Belgium
Korea, Rep.
Ireland
Greece
Mexico
Japan
UK (excl. N. Ireland)
Germany (excl. former East)
New Zealand
Netherlands
Norway
Spain
Denmark
Italy
Switzerland
Portugal
Israel

0   50   100   150   200
Kilos per thousand US$ GDP

Source: OECD.

EMISSIONS OF ORGANIC WATER POLLUTANTS, 1997
Kilos per worker per day

- Less than 0.1
- 0.1-0.15
- 0.15-0.17
- 0.17-0.20
- 0.20-0.24
- More than 0.25
- Insufficient data

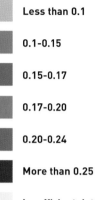

This measure has been taken as an indicator of relative levels of industrial pollution because data on water pollution are more readily available than data on other emissions. This is because most industrial pollution control programs begin by regulating emissions of organic water pollutants.

PRODUCTION OF ORGANIC WATER POLLUTANTS AND RELATIVE SHARE BY TYPE OF INDUSTRY, MID-1990s
Selected countries

	Metric tons per day Mid-1990s	% change since 1980	Primary metals	Paper and pulp	Chemicals	Food and beverages	Textiles	Wood	Other
					% share by type of industry				
China	7 396	119	20.6	11.9	14.2	28.9	14.1	1.0	9.3
USA	2 585	-6	8.8	32.8	10.1	27.3	7.3	2.7	11.0
India	1 664	17	15.5	7.5	8.2	51.5	11.6	0.3	5.4
Russia	1 615	id	18.2	6.8	9.2	44.7	8.0	2.6	10.5
Japan	1 469	1	8.6	21.9	8.9	38.9	6.8	1.9	13.0
Germany	811	id	12.7	16.8	15.5	30.6	4.8	2.2	17.4
Indonesia	728	240	2.4	8.9	8.6	50.2	21.7	5.3	2.9
Brazil	691	-20	19.0	12.6	9.3	41.6	10.9	1.6	5.0
UK	642	-33	7.4	26.3	10.6	35.7	7.5	2.0	10.5
France	585	-20	11.6	21.2	10.8	37.7	6.1	1.8	10.8
Ukraine	540	id	20.5	3.7	7.5	50.7	6.7	1.6	9.3

Source: World Bank.

Source: World Bank.

WORLD CHEMICALS PRODUCTION, 1997
By region

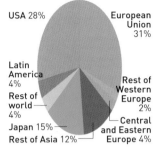

USA 28%

European Union 31%

Latin America 4%

Rest of world 4%

Japan 15%

Rest of Asia 12%

Rest of Western Europe 2%

Central and Eastern Europe 4%

Total value: US$1 231 billion

Source: CEFIC.

CHEMICALS PRODUCTION IN THE EUROPEAN UNION

	1997 production Million US$
Germany	96 786
France	69 413
UK	47 501
Italy	45 275
Belgium	32 924
Spain	26 560
Netherlands	25 907
Ireland	12 051
Sweden	8 256
Denmark	4 922
Finland	4 514
Austria	4 284
Portugal	3 645
Greece	3 283
EU total	**385 321**

Source: CEFIC.

DANGEROUS CHEMICALS INTENSITY IN THE EUROPEAN UNION
Production and imports of dangerous chemicals relative to GDP

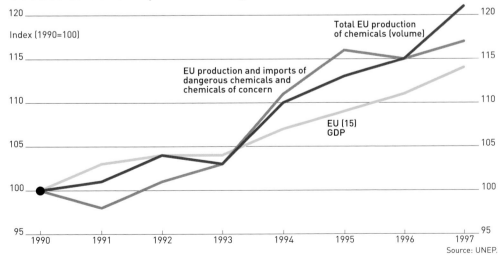

Index (1990=100)

Total EU production of chemicals (volume)

EU production and imports of dangerous chemicals and chemicals of concern

EU (15) GDP

Source: UNEP.

ENVIRONMENTAL EXPENDITURE IN THE EUROPEAN UNION CHEMICAL INDUSTRY
As % of sales

	Operating cost	Capital expenditure
1990	3.9	1.0
1991	3.9	1.0
1992	4.0	1.0
1993	3.8	0.8
1994	3.5	0.6
1995	3.4	0.5
1996	3.5	0.6

Source: CEFIC.

Disposal difficulties

In 1986 *The Khian Sea* left Philadelphia with a cargo of 14 000 tons of incinerator ash containing metals and dioxins. The ship sailed the Caribbean for two years looking for a dumping ground. Most of the load was finally tipped into the sea, while 4 000 tons were off-loaded in Haiti – later to be returned to the United States after an international outcry. The 1972 London Convention has done much to prevent incidents like this.

ESTIMATED NUMBERS OF CHEMICALS, 1990s

Total number including:	**5 000 000**
Chemicals in commerce	100 000
Industrial chemicals (millions of products)	72 000
New chemicals (per year)	2 000
Pesticides (21 000 products)	600
Food additives	8 700
Cosmetic ingredients (40 000 products)	7 500
Human pharmaceuticals	3 300

Source: EPA; EC.

increased dioxin pollution. But a second factor which resulted in a steep increase in their generation was the chlorine industry. Dioxins are generated by many chemical processes involving chlorine and are found in wastes from PVC manufacture, and as contaminants in chlorine-containing products including some pesticides and dyes[5].

Safe disposal of hazardous waste products like PCBs presents a problem. PCBs in landfills may vaporize and turn up in landfill gas or escape to the air. The safest disposal method is by incineration in a purpose-built hazardous waste incinerator. However, even this method has drawbacks. Poorly designed or badly operated incinerators may spread PCBs or other contaminants rather than destroy them. In 1993, an incinerator at Pontypool in Wales was found to have been polluting local soils and food with high levels of PCBs and dioxins[6].

Past disposal of hazardous waste has often been the cause of environmental problems. The dumping of waste at sea was once a widespread practice. It was difficult to regulate and its effects on the marine environment impossible to monitor. However, international agreements made under the 1972 London Convention have gradually succeeded in reducing the number of countries dumping at sea. Many European nations have not only agreed to stop the sea disposal of industrial waste, but also the dumping of sewage sludge – contaminated with toxic metals and dioxins – and radioactive wastes.

Hazardous wastes have also been exported to developing countries which have no facilities to dispose of them, and whose people have little knowledge of the hazards they represent. Efforts to control the trade in hazardous waste began in 1989 with the Basel Convention. A blanket ban on the export of hazardous wastes from developed to developing nations has been agreed and is now applied – although it still awaits formal legal completion.

In developed countries there is increasing control of industrial waste and its disposal. There is good evidence, for example, that emissions of PCBs and dioxins are declining, and so too is human exposure[7]. But there is a clear need for the international community to ensure that developing countries are able to impose sufficient controls on their industries to minimize the generation of hazardous wastes and ensure their correct disposal in order to protect the health of their populations and the global environment.

Many lessons have been learned from the experience of the last 50 years. However, there are an estimated 100 000 chemicals on the market and their ecotoxicity and biodegradability are often poorly studied[8]. Although international rules now require testing of the new chemicals produced in large volumes, there is an enormous backlog of compounds for which full hazard and toxicity data have never been produced. Modern chemical analytical techniques show that sewage sludges and waters receiving industrial and domestic effluents contain cocktails of thousands of chemicals – waste products, by-products and breakdown products of modern chemical goods from fragrances to flame retardants.

Attempts to assess the risks – and to introduce new controls on their use – have proved to be a lengthy and contentious process. Risk assessments are imperfect because they cannot take into account all the possible interactive effects between different compounds[9]. It is also not yet possible to assess the safety of endocrine disrupting chemicals because their effects are not sufficiently understood and test methods still have to be commonly established.

The presence of so many pollutants in the environment begs the question of whether society should adopt a more precautionary approach to the release of chemical wastes. New ideas for regulating chemicals include strategies which give the environment the benefit of the doubt when data on toxicity and environmental fate are lacking. For example, an agreement reached by many countries surrounding the North Sea, under the OSPAR treaty in 1998, aims to reduce levels of manufactured chemicals in the environment by "continuously reducing discharges" of hazardous substances with the aim of achieving environmental concentrations "close to zero" for all synthetic substances by 2010[10].

Agrochemicals

World food production has approximately doubled since 1960, largely as a result of the introduction of new crop varieties and the intensification of agriculture – supported by increased applications of fertilizers and pesticides. But some scientists suggest that population and economic growth worldwide have raised the demand for food beyond levels that can be supported by extensive and environmentally benign farming[1].

At the end of the 20th century an average of 91 kilos of fertilizer were used on each hectare of the world's cropland, an increase of more than a third since the mid-1970s. This masks huge variations, from just 1 kilo in Rwanda or Mongolia, to more than 700 in Switzerland. Since the mid-1980s, use per hectare in the developed world has declined from 121 kilos to around 81 kilos – a time during which its agricultural production remained almost static.

In the developing world between the mid-1980s and mid-1990s, agricultural production and fertilizer use both increased by almost 42 percent, the latter from an average of 63 kilos per hectare of cropland. Consumption of fertilizers and its growth were highest in Asia, while in Africa usage has actually fallen since the 1980s – from 19 kilos per hectare to 18. The Food and Agriculture Organization of the United Nations predicts further rises in the developing world, probably of around 2.8 percent per year[3] from current levels of almost 99 kilos of fertilizer per hectare of cropland.

The benefits are increased supplies of food, but problems arise when significant amounts of fertilizer escape into the wider environment – for example through the leaching and runoff of fertilizers into ground and surface waters. Elevated nitrate levels in drinking water, recognized as a threat to human health, have been found in 6 percent of wells surveyed by the Environmental Protection Agency in the United States; in the United Kingdom, where over a million people's supply was found to have levels in excess of European legal limits; and in the drinking waters of Sao Paulo, Brazil and Buenos Aires, Argentina. As nitrates take many years to penetrate groundwater, these problems could increase as a result of the heavy applications of fertilizers in the recent past.

High nitrate and phosphorus levels in rivers, lakes and coastal waters disrupt the balance of aquatic habitats through the process of eutrophication. In freshwaters, high phosphorus levels encourage excessive algal growth and create murky green waters which shade out bottom-rooting plants, impacting invertebrates and fish that depend on such plants for food and shelter. Similarly in coastal and estuarine waters, excessive nitrate inputs boost algae and turbidity, and promote filter-feeding worms and bivalves – effects that may be particularly damaging for coral reefs.

Massive agglomerations of algae known as blooms cause deaths of aquatic life on a huge scale. In 1996 a bloom smothered invertebrates over several hundred square kilometers off Scotland's west coast[4], and in 1998 a bloom off California poisoned more than 400 sea lions[5]. Filter-feeding shellfish such as mussels and oysters can become toxic as they absorb algae from the water. In most developed countries shellfisheries are now monitored to guard against related outbreaks of poisoning, which are becoming increasingly frequent.

Natural pesticides

In India, seeds of the neem tree are used as a natural insecticide, protecting crops and stored grain from up to 200 species of pest including locusts, maize borers and rice weevils. But the neem does not harm birds, mammals or beneficial insects such as bees.

THE WORLD TRADE IN PESTICIDES

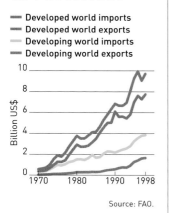

— Developed world imports
— Developed world exports
— Developing world imports
— Developing world exports

Source: FAO.

EXPORTS OF BANNED OR RESTRICTED PESTICIDES FROM US PORTS

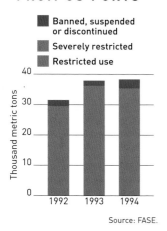

■ Banned, suspended or discontinued
■ Severely restricted
■ Restricted use

Source: FASE.

RESISTANCE TO PESTICIDES

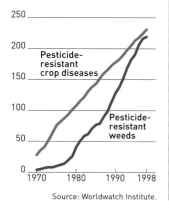

Pesticide-resistant crop diseases

Pesticide-resistant weeds

Source: Worldwatch Institute.

WORLD FERTILIZER USE, 1998
Kilos per hectare of cultivated land

Up to 10

10-20

20-50

50-90

90-300

300-1 000

More than 1 000

Insufficient data

Over the last decade fertilizer use remained static or fell in a number of countries with very high use, such as the United Kingdom or Iceland, but continued to increase rapidly in others, particularly the United Arab Emirates.

AREAS OF HIGH PESTICIDE USE

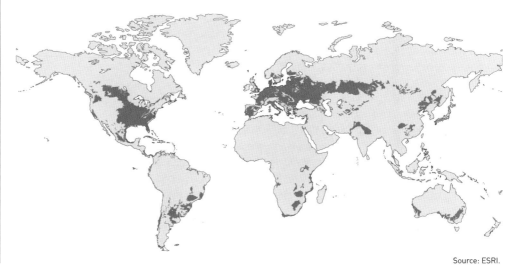

Source: ESRI.

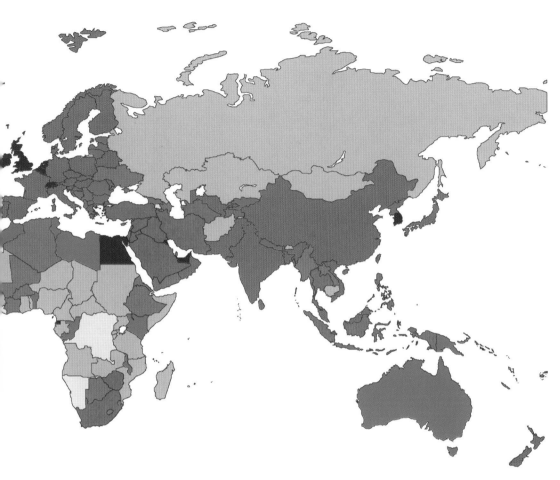

Source: FAO.

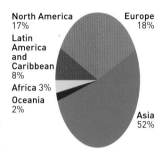

FERTILIZER USE
Regional share, 1997

North America 17%
Europe 18%
Latin America and Caribbean 8%
Africa 3%
Oceania 2%
Asia 52%

Total fertilizer use:
137.25 million metric tons

Regional growth

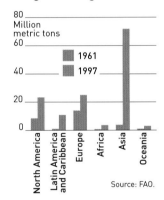

80
Million metric tons
60

■ 1961
■ 1997

40
20
0

North America
Latin America and Caribbean
Europe
Africa
Asia
Oceania

Source: FAO.

THE GROWTH OF FERTILIZER USE
Kilos per hectare of arable and cropland

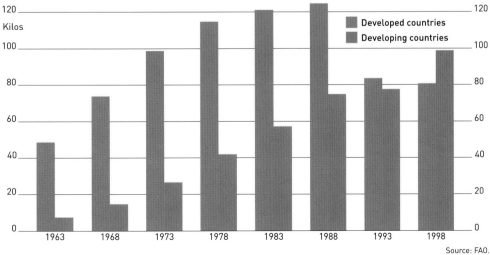

Kilos

■ Developed countries
■ Developing countries

1963 1968 1973 1978 1983 1988 1993 1998

Source: FAO.

FERTILIZER USE AND CEREAL YIELDS
Selected countries

	Fertilizer use Kilos per hectare		% increase in yield
	1968	1998	1968-98
Papua New Guinea	2	22	108
Kenya	8	28	21
India	11	99	114
China	26	259	153
Italy	76	158	101
USA	77	110	77
Israel	113	277	23
Egypt	115	337	87
Denmark	204	170	51
Korea, Rep.	206	458	91
UK	243	330	93
Ireland	258	520	58
Switzerland	348	749	76
Japan	365	290	11
Netherlands	622	494	78
World	**43**	**91**	**77**

Source: FAO.

Carnivorous algae

Fish farmers suffered major economic losses in the Neuse estuary in North Carolina, United States, when a billion fish were killed by a recently discovered carnivorous species of alga. *Pfiesteria* chemically senses fish and produces lethal toxins which kill in only a few hours, and then feeds off their decaying remains. The toxins can also cause skin ulcers on people exposed to them.

When blooms die back and decay they exhaust supplies of dissolved oxygen, suffocating fish and other aquatic species. Oxygen deficiency has been reported as damaging wildlife in the coastal waters of the Gulf of Mexico, Chesapeake Bay and Long Island Sound in the United States, and the Baltic Sea, while in the United Kingdom some 150 tons of farmed fish were suffocated in 1998 by starch-like chemicals released by algae[6].

Alongside nitrogen oxide emissions from burning fossil fuels, nitrogen fertilizers lead to an increase in nitrogen-containing emissions from plants and soils, adding to the nitrogen load in the atmosphere. Additional deposition of nitrogen compounds over land disturbs upland ecosystems which are naturally constrained by low nitrogen levels. Atmospheric deposition to the world's oceans, which is estimated to exceed the total nitrogen input from rivers, may also trigger algal blooms[7]. Nitrogen fertilizers also contribute to emissions from soil of nitrous oxide – the third most significant greenhouse gas. Similarly, nitrogen in rivers results in emissions of the gas from estuaries, but human impacts on the scale of this natural process are still little understood[8].

Although the use of pesticides increased more than 30 times between 1950 and the end of the 1980s, pests still cost the world billions of dollars annually in lost agricultural production, and more species of weeds, diseases and insects are becoming resistant, up from under 100 in the 1950s to more than 700 today. Use of pesticides in the developed world is now decreasing, in part as a result of the substitution of new more powerful chemicals which are used in much smaller amounts. However, it is still increasing in developing countries, which currently account for more than a quarter of the world's consumption – with a total estimated value of US$25 to US$32 billion annually[9], up from US$16 billion in 1986.

Applications of pesticides inevitably lead to residues in soils which may evaporate to the air or be washed into watercourses, causing contamination of food and the environment, and endangering human health. In the early 1990s, the World Health Organization estimated that 3 million people a year suffered from acute pesticide poisoning with as many as 200 000 of them dying. Most are in the developing world, where village conditions virtually prohibit the safe use of dangerous pesticides. A 1993 study in Indonesia showed that 21 percent of spraying operations resulted in three or more symptoms associated with pesticide poisoning. Eighty-four percent of farmers were also found to be storing chemicals in their homes, in unsafe conditions where children could reach them[10].

Groundwater contamination is particularly serious as it is long-lived and expensive or impossible to remedy. Spray drift into streams and rivers, and contamination from spillages, tank washings or discarded pesticide containers also present a real threat to watercourses. It has been estimated that up to 50 million United States citizens may be drinking pesticide-polluted water, while in England and Wales, reducing pesticides in public drinking water supplies to a precautionary level of 0.1 micrograms per liter is estimated to have cost water companies in excess of US$1.2 billion[11]. Despite the efforts of chemists to design products which bind to soil or crop surfaces, water contamination appears to be unavoidable[12]. Some pesticides are also persistent organic pollutants (POPs), including DDT, hexachlorocyclohexane, toxaphene and dieldrin, and are transported through the atmosphere to be redeposited in cooler regions.

Concern over pesticide residues has prompted the development of integrated pest management (IPM) – the use of a variety of controls including the conservation of existing natural enemies, crop rotation, intercropping, and cultivation of pest-resistant varieties. Pesticides may still be used, but selectively and in greatly reduced quantities. This approach is producing striking results: in Indonesia rice yields have increased by 13 percent alongside a drop in pesticide use of 60 percent, while a study of fruit growers using IPM in New York State and California showed falling costs alongside increased yields.

The revival of organic farming may also prove significant. This already accounts for 10 percent of the food system in Austria and Switzerland, and is growing at 20 percent a year in France, Japan, Singapore and the United States. Whether this represents limited idealism or the presaging of widely accepted agricultural practices that embrace more holistic approaches to the wider environment remains to be seen.

Population and ecosystems

COSYSTEMS sustain life on Earth. They provide vital "ecological services" by cleaning up and absorbing pollution, protecting coastlines, supplying "wild" food from fish to bushmeat, conserving genetic resources needed for crops and pharmaceuticals, maintaining soils and hydrology, pollinating crops and much more. But the demands of rising human populations in many regions are now impacting most of the world's ecosystems.

Humans have been altering their environment for thousands of years. The process probably began with the setting of fires in savannah grassland to aid hunting. Most forests contain the marks of human-set fires, clearance and tree planting, and little strictly "virgin" vegetated land surface now remains.

In the past 10 000 years the dominant technological influences have been the use of timber for building and the spread of crop cultivation. This has accelerated, particularly in the past 150 years during which time the rising population has doubled the area of arable land in use on the Earth's surface.

During this period the burning of fossil fuels has for the first time had a major impact on ecosystems, through pollution and, most recently, climate change. In the past three decades, the widespread saturation of ecosystems with nitrogen compounds, such as ammonia and nitrogen oxides from agricultural fertilizers and air pollution, has emerged as a new global-scale threat.

The extent of ecosystem loss and alteration is closely related to population density, which is very uneven across the planet. Today, one half of the human population lives on less than 10 percent of the Earth's land, and three quarters on only 20 percent[1].

For much of human history, the most heavily populated regions of the planet, and the most ecologically disturbed, have been Europe and South and East Asia – and that remains the case. The population densities of the Americas and Africa have only now risen to those achieved in Europe and India by 1750[2]. In India today, population density is more than 300 people per square kilometer, seven times the global average; little land is unused by humans; and almost 80 percent of the original forest cover has been lost. In particularly uninhabitable parts of the planet population density is very low. In Alaska, for example, it is less than a tenth of the global average, and most of the landscape remains untouched.

Land affected by human activity can be divided into areas transformed – notably by agriculture, which in some parts of the world such as the North American prairies is characterized by low population density but high ecosystem loss – and areas degraded and fragmented by pollution, sporadic human activity including hunting and tourism, or infrastructure development such as high-ways and pipelines.

The extent of forests, which once covered a large part of the planet, is one good measure of ecosystem survival. Overall, at least half of the world's forests have disappeared at the hand of humankind – three quarters of these in the past 300 years and the majority within the past century.

PLANET EARTH

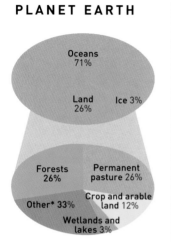

Oceans 71%

Land 26%   Ice 3%

Forests 26%

Permanent pasture 26%

Other* 33%

Crop and arable land 12%

Wetlands and lakes 3%

* Includes arid areas, wastelands, urban areas, roads, rivers and grasslands not used as permanent pastures

Source: WRI; FAO.

MAIN LANDCOVER TYPES AND OCEAN PRODUCTIVITY

Forest

Shrub

Savannah/grass

Cropland

Wetland

Snow/ice

Barren/desert

Insufficient data

Marine chlorophyll concentration

High

Low

The map shows a simplified image of landcover types and ocean productivity. Ongoing in-depth study of these is crucial to understanding the roles played by the various ecosystems in the overall well-being of the planet.

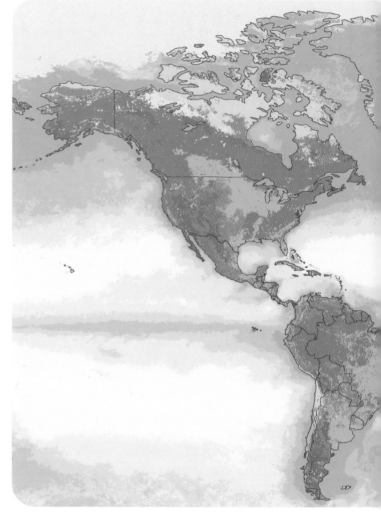

CLIMATIC REGIONS OF THE WORLD

Polar
Ice cap and tundra

Cooler humid
Subarctic and continental

Warmer humid
Marine west coast, humid subtropical and Mediterranean

Dry
Steppe and desert

Tropical humid
Savannah and rainforest

Source: Times.

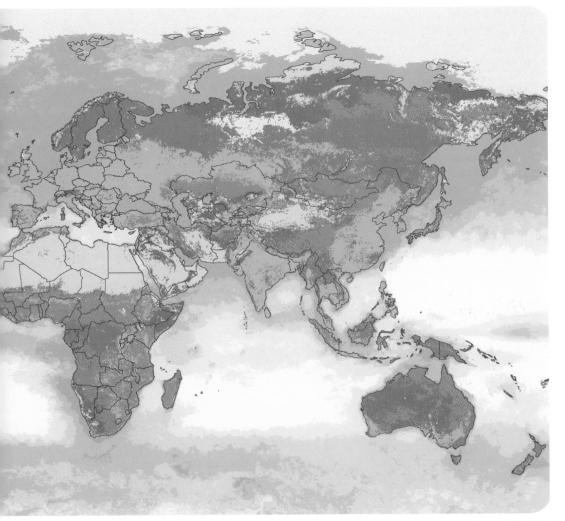

Source: NASA; USGS.

THE LIVING PLANET INDEX, 1970-99

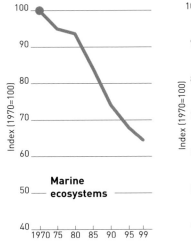

Marine
ecosystems

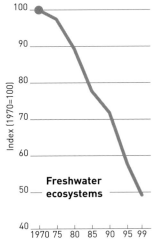

Freshwater
ecosystems

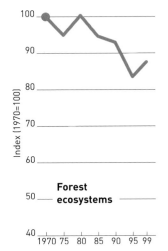

Forest
ecosystems

The Living Planet Index,
developed by the World
Conservation Monitoring
Centre (UNEP–WCMC) and
WWF, the conservation
organization, provides an
indicator of the health of the
three major ecosystem types
of the planet. Based on the
population trends of marine,
freshwater and forest species,
it shows that there has been
a considerable decline in the
health of all three ecosystem
types since 1970.

Their survival is lowest where population density is highest. The Asia/Pacific region has lost 76 percent of its original forest cover, mostly to agricultural development but also to urbanization and mineral exploitation. Losses in Europe (excluding Russia) average 75 percent, in Russia 24 percent, in Africa 68 percent, and in the Americas 35 percent, but with much higher rates in more densely populated areas such as the coastal regions and Central America[3].

The largest tracts of wilderness survive only in the less populated areas of the world, which for various reasons have proved hard for humans to colonize in any numbers. These include the jungles of the Amazon basin and Central Africa; the frozen taiga regions of Siberia and remote areas of North America; and some desert, mountain and wetland regions. Examples of the latter types include the African Sahara, the mountainous Himalayan regions of otherwise densely populated South Asia, and the Florida Everglades, nature's largest preserve on the eastern coast of the United States[4].

Often, rising wealth and economic activity among human populations intensify their impact on local ecosystems by increasing demand for natural resources and generating pollution from industry and energy generation. But not always. Wealth can provide the resources for a clean-up of pollution, as occurred with a number of European rivers in recent years. Likewise, many European countries are replacing farmland and old industrial developments with quasi-natural forests. This is possible because they have the wealth to buy food from elsewhere or to invest in high-input intensive agriculture to grow more food from less land, and have the desire to restore ancient habitats[5]. The United Kingdom, for instance, is planting a "national forest" in the heart of a former Midlands mining and industrial zone.

Some technological advances are more ambiguous. The development of coal burning in the 18th century was initially heralded in Europe as a solution to a growing shortage of fuelwood, and slowed deforestation across the continent. Only later did the environmental downside of fossil fuels emerge.

The link between population density and environmental damage is also disrupted when prosperous or powerful communities, either deliberately or accidentally, buy local ecological conservation at the expense of damage to other areas. Such transference has a long history. The ancient city of Rome turned North Africa into a grain-growing "breadbasket" to supply its million-plus population, until most African soils were exhausted. The grain, meanwhile, was transported across the Mediterranean aboard a fleet of a thousand ships made of wood cut from the Levant.

In the modern era, Japan's demand for timber has deforested much of Southeast Asia, while East African forests have been cleared to grow tea, coffee and other cash crops for export to Europe, and South American pampas grasslands have all but disappeared to provide pasture for meat supplying Europe and North America[6].

Additionally, ecological damage may occur despite low population densities where key environmental resources are in locally short supply. One example is the extreme stress on fluvial ecosystems resulting from water shortages in the arid Middle East where, despite recent increases, overall population density is low by world standards.

Human activity has also created a series of long-distance threats to ecosystems, some of them global in extent. These include acid deposition, the thinning ozone layer, the spread of persistent organic pollutants (POPs), climate change and the spread of nitrogen compounds through soils and fluvial ecosystems[7].

Mountains

MOUNTAINS occupy a fifth of the Earth's land surface but contain only a tenth of its human population[1], making them refuges for many of the planet's rarest animal and plant species and wildlife habitats. Yet these refuges are increasingly threatened by advancing landuse changes, and, potentially, by changing climate patterns.

Mountains are vital economic and ecological resources, high in biodiversity and minerals alike. Their height triggers heavy precipitation which, coupled with the water-storing capacity of glaciers, gives them a vital hydrological role. Mountain regions are the sources of most of the world's major rivers and half the world's population is reliant on mountain water. A billion Chinese, Indians and Bangladeshis drink from rivers flowing out of the Himalayas. In arid countries such as Egypt, mountain sources provide more than 90 percent of the available water[2].

Their elevation allows mountains to harbor a great diversity of species and habitats within a small area, often forming islands of biodiversity that take their own evolutionary path and create high levels of endemism, such as in the Peruvian Andes. More than half the world's endemic bird species occur in tropical mountain regions[3]. Mountains also provide natural refuges for species during times of climatic change and stress.

Mountain terrain has deterred dense human occupation, for cities have nowhere to spread and access is difficult. Mountain communities have traditionally been isolated, developing particular skills to survive – such as transhumance pastoralism and cutting terraces on hillsides to protect soils, conserve water and provide flat land for cultivation. But such communities have often remained poor and at the margins of society. Mountain nations such as Bhutan, Lesotho, Nepal, Rwanda, Burundi and Ethiopia are among the poorest 20 in the world[4]. Within nations, mountains are often home to tribal groups and other minorities, such as the Tibetans, the Quecha in the central Andes and the Kurds in Turkey and Iraq. While some such groups find themselves increasingly marginalized, there are also opposite trends towards social and economic integration with the lowlands.

In countries with land shortages and growing populations, lowlanders may invade hill regions, causing deforestation and cultivating erosion-prone soils. Areas containing tropical mountain forests have had the fastest rates of both annual population growth and deforestation in recent years[5]. Examples include the Guatemalan Highlands and the Bolivian Altiplano.

Elsewhere, mountain regions are being abandoned by farming communities who tire of the meagre earnings and hard work. This is as true in developing countries such as Peru as in the European Alps and Pyrenees. Abandonment does not necessarily reduce environmental degradation but may increase it. Left untended, terraces on steep hillsides swiftly start to crumble away.

But mountains have other attractions for lowlanders. Some contain valuable minerals. And many are scenically beautiful, enticing skiers, mountaineers, trekkers and environmentalists, and offering alternative livelihoods to local communities. The Alps accommodate 100 million visitor-

The movement of ecological zones
As the world warms, climatic zones rise up mountain sides, dragging ecological zones with them. The species associated with them occupy ever smaller areas ever further uphill until, eventually, even the mountain top becomes too hot for some and they disappear altogether.

Andes

LARGE MOUNTAIN RANGES

Peaks up to 2 500 meters

Peaks up to 8 000+ meters

∧∨ Rivers

■ Cities of more than
1 million people in or near
mountains, 1999

World Heritage Sites in
mountain regions, 2000
▲ Cultural
▲ Natural
▲ Cultural /Natural
Administered by UNESCO
under the 1972 World
Heritage Convention

Population density in mountain ranges tends to be relatively low owing to the
inhospitable terrain. Nonetheless, they are becoming increasingly subject to
anthropogenic change as tourism and transport networks expand and
communities move into them to relieve pressure on overpopulated lands in
the surrounding area.

POPULATION DENSITY AND ROAD NETWORKS
IN THREE OF THE WORLD'S MOUNTAIN RANGES, 1999

Population density per square kilometer

0	25-250	∧∨ Major roads
1-25	250-200 000	■ Cities of more than 250 000 people in or near mountains

Alps

Himalayas

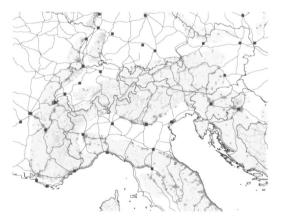

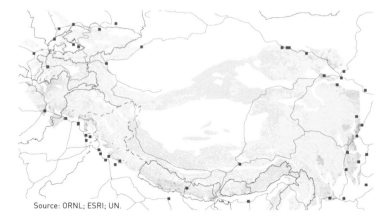

Source: ORNL; ESRI; UN.

Source: ESRI; UNESCO; UNPD.

World Heritage

A natural World Heritage
Site may exemplify a stage
of the world's geological or
biological evolution, or
contain the natural habitats
of endangered animals. It may
be a scene of exceptional
beauty or a reserve for large
numbers of wild animals.
A cultural monument may be
a masterpiece of creative
genius or have exerted great
architectural influence, or it
may be an outstanding
example of a certain culture.
There are some 630 sites
overall, 150 of which fall
within or near mountain
regions, representative of
both the historical and
natural value of mountainous
areas and the qualities that
attract millions of tourists
every year.

WORLD TOPOGRAPHY

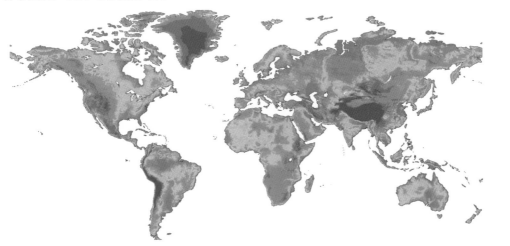

Meters above sea level

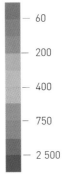

— 60

— 200

— 400

— 750

— 2 500

Source: NOAA.

days a year. In the Himalayas, more than 250 000 pilgrims and trekkers climb to the Gagotri glacier, sacred source of the River Ganges, each year.

The impact of tourism on ecosystems can be double-edged. On the one hand, ski slopes and roads have to be constructed, water and fuelwood found, and rubbish disposed of – all of which can cause environmental damage. On the other hand, there is an economic incentive to protect the wildernesses many come to see – and the revenue to accomplish it.

Valleys within mountain ranges have their own vulnerabilities. They become transport arteries and sites for urban development, where the surrounding mountains can trap urban air pollution. Valleys are also attractive sites for building reservoirs to supply water, generate hydroelectricity or provide flood protection. But reservoirs not only flood valleys and disrupt fluvial ecosystems, they also force displaced inhabitants into the hills, where they may cause further environmental damage. The Three Gorges dam currently being constructed on the River Yangtze in China is expected to displace up to 3 million people into surrounding hills.

Mountain ranges often become zones of conflict, particularly as many contested national borders run through them, for instance in Kashmir. Mountains also play host to disputes between national governments and ethnic minorities such as the Chechens in Russia, the Kosovans in Serbia and the East Timorese. Their rugged terrain may serve to house refugees from such conflicts as well as providing sanctuary for guerrillas and outlaws. Two thirds of the 34 armed conflicts in the world in 1993 took place primarily in mountain areas[6].

Such conflicts may protect the environment by discouraging organized development and inward migration. But they may equally encourage illegal and environmentally destructive activities, such as logging. In Liberia, Cambodia and the Thai-Myanmar border region, intensive logging helped fund warring groups in the 1990s. Virtually all the world's heroin and cocaine comes from three small mountain regions: on the borders of Pakistan-Afghanistan, Myanmar-Thailand-Laos and Bolivia-Colombia, causing massive deforestation and soil erosion[7].

Mountain ecosystems face a massive test of their robustness from projected climate change. Warming is already melting many glaciers, fundamentally altering hydrology both in the mountain regions and downstream. For instance, glaciers cover 17 percent of the Himalayas and provide two thirds of the flow of the River Ganges. But at their present rate of decline all the glaciers in the middle and eastern Himalayas will have disappeared by 2035. Many mountain valleys are threatened by floods as lakes formed by melting ice are breached[8].

SOIL EROSION IN MOUNTAIN REGIONS

Steep hillsides washed by heavy mountain rains are vulnerable to soil erosion and landslides, especially when vegetation is removed for logging, agriculture or roads. On virgin hillsides, landslides create gaps in forests that can encourage biodiversity[9]. But in inhabited areas, they are dangerous to local populations and may lead to floods.

When Hurricane Mitch hit Honduras in October 1998, some 8 000 people were killed in floods and landslides. Much of the damage was attributed to deforestation and land disturbance caused by road and house construction and mining activity in its mountainous interior. Since 1960, the population of Honduras has quadrupled while its forested area has fallen from 63 percent to 37 percent. The national population density – at 51 people per square kilometer – remains comparatively low, but urbanization in mountainous areas maximizes the number of people at risk in a disaster[10].

While land disturbance incontrovertibly causes localized erosion and landslides, there is less scientific agreement about whether these activities cause downstream problems in large catchments. Deforestation in the Himalayas is frequently accused of causing siltation in northern India and Bangladesh. But there is evidence that most eroded material is deposited locally rather than transported over long distances[11].

Forests

ORESTS are the planet's largest reservoir of biological diversity, containing an estimated half of all the world's plant and animal species. They also play a vital role in maintaining "ecological services" such as the water and carbon cycles, by storing carbon, conserving soils and generating rainfall.

There are probably very few truly virgin forests left on Earth. Most have been burned, replanted or otherwise influenced by humans at various times. Ecologists are replacing their model of natural forests as ancient pristine entities with models that characterize them as dynamic, unstable and short-lived[1]. Nonetheless, the scale and pace of anthropogenic "deforestation" in the past 200 years dwarfs anything seen before. The most endangered ecosystem types include tropical dry forests and mountain forest ecosystems, such as cloud forests.

Overall, human activity has removed roughly half of the world's natural forests, with the greatest losses in densely populated countries. With the exception of Russia, less than 1 percent of Europe's "old-growth" forests remain, while some 95 percent of the continental United States' forests have been logged since European settlement began[2]. Most forest remains in the least densely populated forested regions – the major equatorial rainforests of Central Africa, the Amazon basin and the Southeast Asian islands of Sumatra, Borneo and New Guinea, as well as the boreal forests of Siberia and North America[3].

Pressures on forests include high population growth rates, making demands on land for farming in particular; industrial enterprise based on natural resources, such as for timber and pulp production; and demand for fuelwood and charcoal, which consumed 80 percent of the timber cut in developing countries in 1995[4]. Piecemeal forest removal has also fragmented forest regions, which has a disproportionate effect on species diversity by limiting the ecosystem's ability to recover from catastrophes such as fires and by reducing species mobility[5].

Most of the 10 percent recorded loss of the world's natural forests between 1970 and 1995 occurred in the tropics, where population growth rates are fastest[6]. Between 1990 and 1995, the greatest amount of forests were lost in Latin America, followed by Africa and Asia. Annual deforestation rates were highest in fast-growing and already densely populated countries – exceeding 3 percent in Bangladesh, Pakistan, the Philippines and Jamaica[7].

Poverty and wealth distribution are also important determinants of forest survival. Many poor countries and communities rely heavily for income and exports on exploiting forest products, alongside agriculture, while richer countries and communities may have other sources of income. The fastest destruction often occurs when large numbers of people are forced to migrate into the forests, usually because of urban unemployment, rural land shortages, fast-growing populations, the creation of refugees or a combination of these.

Government policies can also be important. Most forests in tropical countries are state-owned, so migration of people into forests usually requires official sanction as well as government-built infrastructure, such as roads and organized farming programs. The deforestation of the Brazilian

NUMBER OF PEOPLE LIVING IN FOREST ECOSYSTEMS, LATE 1990s

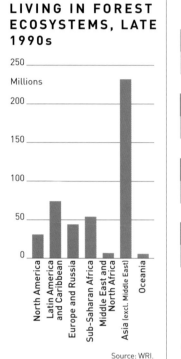

Source: WRI.

CHANGES IN FOREST AREA

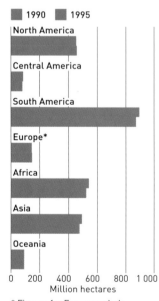

* Figures for Europe exclude the former Soviet Union, for which no comparable data are available. The region is currently estimated to have some 763 500 000 hectares of forest area

Source: WRI.

ORIGINAL AND CURRENT FOREST AREA

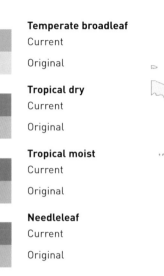

Temperate broadleaf
Current
Original

Tropical dry
Current
Original

Tropical moist
Current
Original

Needleleaf
Current
Original

The map shows current forest cover alongside an estimate of where there would be forest had there been no human intervention and assuming current climatic conditions. This is close to the maximal area of forest some time after the last ice age, around 6 000 years ago.

PROTECTED FOREST AREA, 1997
Thousand hectares

	Tropical forest area	Protected area	Non-tropical forest area	Protected area	Disturbed natural and plantations	Protected area
North America	443	30	683 700	61 074	260	20
Central America	71 893	8 834	21 293	664	1 963	144
South America	620 514	75 907	39 291	6 182	13 259	863
Europe*	0	0	1 019 178	29 588	0	0
Africa	448 197	40 752	8 240	168	41 565	865
Asia	210 720	34 603	145 101	7 462	39 975	2 408
Oceania*	53 560	4 889	27 088	5 068	0	0

* Owing to the difficulty in distinguishing natural forest and plantations in many developed countries, total forest area is not broken down into sub-categories

Source: WRI.

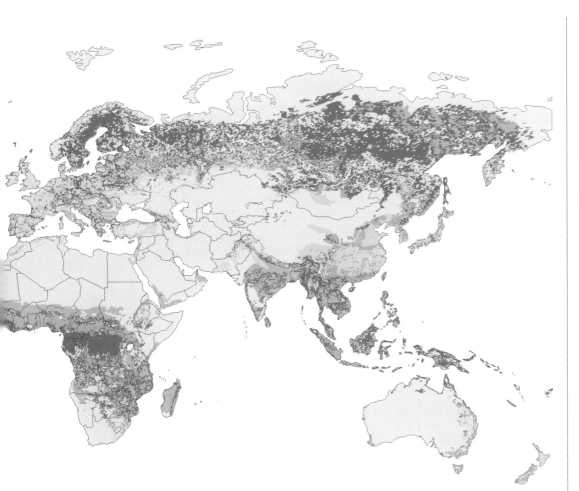

Source: UNEP-WCMC.

SHRINKING FORESTS

While the United States of America and Europe had lost most of their forest by the beginning of the 20th century, Costa Rica, by contrast, saw rapid deforestation during the 20th century.

Costa Rica

1940

1961

1983

Source: Dobson.

COUNTRIES WITH THE HIGHEST RATES OF FOREST LOSS

	Annual % natural forest loss 1990-95	Population growth rate 1990-95	Population density per square kilometer 1995	GDP per capita $US 1995
Lebanon	-10.3	3.3	294.1	3 703
Jamaica	-8.0	0.7	225.9	1 785
Afghanistan	-7.1	5.8	30.9	id
Haiti	-5.2	2.0	260.5	287
Syria	-5.0	3.4	79.8	1 182
Jordan	-4.8	4.9	61.2	1 187*
Philippines	-3.6	2.1	226.7	1 093
El Salvador	-3.5	2.2	278.4	1 673
Pakistan	-3.2	2.8	182.3	445
Bangladesh	-3.1	2.2	925.2	246
World	**+**	**1.6**	**43.6**	**4 896**

* 1994
+ No global annual rate of natural forest loss is available; the global rate of loss including all forest types is -0.3%

Source : FAO; UNPD; WRI; World Bank.

CARBON IN LIVE VEGETATION
Actual carbon estimate

Ecosystem complex	Kilos carbon per square meter
Conifers	13
Tropical/subtropical broad-leaved humid forest	12
Mid-latitude temperate broad-leaved forest	9
Tropical/subtropical dry forest and woodland	6
Northern or maritime taiga, subalpine	5
Tropical savannah and interrupted woodland	3
Wooded tundra	2

Source: CDIAC.

In the 1990s forests were estimated to be soaking up a third of all CO_2 emissions from fossil-fuel burning, due to the "fertilization effect" of the extra CO_2 in the air. But this will not last. United Nations scientists warned in the third assessment of the Intergovernmental Panel on Climate Change (IPCC) that warming will soon neutralize this effect by speeding up the decay of plant matter in forests. Warming may also trigger droughts and forest fires that could drastically reduce the forest cover in the tropics.

Amazon has spread from east to west as roads and development projects have penetrated the forest. Much of Indonesia's forest has been converted into farms as a result of the national transmigration program, which has moved some 4 million people from densely populated areas to thinly populated forested provinces such as Kalimantan and Irian Jaya.

Failures of governance also contribute by encouraging resource plundering. In 1999, in the aftermath of the fall of President Suharto, the majority of Indonesian timber on the international market was illegally logged[8]. Globalization of trade in forest products, especially timber, encourages the removal of control over forests from native people, who have the most incentive to maintain forests for future generations. Poor forest management has left natural forests unable to regrow and often vulnerable to forest fires, such as those that spread through Indonesia in the 1990s.

Natural forests – once characterized as "jungle" that required "clearing" – are now increasingly regarded as important ecological and economic resources for both nations and the planet. They stabilize the landscape by generating rainfall and maintaining soil, groundwater and river flows. They are also a major cultural resource as the homelands and direct sources of natural wealth for indigenous peoples, such as the reindeer herders of Siberia and the tribes of the Amazon, Borneo and New Guinea. The economic value of a sustainable harvest of fruits, nuts, rubber, rattan, medicinal plants and meat frequently exceeds the one-off value of clear-felling.

Most countries eventually adopt conservation measures to protect surviving natural forests – often following a natural disaster attributed to deforestation. In 1998, after floods did extensive damage on the River Yangtze, China banned further logging in some watersheds and launched a replanting program. Chinese scientists also partly blame deforestation for the falling water flows in the Yellow River.

In the past two decades, the temperate northern latitudes have seen a modest increase in forest cover. However, this was mainly of commercial forest stands, which have much lower species diversity and ecological value than natural "old-growth" forests. And many European forests are in poor health, primarily because of air pollution.

Moreover, the felling of old-growth forests continues, often with state subsidies – for instance in the northwest of the United States and the temperate rainforests of the Canadian west coast. Western and Japanese timber companies have frequently "exported" their destruction of natural forests to tropical regions: Southeast Asian forests are a major source of hardwood timber for Japan.

The 1990s saw the first worldwide efforts to halt the decline of tropical forests. Studies for the International Tropical Timber Organization (ITTO) at the start of the decade found that less than 1 percent of logging was carried out sustainably (with recovery to a similar ecological value)[9]. Consumer boycotts of tropical timber grew in protest, and by the end of the decade more than 15 million hectares of forestry projects had received certificates of their sustainability from the Forest Stewardship Council, a coalition including foresters, conservation and community groups, timber traders and certification organizations. Certified timber products can command a premium price.

Economists and environmentalists have also sought to give tangible economic worth to the undoubted ecological value of natural forests as watershed protectors, storehouses of biological diversity, and recreational and spiritual assets. The 1992 Convention on Biological Diversity gave countries new rights to the ownership of the genetic resources in their forests, which could find value in pharmaceuticals or new crops, although this has yet to prove profitable. Ecotourism, a fast-growing industry, is being actively encouraged.

The potential commercial value of fast-growing trees planted to soak up carbon dioxide (CO_2) from the atmosphere and act as carbon "sinks" has also been recognized – and backed by the 1997 Kyoto Protocol on Climate Change. Carbon credits earned by planting these forests will be tradeable with countries wanting to offset them against emissions, which are limited under the Protocol. However, management of sink forests to maximize their carbon absorption often reduces their ecological value.

Deserts and drylands

D ESERTS AND DRYLANDS are the largely unfenced, unforested parts of the planet, where low and erratic rainfall makes the land unsuitable for cultivation. The land is used for grazing domesticated animals, set aside for wild animals or simply set aside. Human population density is generally low, except around water sources or the focus of economic activity such as minerals. But sophisticated nomadic and pastoral cultures often thrive in the marginal land, some of which is suitable for cultivation if irrigated, making it a potentially valuable resource where water is available.

Desert margins, generally called drylands, have great biological value. They are the original homes of many of the world's most important food grains – wheat, barley, millet and sorghum – and botanical medicines, resins and oils, as well as many animal and bird species. Dryland soils are unusually vulnerable to degradation. New soil forms only very slowly in these arid environments, and salts tend to build up owing to infrequent rains. The dry sparsely covered topsoil is easy victim to erosion by wind or by the rains when they do come. Regions susceptible to such erosion include the desert margins of North and Southern Africa, the Great Plains and pampas of the Americas, the steppes of Southeast Europe and Asia, the Australian "outback" and the Mediterranean margins.

Degradation, often known as "desertification", may arise from human misuse of the land or climatic change, and may or may not be reversible. Either way it can force people to leave the land. A fifth of the world's drylands, or around a billion hectares, are thought to be affected by human-induced soil erosion, and an estimated 250 million people, including many of the poorest, most marginalized and politically weak citizens[1], are directly affected by land degradation in arid areas. International action to improve management of the world's drylands is concentrated on the 1996 United Nations Convention to Combat Desertification, but it has so far failed to attract substantial funding from donor nations.

There is continuing uncertainty about the processes and definitions of desertification[2]. The term came into wide use in the 1970s with images of the Sahel, a band of semiarid land on the southern borders of the Sahara desert, "marching" south. In places it advanced by up to 100 kilometers between 1950 and 1975, a process seen at the time as an irreversible human-induced phenomenon. But satellite images have now revealed the Saharan advance to have been largely a consequence of short-term climatic change. The desert border has advanced and retreated with the rains several times since 1980[3].

Some historical incidents of desertification, for instance the abandonment of farming in the Negev desert, are now also held to have arisen as much from changing climate as poor land management[4]. In many cases, however, the two go together, with intensified landuse leaving vegetation and soils vulnerable to degradation during drought. The "dust bowl" in the American Midwest in the 1930s had such multiple causes.

GLOBAL LAND AREA

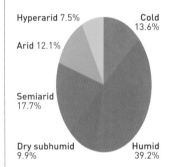

Hyperarid 7.5%

Cold 13.6%

Arid 12.1%

Semiarid 17.7%

Dry subhumid 9.9%

Humid 39.2%

Total land area: 13 049 million hectares

Source: UNEP.

GLOBAL SOIL DEGRADATION, 1990s

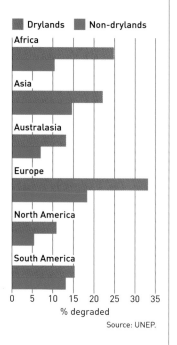

■ Drylands ■ Non-drylands

Africa

Asia

Australasia

Europe

North America

South America

0 5 10 15 20 25 30 35
% degraded

Source: UNEP.

SOIL DEGRADATION IN THE WORLD'S DRYLANDS, 1990s

Dry subhumid
Strong/extreme

Moderate/light

Semiarid
Strong/extreme

Moderate/light

Arid
Strong/extreme

Moderate/light

Non-degraded susceptible drylands

Hyperarid lands not generally susceptible to degradation

Owing to the erratic rainfall in arid regions, drylands themselves are difficult to define, and areas have to be studied for a number of decades before it can be said with certainty that desertfication, rather than natural variability, has taken place. It is this high degree of variability that makes drylands more susceptible to degradation than other regions, and more pressing the need for monitoring and understanding the underlying causes of dryland degradation.

HUMAN-INDUCED SALINIZATION IN SUSCEPTIBLE DRYLANDS, 1990s

	Million hectares
North America	1.8
South America	1.0
Europe	3.0
Africa	5.8
Asia	35.4
Australasia	0.9
Total	**47.9**

Source: UNEP.

SOIL DEGRADATION BY REGION IN SUSCEPTIBLE DRYLANDS, 1990s
Million hectares

	Water erosion	Wind erosion	Chemical deterioration	Physical deterioration	Total
North America	38.4	37.8	2.2	1.0	79.4
South America	34.7	26.9	17.0	0.4	79.0
Europe	48.1	38.6	4.1	8.6	99.4
Africa	119.1	159.9	26.5	13.9	319.4
Asia	157.5	153.2	50.2	9.6	370.5
Australasia	69.6	16.0	0.6	1.2	87.4
Total	**467.4**	**432.4**	**100.7**	**34.7**	**1 035.2**

Source: UNEP.

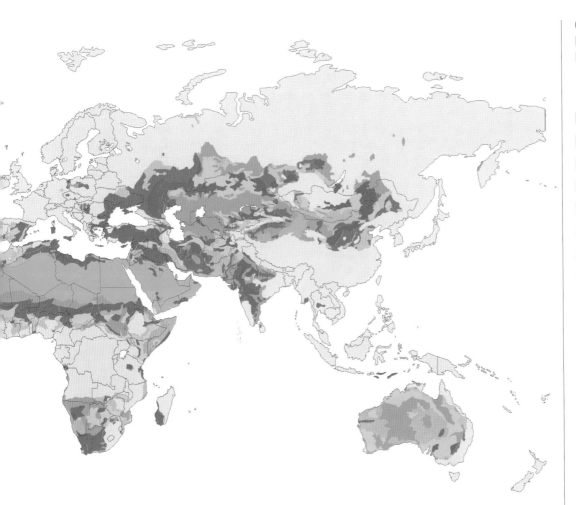

Source: UNEP.

COUNTRIES WITH LARGE AREAS OF DRYLANDS

	Population growth rate 1995-2000	Population density per km² 1995	GDP per capita $US 1995
Afghanistan	5.3	30.9	id
Albania	0.6	125.6	648
Algeria	2.3	11.7	1 474
Angola	3.3	8.9	344
Argentina	1.3	12.6	8 084
Armenia	0.2	126.7	783
Australia	1.1	2.4	19 522
Azerbaijan	0.8	87.8	461
Botswana	2.2	2.6	2 978
Bulgaria	-0.5	79.3	1 453
Burkina Faso	2.8	37.7	222
Chad	2.8	5.1	180
China	0.9	131.0	572
Egypt	1.9	63.2	763
El Salvador	2.2	278.4	1 673
Eritrea	3.7	35.0	id
Ethiopia	3.2	50.0	94
Greece	0.3	81.1	8 662
India	1.6	314.7	349
Iran	2.2	41.1	1 756
Iraq	2.8	46.8	2 755
Israel	1.9	273.0	16 645
Jordan	3.3	61.2	1 187
Kazakhstan	0.1	6.4	1 273
Kenya	2.2	49.7	335
Kuwait	3.0	86.8	15 760
Kyrgyzstan	0.4	24.8	685
Lebanon	1.8	294.1	3 703
Libya	3.3	3.1	4 984
Macedonia	0.7	85.1	937
Madagascar	3.1	25.4	215
Malawi	2.5	118.3	151
Mali	3.0	8.8	225
Mauritania	2.5	2.2	470
Mexico	1.6	49.1	2 743
Moldova	0.1	134.4	793
Mongolia	2.1	1.5	349
Morocco	1.8	60.6	1 222
Mozambique	2.5	20.4	85
Namibia	2.4	1.9	1 974
Niger	3.3	7.2	203
Nigeria	2.8	122.7	362
Oman	4.2	10.2	5 483
Pakistan	2.7	182.3	445
Romania	-0.2	99.1	1 563
Russia	-0.3	8.6	2 333
Saudi Arabia	3.4	8.3	6 875
Somalia	3.9	14.7	106*
South Africa	2.2	34.0	3 281
Spain	0.1	79.3	14 097
Sudan	2.2	11.8	239
Syria	2.5	79.8	1 182
Tajikistan	1.9	42.8	343
Turkey	1.6	80.5	2 709
Turkmenistan	1.9	8.4	961
UAE	2.0	22.8	17 696
Ukraine	-0.4	88.7	1 548
USA	0.8	27.5	26 026
Uzbekistan	1.9	53.7	947
Venezuela	2.0	24.8	3 434
Yemen	3.7	27.5	319
Zimbabwe	2.1	29.1	583
World	**1.4**	**43.6**	**4 896**

*1990   Source: WRI.

SOIL DEGRADATION BY DEGREE IN SUSCEPTIBLE DRYLANDS, 1990s
Million hectares

	Water erosion	Wind erosion	Chemical deterioration	Physical deterioration	Total
Light	175.1	197.2	44.3	10.8	427.3
Moderate	208.5	215.4	31.4	15.0	470.3
Strong	79.0	18.0	24.2	8.9	130.1
Extreme	4.8	1.8	0.8	0.0	7.5
Total	**467.4**	**432.4**	**100.7**	**34.7**	**1 035.2**

Source: UNEP.

The movement of "lost" soils can be dramatic, as seen in this satellite image of a dustcloud off the west coast of Africa, taken in February 2000. Up to 100 million tons of dust cross the Atlantic annually from West Africa to the Caribbean[11]. In 1998, a dust storm originating in China could be tracked as it crossed the United States[12].

By some estimates, the world loses 24 billion tons of topsoil each year[13], with South Africa alone estimated to lose 300-400 million tons annually. The decline in soil and vegetation reduces the ability of the land to hold water after infrequent rains, accelerating desertification and flooding, since surface runoff increases.

Photo: NOAA/Operational Significant Event Imagery.

In most cases "desertification" does not involve advancing desert sands, but rather a progressive decline in the productivity of the land. The largest single cause worldwide is the overgrazing of pastures[5]. Plants in semiarid regions are adapted to being eaten by large grazing animals at low densities, with regular nomadic stock movements maintaining this vegetation. But the trend towards sedentarization, the use of fences to separate domesticated animals from wildlife and the concentration of animals around water boreholes have often caused loss of vegetation followed by soil erosion.

Many governments exacerbate these problems by trying to halt nomadism, particularly across national borders. They also try to concentrate wildlife within national parks, such as Amboseli in Kenya, which is being overgrazed by elephants and other large herbivores[6]. Other threats to natural vegetation and soils include deforestation and the collection of wood for fuel, cultivation of marginal land and poor irrigation practices, which can lead to an accumulation of salt in soils and eventual abandonment of the land.

While not generally densely populated, the world's arid lands have some of the fastest population growth rates in the world. This growth tends to extend and intensify cultivated land and squeeze out nomadic groups. In the Sahel region of Africa, population has risen fourfold since 1930 and is expected to double again in the next 30 years, even allowing for the migration of some 20 million people to coastal areas[7].

Desertification makes 12 million hectares of land useless for cultivation every year. Since 1965, one sixth of the populations of Mali and Burkina Faso have lost their livelihoods and fled to cities. In Mauritania between 1965 and 1988, the proportion of the population who were nomads fell from 73 percent to 7 percent, while the proportion of the population in the capital Nouakchott rose from 9 percent to 41 percent.

But desertification is not exclusively a problem of the developing world. Commercial agriculture and livestock farming can cause as much damage to arid ecosystems as pastoralism and subsistence agriculture. Australia, one of the world's richest but least densely populated countries, has one of the most serious land degradation problems.

The simple view of population pressure in a fragile environment causing permanent environmental degradation has been subject to re-evaluation. In the Yatenga province of Burkina Faso, farmers rescued their fields from imminent desertification by erecting low stone walls along the contours of hillsides to keep soil and water on the land. The Dogon people of eastern Mali practice some of the most intensive irrigated agriculture in Africa to feed a rapidly rising population in an era of declining rainfall – but do so without causing desertification[8]. Elsewhere in the Sahel communities have adopted rainwater harvesting methods to halt soil loss and improve the productivity of their lands.

The Machakos district in Kenya was considered to be on the verge of desertification in the 1930s. But in the ensuing decades, even with a fivefold population increase, water and soil conservation measures, such as cutting hillside terraces and digging water-storage ponds, are generally held to have improved the environment[9]. Similarly, adaptive farming methods have maintained a productive agricultural landscape despite a very high population density in semi-arid northern Nigeria[10]. Critics of these studies point out that in both cases large urban areas nearby (Nairobi and Kano respectively) mean the areas are far from typical of drylands under population pressure.

Freshwater wetlands

WETLANDS are the fragile interface between land and water. Throughout history, humans have separated these two elements with dykes, dams and drains – and wetlands have been the prime victims. Growing recognition of their value to ecology and human systems alike, however, has led to widespread restoration of wetland habitats in recent years.

Freshwater wetlands take many forms: marshes like the prairie potholes of North America; peatland bogs, fens and mires; swamps such as the swamp forests of the Amazon and Borneo; as well as river deltas, ponds, Australian billabongs, lagoons, mudholes and river floodplains. They are distinguished by being land that is, at least seasonally, waterlogged, whether fed by precipitation, groundwater or rivers. They have vital hydrological roles as sources, reservoirs and regulators of water within river basins, and they are among the richest and most distinctive ecosystems, often compared with rainforests and coral reefs.

Wetlands typically have a high concentration of nutrients, making them rich habitats for the many small organisms on which fish and other water life feed, in turn attracting mammals and birds. Many, such as acidic peatland bogs, provide unique ecological niches for wildlife.

Wetlands now cover just over 6 percent of the world's land area, perhaps half their original extent. Some specialized communities still live in and exploit these ecosystems – for example the Marsh Arabs of Iraq and the 300 000 inhabitants of the Sundarbans of Bangladesh. But for most humans, wetlands have been regarded as disease-ridden wastelands fit only to be drained. Population density is a key determinant of the scale of wetland loss: when land or water are in short supply, wetlands are an obvious source[1].

Humans have damaged wetlands by damming, dyking and canalizing rivers, converting floodplains to aquaculture, planting trees on bogs, draining marshes for agriculture, forestry and urban development and "mining" them for peat, often with heavy state subsidy. But throughout history, agricultural activity has been the most important single cause of damage, with wetlands, including traditional wet pastures, drained to provide croplands.

In the 19th and 20th centuries, wetlands suffered because of the large-scale damming of rivers and pumping of groundwater to meet increasing demand for water. Thus the arid and heavily populated state of California has lost 91 percent of its wetlands in the past 200 years[2]. The United States as a whole has lost 50 million of the 90 million hectares of wetlands it had 500 years ago.

Wetlands along the flood-prone Mississippi once stored 60 days of the river's floodwater; today they are so reduced that they can only store 12 days' worth. Those around the edge of Lake Victoria, the world's second largest freshwater lake, have degraded so much in recent decades that they can no longer filter the nutrients such as nitrates and phosphates that flow into the lake from surrounding land. The result has been eutrophication and an explosive growth of water hyacinth that is clogging the lake.

NUMBER OF PEOPLE LIVING IN THE TEN LARGEST RIVER CATCHMENTS, LATE 1990s

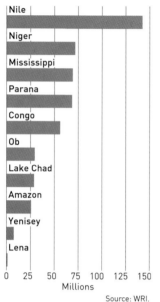

Millions

Source: WRI.

MAJOR INLAND WATERS AND RIVER CATCHMENTS OF THE WORLD

- Freshwater marshes and floodplains
- Inland open waters
- Peatlands
- Saline systems
- Seasonally flooding inland systems
- Swamp forests
- Tidal/coastal systems
- Unclassified wetlands
- **River catchment** (see table below)

Recognition of the significance of wetland ecosystems as ecological regulators has been relatively slow to emerge. At the time of the establishment of the Ramsar Convention on Wetlands of International Importance in 1971, it was for their role as sites for migrating and overwintering bird populations that wetlands were recognized by the conservation community as in need of specific protection measures.

RAMSAR SITES: WETLANDS OF INTERNATIONAL IMPORTANCE, 1997
By regional share

North America 23%
Europe 21%
Central America 2%
Asia 8%
South America 16%
Oceania 9%
Africa 21%

Total: 66 840 000 hectares over 891 sites

Source: Ramsar Bureau.

DEFORESTATION AND POPULATION DENSITY IN THE WORLD'S LARGEST RIVER CATCHMENTS, LATE 1990s

River catchment	% original forest lost	Population density per square kilometer
1. Yukon	23	0.2
2. Mackenzie	8	0.2
3. Nelson	24	2.2
4. Mississippi	52	21.5
5. St. Lawrence	23	41.6
6. Amazon	13	4.3
7. Parana	71	23.5
8. Niger	95	31.2
9. Lake Chad	100	11.0
10. Congo	46	14.5
11. Nile	92	42.7
12. Zambezi	43	17.7
13. Volga	53	41.4
14. Ob	38	191.9
15. Yenisey	19	2.3
16. Lena	19	1.3
17. Kolyma	56	0.5
18. Amur	33	35.2
19. Ganges/Brahmaputra	78	296.4
20. Yangtze	85	223.7
21. Murray-Darling	64	2.1

Source: WRI.

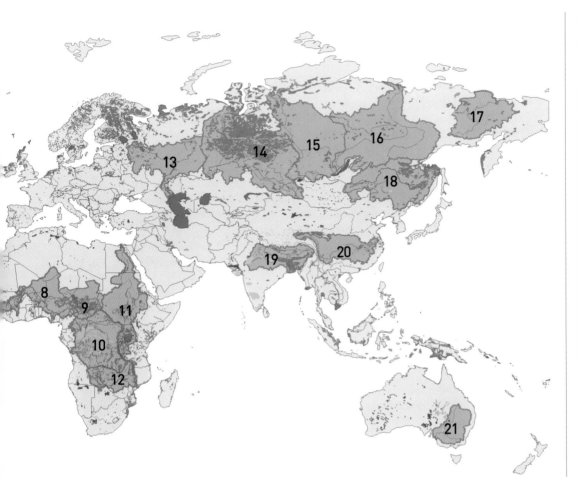

Source: UNEP-WCMC; WRI.

FRESHWATER FISH SPECIES THREATENED, 1996

Madagascar
Portugal
Croatia
South Africa
Spain
Italy
Mexico
Greece
USA
Hungary
Australia
Romania
Bulgaria
Moldova
Slovakia
Turkey
Germany
Sri Lanka
Canada
Papua New Guinea
Japan

Countries whose fish populations have been evaluated and which have the largest numbers of threatened species

0   10   20   30   40
% threatened

Source: IUCN.

HUMAN ACTIONS LEADING TO WETLAND LOSS

Cause of loss	Floodplains	Rivers	Lakes	Peatlands	Swamps
Drainage for agriculture, forestry and mosquito control	•	•	+	•	•
Dredging and channelization for navigation and flood protection	O	+	O	O	O
Filling for solid waste disposal, roads and commercial, industrial or residential development	+	+	+	O	O
Conversion for aquaculture	•	•	+	O	O
Construction of dykes, dams and seawalls for flood and storm control, water supply and irrigation	•	•	•	O	O
Discharge of pesticides, herbicides, domestic and industrial waste, agricultural runoff and sediment	•	•	•	O	O
Mining of wetlands for peat, coal, gravel, phosphate and other materials	+	O	•	•	•
Logging and shifting cultivation	•	+	O	•	•
Groundwater abstraction	+	•	O	O	O
Fire	•	+	O	•	•
Sediment diversion by dams, deep channels and other structures	•	•	+	O	O
Hydrological alteration by canals, roads and other structures	•	•	•	+	+
Subsidence due to extraction of groundwater, oil, gas and other minerals	•	•	O	O	O

• **Common and important cause of loss** + **Present but not a major cause of loss** O **Absent or exceptional**

Source: UNEP.

POPULATION TRENDS IN A SAMPLE OF FRESHWATER SPECIES

Increasing
Stable
Decreasing

1970-79   1980-89   1990-99
9%   11%   13%
59% 32%   55% 34%   52% 35%

Source: WWF.

THE RISE OF AQUACULTURE IN FRESHWATER FISH PRODUCTION

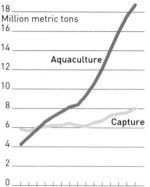

Source: FAO.

People have created artificial wetlands for specific purposes such as rice paddies, farm ponds, and reservoirs on dammed rivers, but this has often been at the expense of natural wetlands. In peninsular Malaysia, 90 percent of freshwater swamps have been drained for rice cultivation.

Conservationists have ensured that more than 800 of the world's most important wetlands in around a hundred countries are protected as wildlife habitats under the 1971 Ramsar Convention. But there is an increasing realization that they have a large economic value to human society as well. They cleanse water of organic pollutants; soak up floodwaters, so preventing inundation downstream; protect riverbanks and seashores against erosion; recycle nutrients; capture sediment and recharge groundwater.

A study of the large Hadejia-Nguru wetland in arid northern Nigeria found that water in the wetland yielded a profit in fish, firewood, cattle grazing lands and natural crop irrigation that was 30 times greater than the yield of water being diverted from the wetland into a costly irrigation project[3]. A recent attempt to put a dollar value on the "ecological services" provided by different ecosystems worldwide put wetlands top at almost US$15 000 per hectare per year, seven times that of tropical rainforest[4]. Much of this value comes from flood prevention.

Wetlands store very large amounts of carbon in organic matter. Peat bogs in Siberia, North America and Scandinavia contain a third of all the carbon in the world's soils. Scottish peat bogs contain more than 90 percent of the carbon in British soils and forests.

Much of the carbon in wetlands is released as methane by natural processes, accounting for roughly half of the methane currently released into the air. Molecule for molecule, this is a much more potent greenhouse gas than carbon dioxide[5], and much more could be released if climate change warms and dries the northern peatlands, triggering slow destruction or catastrophic burning. Wetland maintenance is therefore significant in helping to moderate global climate change.

The world's largest wetland restoration project will spend US$700 million over two decades to revive the Florida Everglades. It will include a series of six artificial wetlands known as "storm water treatment areas", which will receive and clean up excess nutrients that enter the wetland from neighboring farming districts[6].

THE MEDITERRANEAN

Among the world's most threatened wetlands are those around the Mediterranean, which for two millennia has been one of the most densely populated regions on Earth. Draining of wetlands and floodplains for agriculture – and more recently for urban areas, tourist developments and to eradicate malarial mosquitoes – has been among the largest engineering endeavors of the region. More recently, rising demand for water from the 160 million people who live on the Mediterranean coastline and the similar number of tourists who visit each year has caused a general water shortage in the region that peaked with a series of droughts in the 1990s. It left little water to be "set aside" in wetlands.

Both Spain and Greece have drained 60 percent of their wetlands in the last century. Pumping of groundwater for agricultural irrigation is drying up Spanish wetlands such as the Doñana reserve, one of Europe's top sanctuaries for wintering birds, where the water table is falling by a meter every two years[7].

Other wetland ecosystems have become convenient cesspits for large cities, overwhelming their natural cleansing capacities and leaving stagnant water clogged with algae. Examples include the Lac du Tunis, outside the Tunisian capital, the Manzalah lagoon outside Cairo, and wetlands on the River Po, which runs through many of northern Italy's industrial cities.

Mangroves and estuaries

MANGROVES protect coastlines by absorbing the force of storms, and provide sufficient nutrients to nurture most of the world's marine life. Many have been lost, largely through conversion to rice paddies and shrimp farms, and with coastal regions set to double their human populations over the next 25 years, coastal ecosystems such as mangroves, estuaries, mud flats and seagrass beds are coming under increasing threat.

Mangroves are forests of salt-tolerant trees and shrubs that grow in the shallow tidal waters of estuaries and coastal areas in tropical regions. They require slow currents, no frost and plenty of fine sediment in which to set their roots. Their muddy waters, rich in nutrients from decaying leaves and wood, are home to sponges, worms, crustaceans, molluscs and algae, and provide shelter for marine mammals, snakes and crocodiles. They act as fish nurseries and help feed life further out to sea. Queensland's mangroves, for instance, do much to sustain the Great Barrier Reef, the world's largest coral reef system. Mangroves are also strongly correlated with the presence of shoals of shrimp further offshore.

Mangroves extend over 18 million hectares worldwide, covering a quarter of the world's tropical coastline[1]. They dominate the river deltas and tidal creeks of Southeast Asia from Thailand, Myanmar and Vietnam through Malaysia to Indonesia, with more than 5 million hectares around the thinly populated islands of New Guinea and Borneo alone[2]. The largest single system is the 570 000 hectares of the Sundarbans of Bangladesh, which harbor the Bengal tiger and sustain some 300 000 people.

Mangroves have many uses, providing large quantities of food and fuel, building materials and medicines. One hectare of mangroves in the Philippines can yield 400 kilos of fish, shrimps, crabmeat, molluscs and sea cucumbers annually, and help feed a further 400 kilos of fish and 75 kilos of shrimps that mature elsewhere[3]. The majority of the world's marine species, including most fish catches, depend on coastal wetlands such as mangroves for part of their life cycle. The seedlings of the main tree species, *Rhizophora*, cure a sore mouth and are said to have aphrodisiac powers. Filipinos use *Nypa* foliage to thatch roofs, while its fermented sap produces an annual 10 000 liters of alcohol per hectare of mangroves[4].

But mangroves are nonetheless under grave threat. Their many communal benefits are no match for the quick cash profits that can be made from chopping them down for timber for firewood, draining them for urban development and farming, or converting them into salt pans and brackish shrimp ponds[5]. Most Caribbean and South Pacific mangroves have disappeared, while India, West Africa and Southeast Asia have all lost half their mangroves[6]. Growing population density is a major factor. Most of the Philippine mangroves that survive are on the least populated island of Mindanao, while the heavily populated Indonesian islands of Java and Bali have lost almost all theirs. But the increasing international trade in timber and shrimps has also been critical.

MANGROVES OF THE WORLD, MID-1990s
By regional share

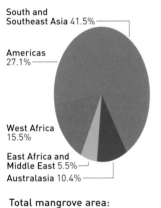

South and Southeast Asia 41.5%

Americas 27.1%

West Africa 15.5%

East Africa and Middle East 5.5%

Australasia 10.4%

Total mangrove area: 18 107 700 hectares

Source: ISME.

MANGROVE AREAS AND COASTAL AND ESTUARY CITIES, LATE 1990s

● Mangrove

/\/\ Major inland waterway

● Coastal and estuary cities of more than 1 million people

Mangroves are only able to grow in coastal areas such as estuaries that are free from wave action, making them particularly vulnerable to transformation by human populations, who favor similar sites for development.

THE WORLD'S MAJOR SHIPPING PORTS, 1997

Port	Approximate shipping volume Gross tons
Singapore	768 000 000
Rotterdam	315 500 000
Kaohsiung	310 038 615
Chiba	173 600 000
Hong Kong	169 229 000
Nagoya	143 000 000
Antwerp	120 000 000
Yokohama	117 800 000
Hamburg	76 000 000
Long Beach	60 000 000
Los Angeles	60 000 000
Busan	46 500 000
Kobe	41 910 796
South Louisiana	33 000 000
Ulsan	31 000 000
Dubai Ports	28 000 000
Shanghai	3 600*

*Number of vessels

Source: ISEL; Fairplay.

HUMAN ACTIONS LEADING TO COASTAL DEGRADATION

Cause of degradation	Estuaries	Mangroves	Open coasts
Drainage for agriculture, forestry and mosquito control	●	+	●
Dredging and channelization for navigation and flood protection	●	●	O
Filling for solid waste disposal, roads and commercial, industrial or residential development	●	●	+
Conversion for aquaculture	●	●	●
Construction of dykes, dams and seawalls for flood and storm control, water supply and irrigation	●	●	●
Discharge of pesticides, herbicides, domestic and industrial waste, agricultural runoff and sediment	●	●	●
Mining of wetlands for peat, coal, gravel, phosphate and other materials	+	O	+
Logging and shifting cultivation	+	●	O
Fire	+	+	O
Sediment diversion by dams, deep channels and other structures	●	●	●
Hydrological alteration by canals, roads and other structures	●	●	●
Subsidence due to extraction of groundwater, oil, gas and other minerals	●	O	+

● **Common and important cause of degradation** + **Present but not a major cause** O **Absent or exceptional**

Source: UNEP.

Source: UNEP-WCMC; UNPD.

SOME MANGROVE LOSSES

Thailand: 185 000 hectares between 1960 and 1991, to shrimp ponds

Malaysia: 235 000 hectares between 1980 and 1990, to shrimp ponds and clearance for agriculture

Indonesia: 269 000 hectares between 1960 and 1990, to shrimp ponds

Vietnam: 104 000 hectares between 1960 and 1974, to US Army defoliants

Philippines: 170 000 hectares between 1967 and 1976, largely to shrimp ponds

Bangladesh (Chokoria): 74 000 hectares since 1975, largely to shrimp ponds

Guatemala: 9 500 hectares between 1965 and 1984, largely to shrimp ponds and salt farming

Source: Choudhury; ISME.

COUNTRIES WITH LARGE AREAS OF MANGROVE

	Mangrove area Square kilometers	As % of total land area	As % of total forest area 1995	Population density per square kilometer 1995	GDP per capita US$ 1995
Indonesia	42 550	2.23	3.88	109.1	1 003
Brazil	13 400	0.16	0.24	19.1	4 327
Australia	11 500	0.15	2.81	2.4	19 522
Nigeria	10 515	1.14	7.63	122.7	362
Cuba	7 848	7.07	42.60	100.5	id
India	6 700	0.20	1.03	314.7	349
Malaysia	6 424	1.95	4.15	61.3	4 236
Bangladesh	5 767	4.00	57.10	925.2	246
Papua New Guinea	5 399	1.17	1.46	9.5	1 139
Mexico	5 315	0.27	0.96	49.1	2 743

Note: The mangroves in these countries represent 64% of world mangroves.

Source: ISME; WRI.

RISING SHRIMP AND PRAWN PRODUCTION

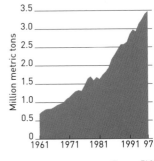

Source: FAO.

THE REVIVAL OF CHESAPEAKE BAY
Phosphorus content

1984-87

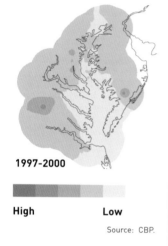

1997-2000

High　　　　　Low

Source: CBP.

Following the initiative to rehabilitate Chesapeake Bay in the United States, there has been a marked decrease in the levels of phosphorus found in the waters of the bay and surrounding areas. Levels of nitrogen and suspended particulates have not declined to the same degree. However, there has been an improvement in the health of wildlife in and around the bay, even while the human populations have increased considerably. Future population growth and sprawl represent the biggest challenges to the health of Chesapeake Bay.

The fate of mangroves shows in stark relief the crisis facing the world's coastal regions, which have the fastest rates of both urbanization and population growth. Half the world's population, some 3 billion people, live within 200 kilometers of the coast. By 2025 that figure may double, rising to three quarters, or 6 billion people[7].

Thirteen of the world's 16 largest cities are on the coast[8], as are most of the fastest growing Asian cities: Bangkok, Jakarta, Karachi, Manila, Mumbai and Shanghai. An estimated 80 million Chinese have moved to coastal cities in recent years; in the United States people are moving to the coast at the rate of 3 600 a day and the five fastest growing states are all coastal; in Australia, 90 percent of all building activity is in the coastal zone.

Coasts offer fertile soils for tilling, flat land for urban development and sites for trading ports. A detailed analysis by the World Resources Institute[9] found 51 percent of the world's coastlines under "moderate" or "high" threat from development activities. The study found a strong correlation between mangrove loss and the growth of cities and ports, and a moderate relationship with population density. Development for tourism was found to be a major threat to coastal ecosystems in the Caribbean.

People also bring pollution. The most serious sources of coastal pollution are nutrients from farming, land clearance and sewage disposal – a problem often made worse by the loss of natural filters such as mangroves. One result of the consequent overfertilization of coastal waters is "red tides" of toxic algae, such as the explosive growth that covered much of the South China coast, including all of Hong Kong, in 1998, decimating fish farms and causing seafood poisoning[10]. Other outbreaks of toxic algae are thought to have caused mass mortalities of sea mammals, such as the 100 critically endangered Mediterranean monk seals found dead on the Mauritanian coast in 1997[11].

The world's seagrasses are also under threat because of urban pollution and the invasion of alien species. In recent years Australia has lost 450 square kilometers of seagrasses and the United States 900 square kilometers[12]. Meanwhile the habitat of Mediterranean seagrasses along the French and Italian Riviera has been invaded by tropical algae, *Caulerpa taxifolia*, thought to have escaped from the Monaco Oceanographic Observatory[13].

Many governments find it hard to secure communal benefits from the protection of habitats such as coastal wetlands in the face of the private profit motive. To be successful requires complex coastal management programs. The United States has begun a long process of rehabilitating its largest brackish estuary, Chesapeake Bay, by cutting pollution, including from nutrients in the surrounding catchment, and restricting coastal development. Popular local support is vital to such programs. Ecuador has discouraged the further destruction of its mangroves by giving shrimp farmers incentives to restore them[14]. Bangladesh employs villagers in its Sundarbans reserve in a program of mangrove planting on coastal mudflats. More than 100 000 hectares have been planted so far.

STORM PROTECTION
Mangroves protect shorelines from devastation by storms. The trees both shield the land from wind and trap sediment in their roots, maintaining a shallow slope on the seabed that absorbs the energy of tidal surges. Their loss can prove disastrous. In the Indian state of Orissa, where the low-lying coastline has been stripped of mangroves to make way for tiger-prawn farms, a cyclone came ashore in 1999, drowning an estimated 10 000 people[15].

Coral reefs

ORAL REEFS are among the most ancient and biologically rich of the planet's ecosystems. Often called "the rainforests of the oceans", they first emerged more than 200 million years ago. A number of living coral reefs are believed to be more than 2 million years old, though most began growing within the last 10 000 years. Their rich fish stocks alone feed a billion people annually, but they now face the combined threats of local assault from destructive fishing methods and coastal development, and the global phenomenon of climate change.

The coral polyp is a tiny invertebrate creature related to the jellyfish. For most of its food and energy it depends on algae that live inside it, and when it dies its skeleton forms the calcium carbonate structure on which new coral grows. Over hundreds of years, this symbiotic relationship has created the vast coral reefs that could cover as many as 600 000 square kilometers of the world's oceans. Many of these are in warm tropical waters, but deep, cold waters have their own coral reef systems, such as those recently discovered in the North Atlantic.

The global area of the most biologically productive near-surface reefs has been estimated at 255 300 square kilometers[1]. These are among the most biologically diverse ecosystems on Earth, calculated to contain more than a million species. Around a quarter of all the world's sea fish feed, grow, spawn and hide from predators in their labyrinths. Hotspots for fish include most of the Philippines and much of Indonesia, as well as Tanzania and the Comoros in Africa, and the Lesser Antilles in the Caribbean[2].

For millennia humans have taken fish from reefs without destroying them. But conventional nets get torn on reefs and more destructive fishing methods have become widespread. Some fishers dynamite reefs to capture fish; others use a cyanide solution to catch live fish for East Asian restaurants. This stuns the target fish, such as the large grouper, but also kills many of the surrounding invertebrates and smaller fish. In the past three decades an estimated million kilos of cyanide have been deposited onto the reefs of the Philippines alone.

Coral reefs face many other threats from human activity. They are dismembered by souvenir-seeking divers, mined for building materials and damaged by the anchors of cruise ships. Silt from dredging, deforestation and urban sewage smothers and kills coral, or feeds the growth of suffocating and sometimes toxic algae, which now cover almost all Jamaican reefs.

Attempts to identify the world's threatened coral reefs have found a strong correlation between risk of damage and coastal population density. Most species-rich coral reefs in Southeast Asia face the gravest threats from rising populations, growing reef tourism and rapidly expanding exports of reef fish. Where coastal populations are generally low, however, the risk of physical assault is also lower. Around 60 percent of reefs in the Pacific Ocean – including Australia and atoll nations such as Kiribati and Tuvalu – fall into this category[3].

But there are also remote threats. Dust storms from Africa, spread on the winds across the

THE WORLD'S REEFS AT RISK, 1998

Low risk 42%

High risk 27%

Medium risk 31%

Total area of near-surface reefs: 255 300 square kilometers

Source: WRI.

The disappearance of species

One of the many threats to coral reefs is the overfishing of target species. Entire populations can be eliminated by fishers who "clear" a reef before moving on to a new area. In the Philippines in the late 1980s the sea urchin *Tripneustes gratilla*, which had thrived throughout the 24-square-kilometer seagrass bed of a flat reef in Bolinao, became the target of traders from China. By 1995 the urchin was believed to have disappeared from the reef[4].

NUMBER OF PEOPLE LIVING WITHIN 100 KILOMETERS OF A REEF, 1998

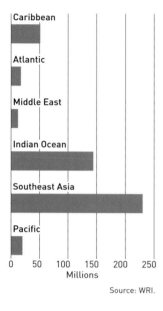

Millions

Source: WRI.

FACTORS THREATENING REEFS

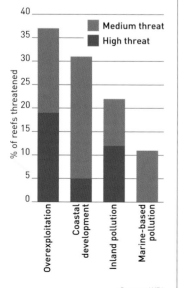

Source: WRI.

DISTRIBUTION OF THE WORLD'S NEAR-SURFACE REEFS, CORAL DISEASE AND BLEACHING EVENTS, 1998

- Coral reef
- Disease
- Light bleaching
- Moderate bleaching
- Severe bleaching
- Coral take, 1997 (kilos)

Western Ce
Atlantic 13 77

Eastern Central
Pacific 907

The map shows the global distribution of coral reefs together with the locations of recent mass bleaching events and disease outbreaks. Coral bleaching is most commonly the result of unusually warm sea temperatures, while the immediate cause of most of the diseases is bacterial infection. There is concern that increasing evidence of these diseases may be related to greater human impacts on reefs.

AREA OF NEAR-SURFACE REEFS AND LEVEL OF THREAT, 1998
Square kilometers

	Total area	Low threat	Medium threat	High threat
Caribbean	20 000	7 800	6 400	5 800
Atlantic	3 100	400	1 000	1 700
Middle East	20 000	7 800	9 200	3 000
Indian Ocean	36 100	16 600	10 500	9 000
Southeast Asia	68 100	12 300	18 000	37 800
Pacific	108 000	63 500	33 900	10 600
Total	**255 300**	**108 400**	**79 000**	**67 900**

Source: WRI.

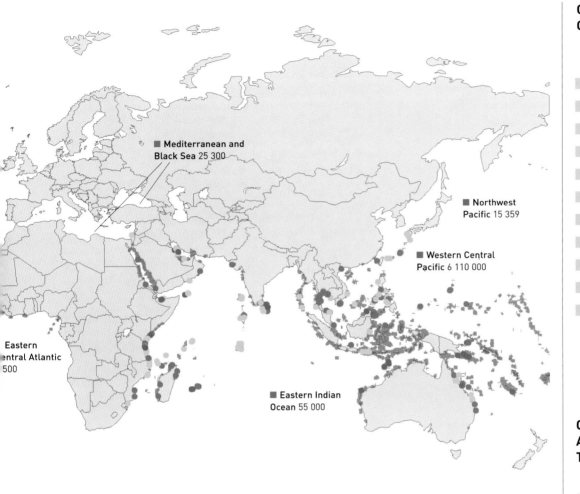

Mediterranean and
Black Sea 25 300

Northwest
Pacific 15 359

Western Central
Pacific 6 110 000

Eastern
Central Atlantic
500

Eastern Indian
Ocean 55 000

Source: UNEP-WCMC; FAO.

CORAL TAKE BY COUNTRY, 1997

	Kilos coral
Malaysia	4 000 000
Indonesia	1 500 000
Philippines	500 000
Fiji	110 000
India	55 000
Haiti	13 000
China	10 245
Spain	8 400
Algeria	5 400
Japan	5 114
Italy	4 100
France	2 500
Croatia	1 600
Morocco	1 600
Tunisia	1 200
Greece	1 100
USA	907
Albania	800
Mexico	775
Turkey	100
Total	**6 221 841**

Source: FAO.

CORAL, PEARL AND SPONGE TAKE, 1997

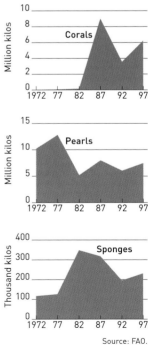

Source: FAO.

COUNTRIES WITH LARGE CORAL REEFS, 1998

	Reef area Square kilometers	Coastal population density per square kilometer	GDP per capita US$ 1998
Australia	48 000	12	19 241
India	6 000	412	439
Indonesia	42 000	93	462
Papua New Guinea	12 000	7	814
Philippines	13 000	174	866
Saudi Arabia	7 000	15	6 227

Note: Half of the world's near-surface reefs are found in these countries.

Source: WRI.

TOURISM IN THE CARIBBEAN, 1997
Selected countries

	Tourists as % of local population	Tourism receipts Million US$	Tourism as % of GNP
Antigua and Barbuda	352	260	53
Aruba	722	666	56
Bahamas	547	1 416	43
Barbados	177	717	41
Dominica	92	37	16
Dominican Republic	27	2 107	16
Grenada	119	61	21
Haiti	2	97	4
Jamaica	47	1 131	28
Puerto Rico	86	2 046	8
St Kitts and Nevis	226	72	29
St Lucia	168	282	49
St Vincent	58	70	25
Trinidad and Tobago	25	108	2
World	**10**	**435 981**	**1**

Source: World Tourism Organization; UNPD; World Bank.

Atlantic, may have introduced bacterial infections from soils to Caribbean reefs[5]. On a global level, no reef can escape the threat posed by the build-up of greenhouse gases in the atmosphere. This works in three ways. Firstly, higher concentrations of carbon dioxide in the air make surface waters more acidic and reduce coral growth rates[6]. Secondly, a warming of the oceans could cause sea-level rise at a rate that coral reefs cannot match as they grow – threatening the survival of atoll nations. Thirdly and most immediately, the rise of ocean temperatures by half a degree or more in recent decades has already placed many reefs at the top end of temperature ranges they can tolerate without undergoing "bleaching".

Bleaching occurs when high temperatures expel the algae in coral, removing their distinctive color – hence the coral appears bleached. If bleaching persists and new algae do not appear, the coral will starve and die, and the reef will become brittle and break up.

As a result of an epidemic of bleaching in the 1990s, which peaked with the El Niño induced warming of 1998, more coral is believed to have died in the last few years of the 20th century than from all human causes to date[7]. A US State Department study in 1999 concluded that two thirds of all the world's coral reefs were deteriorating[8].

Until recently scientists believed that reefs in good general health and remote from human activity were not vulnerable to bleaching. But that view was thrown into question when one of the largest, most remote, pristine and biodiverse coral atolls, at the Chagos Islands in the Indian Ocean, was found extensively bleached[9]. Investigators found an area the size of New Jersey strewn with dead and broken coral. Most of the reef fish had disappeared.

Coral reefs are a major global biological and economic resource for both fisheries and tourism, and because they protect vulnerable coastlines from wave action and storms. Countries such as Barbados, the Maldives and the Seychelles rely on reef tourism for much of their foreign income. Florida's reefs attract annual tourism revenues of US$1.6 billion. One estimate puts the global annual value of coral reefs in fisheries, tourism and coastal protection at US$375 billion. That is US$60 for every member of the human race[10].

Worldwide, there are more than 400 protected coral reefs. The overwhelming number are in Australia and Indonesia, the two countries with the most reefs overall. But most reserves are small and at least 40 countries with reef systems – in both the industrialized and developing world – lack any marine protected areas. Nonetheless, there are several examples of good management and planning. Bermuda, for example, closed its pot-fishing industry for the benefit of biodiversity and the lucrative reef-based tourism. The Philippines has organized locally managed marine reserves to protect reefs from cyanide fishing on Apo Island, and developed scuba-diving tourism. Australia's Great Barrier Reef World Heritage Site has imposed "no take" fishing zones as well as local bans on mining and tourism infrastructure[11].

Regional seas

THE REGIONAL SEAS, hugging the coasts and largely surrounded by land, have been the cradles of many ancient civilizations and lent their names to many of the world's regions, for example the Mediterranean, Caribbean and Baltic. With major trading cities and states huddling around their shores they have been routes for the exchange of goods, information and culture, and have supplied large populations with food, raw materials and, increasingly, entertainment and leisure.

Mostly occupying shallow continental shelves and closely tied to coastal ecosystems such as mangroves and coral reefs, regional seas are naturally rich in marine life. They have been viewed as an endless supply of fish, as well as a bottomless pit for garbage. But their capacity to absorb the impacts of human exploitation is in many cases being stretched to the limit.

Urbanization and rising population densities along their shores are turning many of these seas into reservoirs of undispersed pollution. Their sediment flows are becoming impoverished, their ecosystems are overfished and invaded by alien species, and sometimes even their circulation patterns are disrupted.

The Mediterranean, home to the Egyptian, Phoenecian, Greek and Roman empires, now has 160 million residents on its shores and a similar number of annual visitors. More than 500 million tons of sewage are poured into the sea each year, along with 120 000 tons of mineral oils, 60 000 tons of detergents, 100 tons of mercury, 3 800 tons of lead and 3 600 tons of phosphates[1]. One fifth of all the world's oil spills have occurred in its waters[2]. It was the first sea to have its own treaty and an action plan to reduce pollution and protect coastal ecosystems – so far with only moderate success.

About 75 percent of marine pollution worldwide originates on land, reaching the sea either directly, down rivers or via the fallout of atmospheric pollution. Nutrients from agricultural run-off and sewage discharge are causing algal blooms that starve the waters of oxygen and drive away sea life – a process known as eutrophication. Inputs of nitrates to the North Sea in Northern Europe have risen fourfold and phosphate inputs eightfold since the 1970s[3], causing eutrophication on its eastern shores and tides of toxic algae that have killed stocks in offshore fish farms.

One consequence of eutrophication can be the formation of "dead zones" on the seabed. As excessive amounts of algae die and decay, the water's oxygen levels drop, depriving other species of the oxygen they need to survive. The collapse of the Baltic Sea cod fishery in the early 1990s is blamed on oxygen loss in deep waters, which interfered with cod reproduction. One of the largest dead zones has formed along the United States shoreline of the Gulf of Mexico[4], where increasing volumes of fertilizer wash into the Gulf from the Mississippi river system. The river water is rich in nutrients from both pollution and natural sources which, along with the algae that feed on it, consume all the available oxygen. This hypoxic zone was first documented in 1972.

Offshore mining and the extraction of oil and gas reserves from the continental shelf are a

NUMBER OF PEOPLE LIVING WITHIN 100 KILOMETERS OF THE COAST, LATE 1990s

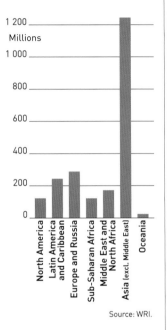

Source: WRI.

COASTAL POPULATIONS, MARINE PROTECTED AREAS AND LARGE MARINE ECOSYSTEMS

Proportion of the population living within 100 kilometers of the coast, 2000

More than 90%

70-90%

50-70%

30-50%

15-30%

1-15%

0%

Marine protected areas, 1997
- Smaller than 100km^2
- 100-1 000km^2
- 1 000-5 000km^2
- Larger than 5 000km^2

Large marine ecosystems
Closely linked to the regional seas, several large marine ecosystems, each with distinct characteristics, have been identified in response to the need for a comprehensive approach to marine management. Unmarked coastal areas have yet to be studied.

OIL POLLUTION ACCIDENTS IN THE MEDITERRANEAN
By type of accident

Grounding

Fire/explosion

Collision

Terminal operations

Sinking

Other

1981-90
1991-95

Source: EEA.

OIL AND GAS RESERVES OF THE REGIONAL SEAS

- Oil reserves
- Gas reserves
- Oil/gas reserves

Source: ESRI.

COASTLINES UNDER THREAT, 1998

- High threat
- Moderate threat
- Low threat

North and Central America

South America

Europe

Former USSR

Africa

Asia

Oceania

0 % 20 40 60 80 100

Source: FAO.

A recent study by FAO found that more than half the world's coasts are at threat from human development. With coastal populations expected to double in the next 20 or 30 years, the rapid increase in construction and urban and industrial waste output will put enormous stresses onto the regional seas' fragile ecosystems.

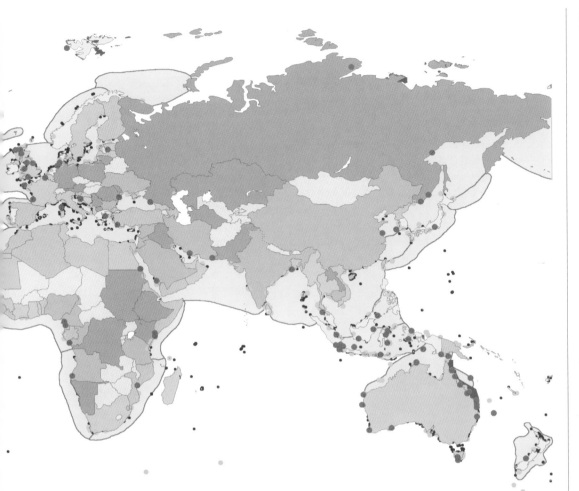

Source: UNEP-WCMC; CIESIN.

THE DIVERSITY OF THE REGIONAL SEAS, 1990s
Numbers of species

	Molluscs	Shrimps and lobsters	Sharks	Seabirds	Marine mammals	Endemic
East Africa	80	91	73	44	28	7
Southern Africa	145	42	93	39	36	9
West and Central Africa	238	47	89	51	44	8
Antarctica	7	3	0	51	20	22
Arctic	44	9	5	27	23	0
South Asia	246	117	58	26	29	6
North Atlantic	432	77	87	56	48	12
Southwest Atlantic	299	46	68	33	49	11
Southwest Australia	197	25	64	22	43	9
Black Sea	6	7	1	17	4	1
Caribbean	633	68	76	23	31	23
East Asian seas	1 114	210	140	39	29	31
Kuwait marine area	66	26	34	21	27	1
Mediterranean Sea	138	42	43	22	17	1
Northeast Pacific	517	45	57	66	50	28
Northwest Pacific	404	128	93	69	45	27
South Pacific	984	105	128	115	52	98
Southeast Pacific	393	33	67	68	47	36
Red Sea and Gulf of Aden	57	38	39	22	26	26

Source: WRI.

SEDIMENTATION AND EROSION IN THE MEDITERRANEAN, 1998

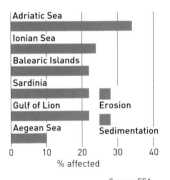

Adriatic Sea

Ionian Sea

Balearic Islands

Sardinia

Gulf of Lion — Erosion

Aegean Sea — Sedimentation

0 10 20 30 40

% affected

Source: EEA.

further pollution threat to regional seas. The North Sea hydrocarbon industry, for instance, has left hundreds of piles of drill cuttings on the seabed. Contaminated with metals such as boron and cadmium as well as diesel used to lubricate drilling, there is an estimated 2 million tons of this debris spread across hundreds of square kilometers.

Enclosed seas, cut off from the wider ocean, have seen some of the worst ecological damage, including the loss of water itself. Forty years ago the Aral Sea in Central Asia was the fourth largest inland sea in the world. Its fisheries were sufficiently plentiful to feed the Soviet empire. But since then more than 90 percent of the water from the Amu Darya and Syr Darya rivers that feed it has been diverted to irrigate cotton fields in Uzbekistan and Turkmenistan. The sea has lost two thirds of its volume and almost all native organisms, including its 24 known fish species, have died out[5]. This decline has triggered further environmental damage as winds whip up sand on 3 million hectares of exposed salt and pesticide-impregnated seabed, contaminating ecosystems, water supplies and food over a wide area. Local doctors blame it for epidemics of anemia, kidney disease, cancer and other health problems[6].

Increasingly, countries are banding together in an effort to save their seas. The environmental action plan for the Mediterranean has been followed by others for the Black, Aral, Baltic and North Seas. The North Sea programs have had conspicuous success in reducing the discharge of many pollutants and in lowering fish catch limits, though others have fared less well.

FISH CATCH* OF THE COUNTRIES BORDERING THE BLACK SEA

* Includes the Mediterranean and Black Sea catch

Source: FAO.

THE BLACK SEA

The fish of the Black Sea once supported the ancient Persian and Byzantine empires. In the 20th century, its beaches played host to both holiday-making Russians and the great Soviet Black Sea navy. But fertilizers, sewage and toxic effluents from 170 million people in 13 countries of Eastern and Central Europe wash into the sea down great rivers such as the Danube and Dneiper at levels ten times those of half a century ago[7]. The pollution has smothered sea meadows in the northwest of the sea, inhibiting oxygen generation. The result has been massive eutrophication, with thick mats of algae invading beaches, and fisheries diminished. Into this badly disrupted ecosystem an Atlantic comb jelly, a kind of jellyfish, was accidentally released from a ship's ballast water in the early 1980s. Feeding on native fish eggs and larvae, it reached a biomass of 900 million tons within a decade, triggering a 90 percent decline in fish stocks at a cost of hundreds of millions of dollars[8].

Oceans

T HE OCEANS cover 70 percent of the planet's surface and make up some 90 percent of space habitable by life forms. Most of their volume is far from land and locked deep beneath the surface, away from contact with the atmosphere. Less than a tenth of it has ever been explored; even so the human hand is increasingly evident.

Beyond the regional seas and the continental shelves lies the deep ocean – the most widespread natural habitat on the planet. Once dismissed as a marine desert, the deep ocean is now emerging as a center of vast biological richness. The seabed is peppered with "black smokers", volcanic vents that are home to a huge variety of marine life. A fantastic range of invertebrates has been found occupying the sediment on the ocean floor[1].

Historically, fisheries have been the most abundant resource of the oceans. However, our over-exploitation is threatening some of the world's largest fish stocks. Such is the intensity of this assault that we may so reduce stocks that we will have to "farm" the bulk of our marine fish just as we do our livestock on land.

Other human activities are beginning to impinge on the ecological health of the vast expanse of oceans. Oil exploration is a major activity in such regions as the Gulf of Mexico, the South China Sea and the waters around the British Isles. The threats vary. There is growing evidence of widespread toxic effects on benthic communities on the floor of the North Sea in the vicinity of the 500-plus oil production platforms in British and Norwegian waters[2]. Meanwhile, oil exploration in the deep waters of the North Atlantic, northwest of Scotland, threatens endangered deep-sea corals. There is evidence, too, that acoustic prospecting for hydrocarbons in these waters may deter or disorientate some marine mammals[3].

In the future, the biological riches of the "black smokers" face threats from deep-sea mining. The mid-ocean hot springs spew out potentially valuable metal sulfides, such as gold, silver and copper. In the cold water, they are deposited in thick crusts, attracting exploitation. Rights have already been given to one company to prospect for metals on 4 000 square kilometers of the bed of the Bismarck Sea north of Papua New Guinea.

The oceans, like the atmosphere, are fundamental to the health of the planet. They dominate many of its cycling processes as well as being the ultimate sink for a variety of pollutants. They absorb about 2 billion tons of carbon – in the form of carbon dioxide (CO_2) – and disperse an esti-mated 3 million tons of oil spilt annually from ships and, predominantly, from sources on land.

The oceans store a thousand times more heat than the atmosphere and transport enormous amounts of it around the globe. In consequence, they are largely responsible for determining cli-mate on land. The warm Gulf Stream washing up from the tropics in the Atlantic Ocean keeps Europe many degrees warmer in winter than Hudson Bay on the opposite shore. The oscillation between El Niño and La Niña currents in the tropical Pacific Ocean fundamentally changes the weather across the ocean, flipping Indonesia, Australia and coastal South America into and out of

SOURCES OF POLLUTANTS FROM HUMAN ACTIVITIES ENTERING THE SEA

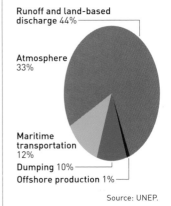

Runoff and land-based discharge 44%

Atmosphere 33%

Maritime transportation 12%

Dumping 10%

Offshore production 1%

Source: UNEP.

FISHING VESSELS
By ownership, 1995

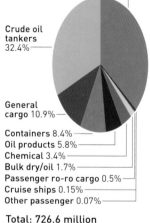

China 23.1%

Russia
12.4%

Japan 6.3%

USA 5.8%
India 4.5%
Other 47.9%

Total: 24 million metric tons

Source: FAO.

OCEAN PRODUCTIVITY
World marine catch, discards and fishery status,
by fishing zone

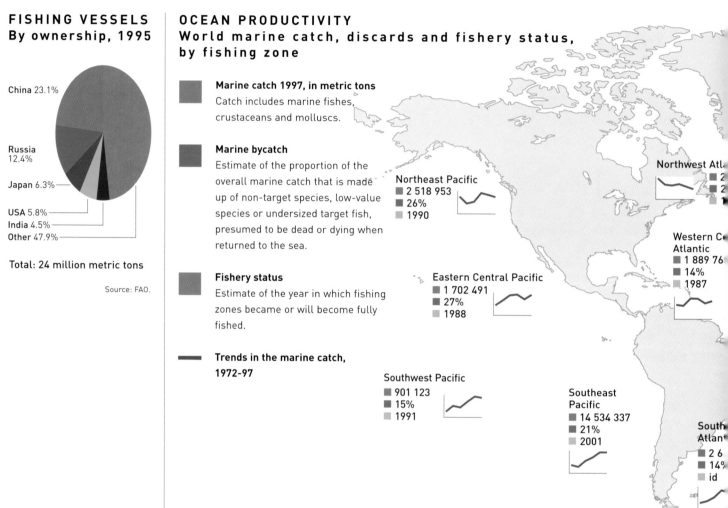

Marine catch 1997, in metric tons
Catch includes marine fishes, crustaceans and molluscs.

Marine bycatch
Estimate of the proportion of the overall marine catch that is made up of non-target species, low-value species or undersized target fish, presumed to be dead or dying when returned to the sea.

Fishery status
Estimate of the year in which fishing zones became or will become fully fished.

Trends in the marine catch, 1972-97

Northeast Pacific
■ 2 518 953
■ 26%
■ 1990

Eastern Central Pacific
■ 1 702 491
■ 27%
■ 1988

Northwest Atl
■ 2
■ 2
■ 1

Western C
Atlantic
■ 1 889 76
■ 14%
■ 1987

Southwest Pacific
■ 901 123
■ 15%
■ 1991

Southeast
Pacific
■ 14 534 337
■ 21%
■ 2001

South
Atlan
■ 2 6
■ 14%
■ id

OCEAN TRAFFIC
By type, 1998

Bulk carriers 36.7%

Crude oil
tankers
32.4%

General
cargo 10.9%

Containers 8.4%
Oil products 5.8%
Chemical 3.4%
Bulk dry/oil 1.7%
Passenger ro-ro cargo 0.5%
Cruise ships 0.15%
Other passenger 0.07%

Total: 726.6 million
deadweight metric tons

Source: Lloyds Register.

OIL TANKER SPILLS AT SEA, WITH SELECTED MAJOR SPILLS

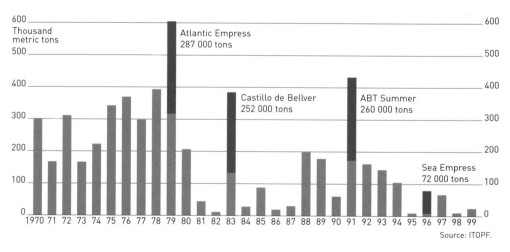

600
Thousand
metric tons

Atlantic Empress
287 000 tons

Castillo de Bellver
252 000 tons

ABT Summer
260 000 tons

Sea Empress
72 000 tons

1970 71 72 73 74 75 76 77 78 79 80 81 82 83 84 85 86 87 88 89 90 91 92 93 94 95 96 97 98 99

Source: ITOPF.

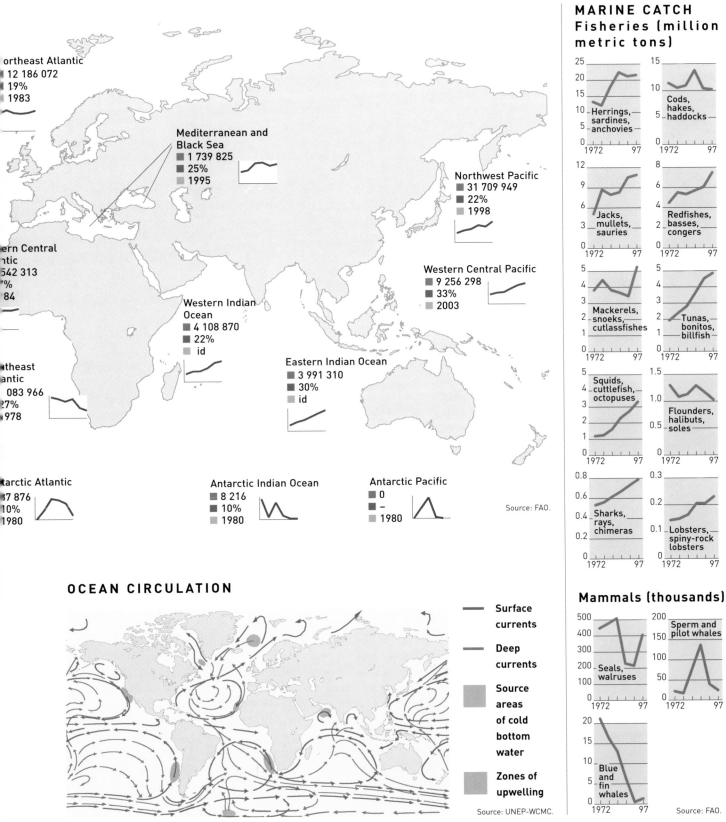

ortheast Atlantic
■ 12 186 072
■ 19%
■ 1983

Mediterranean and
Black Sea
■ 1 739 825
■ 25%
■ 1995

Northwest Pacific
■ 31 709 949
■ 22%
■ 1998

ern Central
tic
542 313
%
84

Western Indian
Ocean
■ 4 108 870
■ 22%
■ id

Western Central Pacific
■ 9 256 298
■ 33%
■ 2003

theast
antic
083 966
27%
978

Eastern Indian Ocean
■ 3 991 310
■ 30%
■ id

tarctic Atlantic
7 876
10%
1980

Antarctic Indian Ocean
■ 8 216
■ 10%
■ 1980

Antarctic Pacific
■ 0
■ –
■ 1980

Source: FAO.

MARINE CATCH
Fisheries (million
metric tons)

Herrings, sardines, anchovies

Cods, hakes, haddocks

Jacks, mullets, sauries

Redfishes, basses, congers

Mackerels, snoeks, cutlassfishes

Tunas, bonitos, billfish

Squids, cuttlefish, octopuses

Flounders, halibuts, soles

Sharks, rays, chimeras

Lobsters, spiny-rock lobsters

OCEAN CIRCULATION

— Surface
currents

— Deep
currents

Source
areas
of cold
bottom
water

Zones of
upwelling

Source: UNEP-WCMC.

Mammals (thousands)

Seals, walruses

Sperm and pilot whales

Blue and fin whales

Source: FAO.

droughts and floods. All these processes now face disruption from the global scale of human activity, particularly climate change. Currently, the oceans moderate climate change by absorbing a third of the CO_2 emitted into the air by human activity. But several studies suggest that global warming will stratify the oceans and reduce their capacity to act as a CO_2 "sink" by 10 to 20 percent over the next century, accelerating warming[4].

Global warming may already be triggering fundamental shifts in the ocean's El Niño oscillation[5]. And if warming continues, climate modellers predict that freshwater from melting Arctic ice may form a cap on the salty waters of the North Atlantic. This could shut down the local plunging of dense, salty water to the ocean depths, which is one of the main engines of the global ocean circulation system known as the conveyor[6]. One effect would be to displace the Gulf Stream, resulting in considerably colder European winters.

There have been some successes in the international handling of the marine environment. The International Whaling Commission's moratorium introduced in the mid-1980s, though not honored by all nations, has helped revive whale stocks. The United Nations Convention on the Law of the Sea, signed in 1982 but only entering into force in 1994, established a framework of law for the oceans, including rules for deep-sea mining and economic exclusion zones extending 200 nautical miles around nation states.

A series of international laws have effectively eliminated the discharge of toxic materials – from drums of radioactive waste to sewage sludge and air pollution from incinerator ships – into the waters around Europe. International public pressure in the mid-1990s forced the reversal by a major oil company of plans to scuttle the Brent Spar, a large structure from the North Sea offshore oil industry, into deep water west of Scotland. European agreements since then have indicated that all production platforms and other structures should be removed from the oil fields at the end of their lives wherever possible.

Efforts have also been made to safeguard marine fisheries. In 1993, more than a hundred nations signed a treaty promising to draw up regional agreements to protect international fish stocks. But progress has been slow, and the failure to reach effective common cause over protecting the planet's fish stocks could arguably be one of the greatest failures of environmental diplomacy.

SEA-LEVEL RISE

One of the more predictable effects of global warming will be a rise in sea levels. It is already under way at a pace of about a millimeter a year – a consequence of both melting land ice and the thermal expansion of the oceans. Current predictions put the likely rise over the coming century at half a meter at the most[7]. But modelling studies suggest that once under way, thermal expansion will last for many centuries after warming of the atmosphere ceases. This is because it will take around a thousand years for the warming at the ocean surface to penetrate to the ocean depths. Even modest global warming over the next half century is likely eventually to raise global sea levels by between 1 and 2 meters – sufficient to drown many coastal areas and atoll islands – from thermal expansion alone[8]. Moreover, the IPCC predicts that a warming of 3°C would trigger the irreversible melting of the Greenland ice sheet, raising sea levels by 7 meters over a thousand years or more.

Polar regions

T HE WORLD'S POLAR REGIONS are its least populated areas. But while Antarctica has no permanent residents, the Arctic has more than 3.7 million inhabitants from eight countries. The prime environmental influences come from outside, whether long-distance tourism or long-distance pollution. But these same influences are also crucibles for new forms of international cooperation.

The Arctic region – defined as the ice-covered Arctic Ocean and surrounding tundra – has a rich history of semi-nomadic communities living off its meagre resources of fish, marine mammals, caribou, berries and mushrooms. These communities live largely in harmony with their environment, creating little pollution and managing their resources sustainably.

Indigenous communities are now outnumbered by migrants from the south in most parts of the region except Greenland and Nunavut (though the Russian migrant population in Siberia is declining). Nonetheless, they remain vibrant societies and are gaining self-governance, culminating in 1999 with the creation of the world's newest autonomous territory, Nunavut in northern Canada[1].

The Arctic's specialized ecosystems and animals, adapted to the cold and dark, are particularly vulnerable to the accumulation of toxic contaminants such as heavy metal, hydrocarbons and persistent organic pollutants (POPs), including polychlorinated biphenyls (PCBs) and pesticides, that accumulate in body fat. Some pollutants have local sources: PCBs leaking from old Canadian military equipment and Siberian oil pipelines and metal refineries, for instance. But levels of most POPs can only be explained by long-range movement from lower latitudes. They reach the region via rivers flowing north into the Arctic, particularly from Siberia; via sea ice transporting contaminants from the coast; via global ocean currents; and by the strong south to north air flows, particularly from Europe.

The cold Arctic air is believed responsible for "capturing" and then depositing passing air pollution, including POPs and mercury, through a process known as "global distillation". The long marine food webs are extremely efficient at increasing the concentrations of such toxins so that birds and animals at the top of the chain receive large doses. Heavy metals such as cadmium and mercury, and POPs such as PCBs, all bioaccumulate in this way. The build-up is made more acute because many of the toxins accumulate in fats, the main food of many polar animals. As a result, studies suggest, polar bears are dying after imbibing PCBs in their mothers' milk[2].

The local people, at the top of the food chain, are among the most heavily exposed populations in the world to such pollutants, which reach dangerous concentrations in the flesh of whales, seals and other mammals. Approaching 17 percent of Greenlanders have potentially harmful levels of mercury in their blood, mostly from eating whale and seal meat. A typical traditional meal of these foods may sometimes exceed maximum daily allowed doses of mercury, PCBs and other toxins. Thus the contaminants directly threaten customary ways of life and cultural traditions.

Arctic ecosystems are particularly vulnerable to contamination, taking a long time to recover.

TOURISM IN THE ARCTIC, EARLY 1990s

Arctic region	Number of tourists per year
Alaska	25 000
Greenland	6 000
Iceland	129 000
Northern Scandinavia	500 000
Northwest Territories*	48 000
Russia	Some tens of thousands
Svalbard	35 000
Yukon*	177 000

*Canada

Source: UNEP.

POPULATIONS OF THE ARCTIC, 1989-94

Arctic region	Total population	% indigenous
Alaska	481 054	15.2
Canada	92 985	50.9
Faroe Islands	43 700	0.0
Finland	200 677	2.0
Greenland	55 419	86.7
Iceland	266 783	0.0
Norway	379 461	9.9
Russia	1 999 711	3.4
Sweden	263 735	2.3

Source: AMAP.

THE TEN TOP FISHING NATIONS IN THE ARCTIC REGION*, 1997

	Marine catch** Metric tons
Norway	2 855 091
Iceland	2 204 553
Denmark	1 825 159
USA	1 191 556
UK	905 448
Russia	828 828
Canada	681 686
Spain	637 382
France	554 560
Netherlands	443 009
Other	2 116 612
Total	**14 243 884**

* Includes Northeast and Northwest Atlantic
** Includes marine fish, molluscs and crustaceans

Source: FAO.

THE ARCTIC

Source: AMAP; UNEP/GRID-Arendal.

— Arctic boundary (AMAP)

Intermittent permafrost

Permafrost

Icesheet

Oil/gas extraction
▲ Gas
▲ Oil
▲ Oil and gas
▲ Exploration

PROTECTED AREAS IN THE ARCTIC, 1997

Arctic region	Number of protected areas	Square kilometers	% of region protected
Canada	48	462 674	8.8
Finland	52	25 905	32.6
Greenland	14	993 023	45.7
Iceland	26	12 165	11.8
Norway	38	41 637	25.5
Russia	31	313 818	4.9
Sweden	44	20 348	21.4
USA	41	331 425	56.1

Source: UNEP.

THE ANTARCTIC

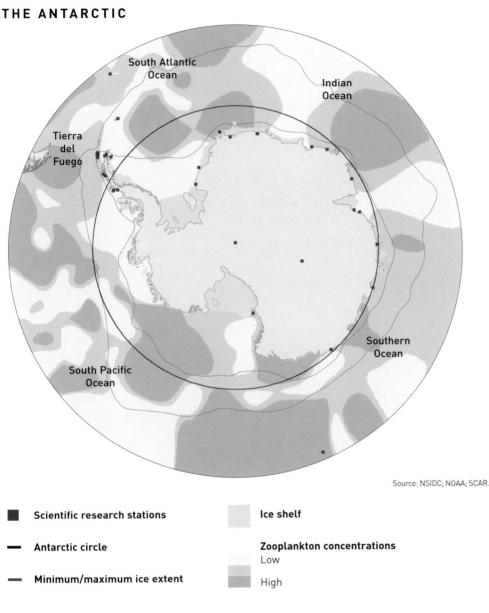

South Atlantic
Ocean

Indian
Ocean

Tierra
del
Fuego

Southern
Ocean

South Pacific
Ocean

Source: NSIDC; NOAA; SCAR.

■ Scientific research stations

— Antarctic circle

— Minimum/maximum ice extent

Ice shelf

Zooplankton concentrations
Low

High

PARTIES TO THE ANTARCTIC TREATY, 2000

Argentina*5	Czech Republic	Japan*1	Slovakia
Australia*3	Denmark	Korea, DPR	South Africa*1
Austria	Ecuador	Korea, Rep.*1	Spain
Belgium	Finland	Netherlands	Sweden
Brazil*1	France*1	New Zealand*1	Switzerland
Bulgaria	Germany*1	Norway	Turkey
Canada	Greece	Papua New Guinea	Ukraine*1
Chile*4	Guatemala	Peru	United Kingdom*2
China*2	Hungary	Poland*1	United States of
Colombia	India*1	Romania	America*3
Cuba	Italy	Russia*6	Uruguay*1

* Countries with research stations and number of stations in 1999   Source: UNEP.

ANTARCTIC FISH CATCH BY COUNTRY, 1997

	Marine fish	Krill
	Metric tons	
Australia	1 088	0
Chile	2 079	0
France	3 680	0
Japan	335	60 898
Korea, Rep.	459	0
Poland	0	19 156
South Africa	2 106	0
Spain	294	0
UK	408	308
Ukraine	1 007	4 246
Total	**11 456**	**84 608**

Source: FAO.

TOURISM IN THE ANTARCTIC

Summer season	Number of tourists
1992/93	6 565
1993/94	8 016
1994/95	8 120
1995/96	9 367
1996/97	7 413
1997/98	9 604
1998/99	10 383

Source: IAATO.

CLAIMS TO SOVEREIGNTY

Argentina, Australia, Chile, France, New Zealand, Norway and the United Kingdom – the seven countries that assert sovereignty over the continent – have all frozen their claims under the Antarctic Treaty. The treaty incorporates the 1972 Convention for the Conservation of Antarctic Seals, the 1980 Convention for the Conservation of Antarctic Marine Living Resources, and the 1991 Protocol on Environmental Protection, which specifically prohibits the exploitation of the region for minerals.

THE PATHWAYS OF PERSISTENT ORGANIC POLLUTANTS TO THE ARCTIC

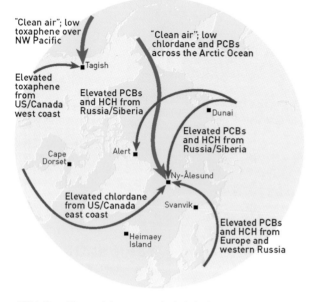

"Clean air"; low toxaphene over NW Pacific

Elevated toxaphene from US/Canada west coast

"Clean air"; low chlordane and PCBs across the Arctic Ocean

Tagish

Elevated PCBs and HCH from Russia/Siberia

Dunai

Elevated PCBs and HCH from Russia/Siberia

Alert

Cape Dorset

Ny-Ålesund

Elevated chlordane from US/Canada east coast

Svanvik

Heimaey Island

Elevated PCBs and HCH from Europe and western Russia

HCH: Hexachlorocyclohexane, particularly in the form of the pesticide lindane

Source: UNEP.

Oil, for instance, breaks down only very slowly in the cold and dark. The oil spill from the *Exxon Valdez* in Alaskan waters in 1989 left 36 000 seabirds and 3 000 sea otters dead and a legacy that lasted far longer than it would have in warmer regions.

Arctic ecosystems have also accumulated radioactive isotopes spread through the atmosphere following the atmospheric testing in the 1950s, and the Chernobyl nuclear accident in Ukraine in 1986. While levels of fallout in the Arctic were no higher than elsewhere, Arctic lichens absorbed large amounts of caesium-137. The lichen is the staple diet of animals such as reindeer, which are eaten by humans. As a result, Arctic inhabitants typically have five times as much of the isotope in their bodies as people to the south, and some reindeer herders have levels 300 times higher. Herders of northern Scandinavia have been prevented from eating and selling reindeer meat because of the fallout from Chernobyl.

Landuse threats to Arctic ecosystems have historically been small, but they do exist. Norwegian reindeer herds have increased threefold since 1950, exhausting lichen cover over an area of several hundred thousand square kilometers. Overgrazing has contributed to severe erosion of the loose volcanic soils in Iceland, and commercial forestry has fragmented the Siberian boreal forests[3].

The Arctic was an important theatre of the Cold War, providing remote sites for military installations and weapons tests, and hiding submarines beneath the sea ice. In the future, its economic role is likely to grow. Long-standing metal smelting in Siberia and coal mining in the far-north island of Svalbard are being joined by oil exploitation in Alaska and the Barents Sea, and plans to reopen the old shipping route north of Norway and Russia. Since the end of the Cold War, the eight Arctic nations have come together to discuss their shared environment. Besides creating nature reserves in the region, they have taken the lead in pushing through a protocol to an existing United Nations convention, curbing 16 POPs in Europe and North America, and have spurred negotiations for a global treaty.

Many of the human-induced environmental threats in the Arctic do not occur in the largely unpopulated Antarctic, where economic activity has declined since the great sealing and whaling expeditions of the 19th century. The main pursuit is now science. The continent has 35 permanently occupied bases, with the oldest, the Argentinean Orcadas base, having been continuously inhabited since 1904. The fastest growing activity is tourism, which now brings more than 10 000 people there annually, mostly by cruise ship.

A certain amount of economic activity is also concentrated on fisheries, and there is concern about large-scale overfishing, particularly of the Patagonian toothfish, which makes up by far the largest share of the finfish catch in the region. In contrast to the rich marine life in the nutrient-filled waters of the Southern Ocean, the largely ice-covered continent has few land species.

Beyond the immediate threat of human activity, the polar regions are falling prey to global threats: notably climate change and the thinning of the ozone layer. The Arctic has lost around 5 percent of its sea ice in the past two decades[4], and land ice could follow. Recent modelling studies suggest that a warming of 3°C would be sufficient to melt the entire Greenland ice sheet, raising sea levels worldwide by 7 meters over a thousand years or more[5].

Warming is already threatening the survival of polar bears around Hudson Bay, because the sea ice from which they hunt is disappearing. And the additional ultra-violet radiation streaming through the Antarctic ozone hole each southern spring is believed to be killing large numbers of fish eggs and larvae floating on the surface of the Southern Ocean by damaging their DNA. It also kills an estimated 15 percent of the phytoplankton in parts of the ocean[6].

Population and biodiversity

NOBODY KNOWS how many species there are in the world – or how fast they are disappearing. Fewer than 2 million have been cataloged and estimates of the total vary wildly, ranging from 7 million to as many as 80 million. The currently accepted working estimate is 13.6 million.

A quarter of the total number of species may be beetles, whose diversity is especially rich high in the rainforest canopy of the Amazon. Many more could be nematodes on the floors of the oceans. As many again could exist among single-cell microbes, whose diversity is beginning to be assessed for the first time using gene-typing[1].

Biodiversity is a term applied to describe the complexity of life. It is generally measured at three levels: the variety of species; the genetic diversity found within members of the same species (what makes you different from your neighbor); and the diversity of the ecosystems within which species live. These three levels are intimately connected. Genetic diversity is essential to the prosperity of the species, giving it the resources to adapt. And the number of species within an ecosystem is closely tied to the health and size of the ecosystem itself[2].

However it is defined, biodiversity is the stuff of life. However far we may be removed from "wild" biodiversity in our daily lives, it remains the source of our food and most of our medicines. In addition, 15 percent of our energy is derived from burning plant materials. Even in the United States, wild species contribute around 4.5 percent of GDP[3].

Some of our uses are direct. Billions of people still harvest wild or "bush" food around the world. Between a fifth and a half of all food consumed by the poor in the developing world is gathered rather than cultivated, while at global level we obtain 16 percent of our animal protein from sea fish caught in the wild. The World Health Organization (WHO) estimates that more than 60 percent of the world's population relies on traditional plant medicines for day-to-day primary health care[4], and 3 000 plant species are used in birth control alone[5].

In the Uxpanapa region in Mexico peasant farmers use 435 wild plants and animals, eating 229 of them[6]. One Thai village was found to eat 295 different local plants and use 119 in medicines. Europe's prime treatment for prostate disorders comes directly from the bark of the African cherry tree, now severely depleted in its homeland in the Central African highlands.

But biodiversity's role extends far beyond these direct uses. We may today only eat a small proportion of the 70 000 plants known to have edible parts[7], but most food crops constantly require an infusion of "wild" genes to maintain their resistance to ever-evolving pests. These raids on nature's "genetic library" enable increases in crop productivity of about 1 percent a year, worth in excess of a billion dollars[8].

Approximately 118 out of the top 150 prescription drugs sold in the United States are laboratory versions of chemicals found by "bioprospectors" in the wild – mostly synthesized from plants but also from fungi, bacteria and extracts from vertebrate animals such as snakes[9]. Aspirin, for instance, derives from an acid first taken from the bark of willow trees. The promising anti-

BIODIVERSITY FOR FOOD

270 000 plants are known to science

of which:

7 000 have ever been used for food

of which:

120 are widely cultivated today

of which:

90 cultivated plant species provide 5% of human food

21 species provide 20% of human food

9 species provide 75% of human food

Source: FAO.

GERMPLASM OF NUTRITIONALLY IMPORTANT CROPS HELD BY CGIAR* CENTERS

	Number of samples held, 2000	% of wild species not yet collected+
Barley	24 218	0-10
Cassava	7 886	80
Chickpea	26 077	50
Common bean	27 595	id
Cowpea	15 001	70
Forages	52 456	id
Groundnut	14 357	30
Maize	19 548	85
Millet	30 300	90-98
Potato	5 057	60
Rice	122 632	70
Sorghum	35 780	90
Soybean	1 909	70
Wheat	110 182	40
Yam	2 878	id

* Consultative Group on International Agricultural Research
+ Global estimate

Source: CGIAR; UNEP-WCMC; FAO.

CENTERS OF PLANT DIVERSITY, GENE BANKS AND GENETIC ORIGINS OF CROPS AND LIVESTOCK

Centers of high plant diversity
Sites and areas identified as important centers of plant diversity at regional and global level

Major gene banks
International centers belonging to the Consultative Group on International Agricultural Research (CGIAR) plus major national plant gene banks

Genetic origins of crops and livestock (see below)

The majority of the world's gene banks are situated in or near the richest regions of biodiversity, from which most of our staple foods originated. These repositories are gaining in importance as wild biodiversity comes under increasing pressure from population growth and landuse change.

GENETIC ORIGINS OF CROPS AND LIVESTOCK

1. North America
Cranberry
Jerusalem artichoke
Muscadine grape
Sunflower
Turkey

2. Mexico/Central America
Avocado
Common bean
Grapefruit
Hemp/sisal
Maize/corn
Papaya
Pecan

Sweet potato
Tabasco pepper
Tomato
Vanilla

3. Andes/South America
Cashew
Cayenne
Cocoa
Groundnut/ peanut
Lima bean
Manioc
Pepper
Pineapple
Potato

Pumpkin
Quinine
Rubber
Upland cotton

4. Mediterranean
Asparagus
Broad bean
Cabbage
Cauliflower
Celery
Common grape
Globe artichoke
Lavender
Mint
Oat
Parsnip

Rape
Sugar beet

Belgium
Brussel sprout

North Africa
Cattle
Marjoram

5. Near East
Alfalfa
Barley
Cabbage
Einkorn wheat
Fig
Goat

Hazelnut
Leek
Lentil
Pea
Pig
Plum
Rye
Shallot
Sheep
Spelt wheat
Sugar beet
Sweet cherry

6. Horn of Africa
Black-eye pea
Bread wheat
Castor bean

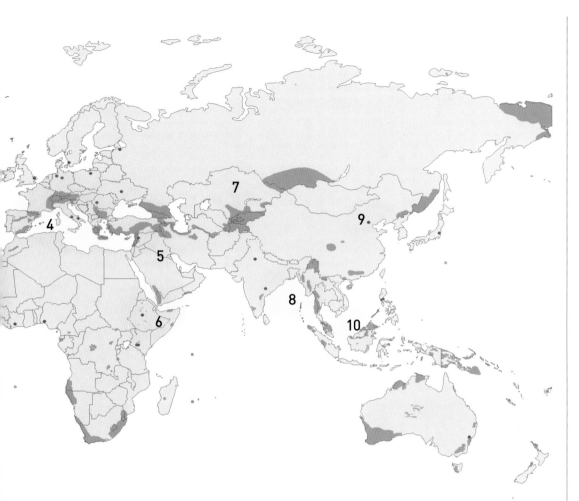

Source: UNEP-WCMC; FAO.

ESTIMATED VALUE OF WILD RESOURCES IN DEVELOPING COUNTRIES, 1990s

Pre-ban ivory exports, Africa: US$35-45 million per year
Tropical non-coniferous forest product exports: US$11 billion per year
Fruit/latex forest harvesting, Peru: US$6 330 per hectare
Sustainable timber harvesting, Peru: US$490 per hectare
Buffalo range ranching, Zimbabwe: US$3.5-4.5 per hectare
Wetlands fish and fuelwood, Nigeria: US$38-59 per hectare
Viewing value of elephants, Kenya: US$25 million per year
Ecotourism, Costa Rica: US$1 250 per hectare
Tourism, Thailand: US$385 000-860 000 per year
Research/education, Thailand: US$38 000-77 000 per year
Tourism, Cameroon: US$19 per hectare
Genetic value, Cameroon: US$7 per hectare
Pharmaceutical prospecting, Costa Rica: US$4.81 million per product

Source: UNEP.

MAJOR DRUGS DERIVED FROM PLANTS

Plant	Application
Amazonian liana	Muscle relaxant
Annual mugwort	Antimalarial
Autumn crocus	Antitumor agent
Belladonna	Anticholinergic
Coca	Local anesthetic
Common thyme	Antifungal
Ergot fungus	Hemorrhage control in childbirth
Foxglove	Cardiotonic
Indian snakeroot	Antihypertensive
Meadowsweet	Analgesic
Mexican yam	Birth-control pill
Nux vomica	CNS stimulant
Opium poppy	Analgesic, antitussive
Pacific yew	Antitumor agent
Recured thornapple	Sedative
Rosy periwinkle	Antileukemia
Velvet bean	Antiparkinsonian
White willow	Analgesic
Yellow cinchona	Antimalarial, antipyretic

Source: WWF.

Coffee	Common	Pear	**9. East Asia**	**10. Southeast**
Cowpea	grape	Watercress	Buckwheat	**Asia**
Date palm	Cucumber		Camphor	Apricot
Egyptian cotton	Flax/linseed	**8. India/**	tree	Banana
Finger millet	Garlic	**Indo-Malaya**	Chive	Cinnamon and
Mustard	Onion	Black pepper	Foxtail millet	cassia
Okra	Rhubarb	Breadfruit	Ginseng	Clove
Pearl millet	Spinach	Cardamom	Lychee	Coconut palm
Short staple		Chick pea	Mulberry	Eggplant
cotton	*European*	Chicken	Peach	Indian almond
Sorghum	*Siberian Region*	Dwarf wheat	Radish	Lemon
Yam	Cattle	Lime	Soybean	Mung bean
	Chicory	Mango	Sweet orange	Sugar cane
	Gooseberry	Moth bean	Tea	Tangerine
7. Central Asia	Kale	Rice	Turnip	
Almond	Lettuce	Safflower	Water	
Apple	Licorice	Sesame	chestnut	
Carrot				

Source: WWF.

cancer drug taxol was first extracted from the wild Pacific yew tree. Globally, it has been estimated that the pharmaceuticals industry gains US$32 billion in profits a year from products derived from traditional remedies[10].

The emerging science of biotechnology offers new potential for using the world's genetic resources, but it is an area of some controversy, yet to be fully developed. Moreover, many of these resources are under threat from human activity. Species are being lost at a rate probably unprecedented outside times of mass extinction millions of years ago. One estimate puts the loss at 27 000 species a year[11]. The United Nations Environment Programme's *Global Biodiversity Assessment* estimates current extinction rates at 50 to 100 times "normal", and anticipates a tenfold or even 100-fold increase over the next quarter century, when between 2 and 25 percent of species could be lost[12].

The primary cause of this loss is not hunting or overexploitation, though these play a part, but loss of natural habitat. Habitat loss is generally greatest where population density is highest. A study of biodiversity data from 102 countries found that in the most densely populated 51 countries (averaging 168 people per square kilometer), 5.1 percent of bird species and 3.7 percent of plant species were threatened. In the 51 less densely populated countries (averaging 22 people per square kilometer), the proportions of threatened species were only half as high at 2.7 percent and 1.8 percent respectively[13].

MASS EXTINCTIONS IN HISTORY

Looked at on a geological timescale, the planet's biodiversity has always been faced with threats of one form or another. Mass extinctions have a history almost as long as biodiversity. There are five known cataclysmic extinctions in the Earth's history. The biggest, at the end of the Permian era 250 million years ago, eliminated between 75 and 95 percent of all species, while the best known, 65 million years ago, saw off the dinosaurs and much else. The extinctions appear to have been caused by massive climatic disruptions, some at least arising from meteor impacts.

Extinction, moreover, is an essential engine for evolutionary progress. Even mass extinctions, by killing large numbers of creatures, open up ecological "niches" to which surviving organisms swiftly adapt. Thus the demise of dinosaurs allowed the rapid evolution, within 10 million years, of bats, whales, horses and numerous other species of mammals and birds. Nonetheless, whatever such benefits to life on Earth may be in the long term, our own immediate future on the planet is jeopardized by the current human-induced mass extinctions.

Species

Humans have been causing the extinction of species for thousands of years. Wherever people have settled they have hunted the local fauna or so altered natural habitats that species within them have suffered. Whether for subsistence or for trade, whether by design or by default, the human impact on the Earth may be bringing about more extinctions than any other single factor since the extinction of the dinosaurs.

The most direct evidence of human-induced extinction comes from North and South America and Australia, where humans are thought to have first arrived around 10 000 to 25 000 years ago. Within a few hundred years, some 70 species of "megafauna" in North America disappeared from the fossil record. These included mammoths and mastodons, giant beavers, sabre-tooth cats, giant ground sloths, horses, camels and more. Climate change may have been partly to blame. But there is abundant evidence that hunting was key[1].

More conjecturally, human alterations to the land have probably caused extinctions dating back as much as 50 000 years – when we have the first evidence of the deliberate use of widespread burning of bush and grasslands to round up wild animals during hunting. By 5 000 years ago, Europeans were deforesting large areas for pasture[2].

Species extinctions occur as a result of human causes ranging from hunting to climate change. The proportions vary with time and place, but one study of animal extinctions since 1600 found that 39 percent arose mainly from the introduction of alien species, 36 percent from habitat destruction, and 23 percent from hunting or deliberate extermination[3].

There have been some spectacular examples of our ability to hunt to extinction even the most populous species. One was the passenger pigeon. In the early 1800s, billions of the birds darkened the North American skies. In September 1914, the last died in a Cincinnati zoo. More recently, the tiger has been under severe threat from the Asian medicinal trade in tiger bones, while primates and other mammals in Central Africa face a booming trade in bushmeat.

But an even bigger cause may be the introduction of non-native species. As people have travelled around the globe, they have taken many other species with them. We have introduced plants that have taken over whole ecosystems and exterminated local species; and predatory animals against which indigenous species had no defence. Sometimes the introductions were deliberate. Plantation crops (such as the rubber plants taken from Brazil to Malaya by British colonial botanists) often thrive best when taken from their natural homes, where there are pests that control them, to new lands where they may be freed from such constraints. Sometimes the introductions have been accidental, and have created widespread ecological dislocation and species extinctions. Many endemic flightless birds have disappeared from the islands of Polynesia and elsewhere following the arrival of humans who, besides hunting, brought rats, cats and other alien species with a liking for birds' eggs.

River and marine ecosystems can be as vulnerable as those on land. One dramatic example

ESTIMATED NUMBERS OF SPECIES, KNOWN AND UNKNOWN, LATE 1990s

	Estimated numbers of described species	Described species as % of total and level of accuracy
Viruses	4 000	1.00 VP
Bacteria	4 000	0.40 VP
Protozoa and algae	80 000	13.33 VP
Vertebrates	52 000	94.55 G
Insects and myriapods	963 000	12.04 M
Arachnids	75 000	10.00 M
Molluscs	70 000	35.00 M
Crustaceans	40 000	26.67 M
Nematodes	25 000	6.25 P
Fungi	72 000	4.80 M
Plants	270 000	84.38 G

Level of accuracy: VP very poor; P poor; M moderate; G good.

Note: Estimates of described species are invariably incomplete because new species are being added all the time. The generally accepted working totals used by scientists are 1.75 million for all described species and 13.62 million for all species, both described and unknown.

Source: UNEP-WCMC; UNEP.

LEVEL OF BIODIVERSITY, BY COUNTRY, 1990s

High

Low

The map illustrates relative biodiversity at country level, taking into account richness and endemism in the four terrestrial vertebrate classes and vascular plants, and adjusting according to country area.

KNOWN VERTEBRATES

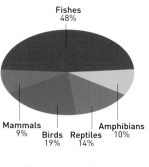

Fishes 48%

Mammals 9%

Birds 19%

Reptiles 14%

Amphibians 10%

Total known vertebrate species: 52 000

Source: UNEP-WCMC.

NUMBERS OF THREATENED ANIMAL SPECIES, 1999
By major biome

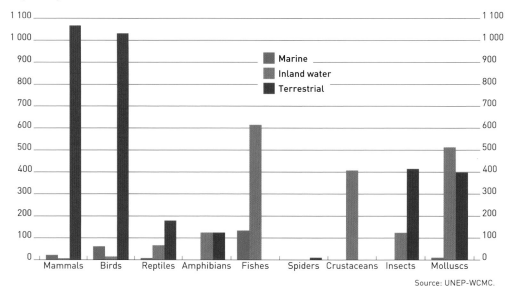

■ Marine
■ Inland water
■ Terrestrial

Mammals   Birds   Reptiles   Amphibians   Fishes   Spiders   Crustaceans   Insects   Molluscs

Source: UNEP-WCMC.

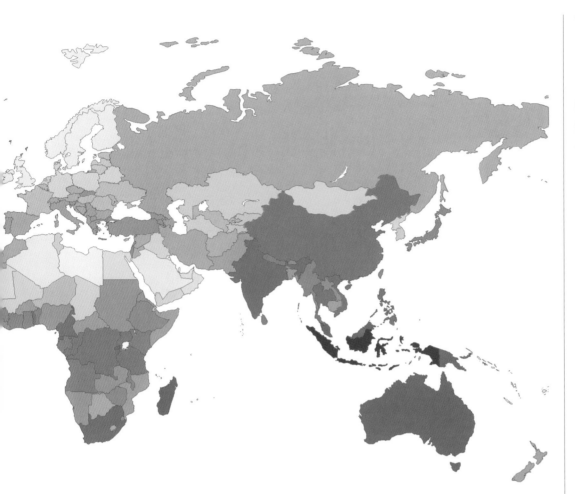

Source: UNEP-WCMC.

WORLD TRADE* IN A SAMPLE OF ENDANGERED SPECIES, 1997

Live specimens

Corals	1 045 342
Orchids	343 801
Snakes	258 714
Parrots	235 771
Tortoises	76 047
Primates	25 692

Skins

Lizard	1 639 244
Snake	1 459 964
Crocodile	850 837

* Includes legal trade only

Source: CITES; UNEP-WCMC.

Trade in wildlife and wildlife products is estimated to be worth up to US$20 billion a year, of which 25 percent is thought to be illegal. Under the Convention on International Trade in Endangered Species (CITES), some species are protected from all international trade (Appendix I), while trade in others that are not immediately threatened with extinction is regulated (Appendix II). CITES also gives countries the option of regulating international trade in some native species already protected within their own borders (Appendix III).

FISH EXTINCTIONS

Global number of freshwater fish species known to have become extinct, by decade

1890s	2
1900s	1
1910s	0
1920s	4
1930s	2
1940s	3
1950s	4
1960s	1
1970s	8
1980s	53
1990s	3

Note: The extinction of 50 species of cichlid in Lake Victoria in the 1980s is largely attributed to the introduction of the Nile perch.

Source: UNEP-WCMC.

THREATENED AND EXTINCT SPECIES, 1999

	Species known to be threatened	Estimated % of total in group threatened	Species known to be extinct	Estimated % of total in group extinct
Mammals	1 096	24	88	2
Birds	1 107	11	107	1
Reptiles	253	3	20	0.3
Amphibians	124	3	5	0.1
Fishes	734	3	172	0.7
Insects	537	0.05	73	0.004
Molluscs	920	1	237	0.3
Crustaceans	407	1	10	0.03
Plants	30 827	11	>400	0.2

Note: Other than mammals and birds, only a small proportion of the total species group has been assessed for threatened status.

Source: UNEP-WCMC.

was the deliberate introduction of the large and carnivorous Nile perch into the rich ecosystem of the world's second largest freshwater lake, Lake Victoria in East Africa, in the 1960s. The result was the extinction of an estimated 50 species of the indigenous cichlid fish within a couple of decades[4].

A recent study by IUCN–the World Conservation Union found that primates, with the exception of human beings, constitute the most endangered order of mammals; some 46 percent are known to be at risk. Overall, a quarter of mammals are endangered, not just "charismatic" animals such as pandas and tigers but many lesser known species of bats, rodents and marsupials. Some 11 percent of birds were found to be threatened. Much less is known about the status of other groups (see table on page 165). While it was estimated that 3 percent of the amphibians and reptiles that have been identified are threatened, a closer study of representative samples of these lesser known groups found a quarter of the amphibians to be at risk, alongside a fifth of the reptiles[5]. The most threatened group was fish, with up to a third endangered. Marine life at risk includes many species of shark and sturgeon, along with other marine animals from the blue whale to sea horses, of which 20 million are harvested annually.

Humans do not always have an entirely negative impact on local biodiversity, however. Our activities, while destructive of some species, create new ecological niches for many forms of wildlife, whether birds nesting in the eaves of houses, rats feeding off waste landfills or mosquitoes breeding in the ruts left by tracks in the mud. With the transportation of species around the world, there are more species of flowering plant in England than ever before, thanks to the country's propensity for planting exotic species in gardens.

Humans have also deliberately added to the genetic diversity within species through thousands of years of plant and animal breeding. As recently as 50 years ago, China grew 10 000 wheat varieties. Andean farmers bred 3 000 varieties of potato[6].

But our plant and animal breeding has in modern times been directed towards the creation of "superbreeds" distributed so widely and universally that others are relegated to gene banks or, worse, lost altogether. China grows only a tenth of the wheat varieties it grew half a century ago, Mexico a fifth of its former corn varieties[7]. More than 6 000 of the 7 000 apple varieties grown in the United States in the 19th century are now extinct, and just two make up half the national crop[8].

Crop genetic resources are disappearing from fields at an estimated 1 or 2 percent a year[9], and domesticated livestock breeds at 5 percent a year[10]. Many traditional plant varieties now live on only in gene banks, where their ability to be transplanted back into fields is sometimes uncertain. This is a biological tragedy. The ability of certain varieties to withstand drought, grow on poor soil, resist insects and disease, prosper in local environments or under global warming, or simply taste better, are contained in these genes. If the genes are lost, so is the future ability to innovate for peasant farmers and global corporations alike.

CLONING

One novel yet controversial approach to protecting individual species is cloning. Species on the verge of extinction, such as the Sumatran rhino or the Yangtze dolphin, could have their DNA captured within a single cell and held within a frozen zoo (like a seed in a gene bank) for eventual cloning[11]. The technique could even bring recently extinct species back to life, using samples of preserved tissue. One proposed candidate is the thylacine, or Tasmanian tiger, which became extinct in 1936.

Ecosystems and conservation

H umankind's greatest assault on the planet's biodiversity comes from the destruction of ecosystems. These are not merely the home to the world's species, they are also the providers of numerous "ecological services" without which life on the planet could not persist.

A conventional measure of biodiversity, the counting of species, produces some remarkable conclusions. Most of the world's known species are contained within an extremely small area. An estimated 44 percent of all plant species and 35 percent of all land vertebrates live exclusively within just 25 "hotspots" that together make up only 1.4 percent of the land surface of the globe, an area roughly the size of Greenland[1]. Most of these hotspots are within the tropics and particularly in tropical rainforests, where biologists estimate that half the world's species live.

There are many reasons for this concentration. Species proliferate best where there is more solar energy to drive natural systems (hence in the tropics); where ecosystems have developed that provide a huge variety of habitats (such as the many layers of a tropical rainforest or the nooks and crannies of a coral reef); or where isolation creates conditions in which, over millions of years, evolution takes a unique course[2]. Thus many islands have species of plants, insects and vertebrates, especially birds, that are found nowhere else. A tenth of the world's bird species evolved in an isolated island environment.

This "endemism" is especially pronounced on large islands cut off for millions of years, such as Madagascar (which has more than 6 000 unique species of flowering plants) and Australia (home of marsupials). But the isolation that creates such biodiversity also makes those species particularly vulnerable to outside interference, both because of their limited spread and because they have little resistance to disease or pests from outside. Birds endemic to individual islands make up more than 80 percent of known species extinctions.

Other hotspots of endemism were, in effect, ecological islands in past eras. Many patches of especially diverse tropical forest, for instance, are ancient forests that survived through the colder and often drier conditions of the ice ages. During those periods evolution pursued its own individual course in forest islands surrounded by savannah. One such "fossil forest" is the Korup rainforest in Cameroon.

One approach to conservation is to concentrate on protecting these hotspots as ecological fortresses[3]. But this runs the danger of ignoring the many other functions of natural ecosystems, particularly in their provisions of vital and diverse environmental management functions.

Ecosystems break down pollutants, purify dirty water, and store and cycle nutrients. They thus maintain chemical equilibrium in both ocean waters and the atmosphere. They create and regenerate soils and regulate rates of erosion. They sustain insects that pollinate most of the world's crops, provide free pest control and disperse seeds[4]. They even help create rain. Half the rainfall in parts of the Amazon basin swiftly evaporates from tree leaves to create rain in the interior[5].

Many of the services offered by genetic, species and ecosystem biodiversity – whether directly

COUNTRIES WITH THE MOST AND LEAST PROTECTED AREAS, 1997-98

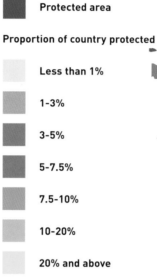

	% of land pro-tected	GDP per capita US$ 1998	Popu-lation density per km²
Ecuador	43.1	1 508	44.0
Venezuela	36.3	4 088	26.3
Denmark	32.2	33 182	124.2
Dominican Republic	31.5	1 926	170.2
Austria	28.3	26 027	98.4
Germany	27.0	25 985	235.2
New Zealand	23.6	13 921	14.2
Slovakia	21.8	3 787	111.8
Bhutan	21.2	177*	42.6
Belize	20.9	2 761*	10.1
Afghanistan	0.3	id	32.7
Lebanon	0.3	5 399	311.9
Myanmar	0.3	id	67.7
Lesotho	0.2	384	67.9
Libya	0.1	4 984+	3.0
Jamaica	0.1	2 529	234.3
Iraq	<0.1	2 755+	49.8
United Arab Emirates	<0.1	20 074	28.1
Yemen	<0.1	256	32.0
Papua New Guinea	<0.1	814	10.2

* GNP   + 1995

Source: WRI; UNPD; World Bank.

PROTECTION OF NATURAL AREAS, 1997

■ Protected area

Proportion of country protected

Less than 1%

1-3%

3-5%

5-7.5%

7.5-10%

10-20%

20% and above

Insufficient data

There is growing concern amongst international organizations, such as The World Bank, that many protected areas are mere "paper parks", enjoying a far greater degree of attention in the world's filing systems than is the case in reality.

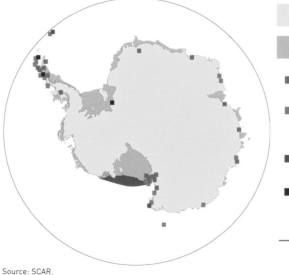

PROTECTION OF NATURAL AREAS, 1997

	Square kilometers protected	As % of total land area
North America	2 147 140	11.7
Latin America and Caribbean	1 438 070	7.2
Europe	1 052 090	4.7
Africa	1 540 430	5.2
Asia	1 628 770	5.3
Oceania	603 820	7.1
World*	**8 410 410**	**6.4**

* Includes areas not included in regional totals; excludes Greenland

Source: WRI.

PROTECTED AREAS IN THE ANTARCTIC, 1997

Land mass

Ice shelf

■ Site of special scientific interest

■ Ecosystem protection and monitoring; entry prohibited without permit

■ Seal reserve

■ Area under management to minimize environmental impact

— **Antarctic Treaty zone** (60° southern latitude) Protects the region from minerals exploitation

Source: SCAR.

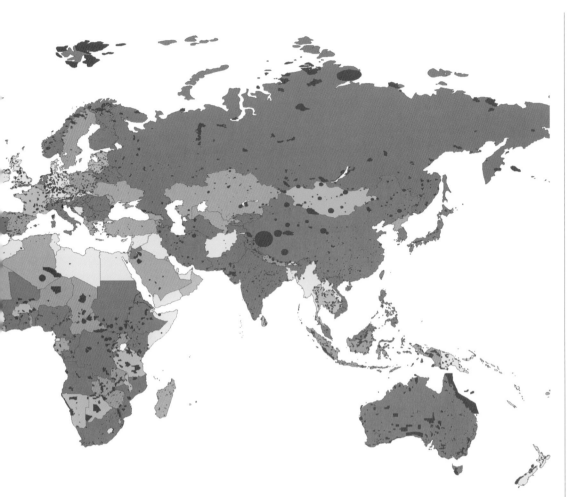

Source: UNEP-WCMC; WRI.

LEVELS OF ENDEMISM, 1990s
Selected countries

Known endemic species
per 100 square kilometers

Source: WRI.

MAJOR COUNTRIES OF ENDEMISM, 1990s

	Mammals – known species		Birds – known species		Higher plants – known species	
	Total	Endemic	Total breeding	Endemic	Total	Endemic
Australia	252	201	649	353	15 000	14 074
China	394	77	1 100	68	30 000	18 000
Colombia	359	29	1 695	63	50 000	1 500
Congo, Dem. Rep.	415	28	929	22	11 000	1 100
Ecuador	302	24	1 388	38	18 250	4 000
Ethiopia	255	31	626	28	6 500	1 000
India	316	45	923	55	15 000	5 000
Indonesia	436	206	1 519	393	27 500	17 500
Japan	132	38	>250	21	4 700	2 000
Madagascar	105	84	202	104	9 000	6 500
Malaysia	286	28	501	9	15 000	3 600
Mexico	450	140	769	89	25 000	12 500
Myanmar	251	6	867	4	7 000	1 071
Peru	344	48	1 538	109	17 121	5 356
Turkey	116	1	302	0	8 472	2 675
USA	428	101	650	69	16 302	4 036
Venezuela	305	17	1 181	42	20 000	8 000

Source: WRI.

REGIONAL SHARE OF THE WORLD'S ENDEMIC PLANTS, 1990s

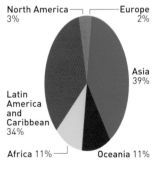

North America 3%
Europe 2%
Asia 39%
Latin America and Caribbean 34%
Africa 11%
Oceania 11%

Source: WRI.

supplied food and medicines, genetic resources or wider environment management services – could not be replaced by human structures or management systems. But because these benefits are not traded in the marketplace, they carry no price tag and can easily be ignored until it is too late[6]. If they were effectively valued and took their place within the prevailing market system, they would be cherished as much as a share portfolio or factory. But since they are not, they are constantly open to being squandered in the name of short-term profit.

Even single species could dramatically change the appreciation of natural resources often deemed by governments as little better than wasteland. When a successful drug against childhood leukemia was developed from the rosy periwinkle, a plant found on the rainforest island of Madagascar, the royalties during the period when the drug came under patent protection exceeded US$100 million, but none got back to the people of the island[7]. Had it done so, the incentive to protect the forests in the interest of finding new pharmaceuticals would have been underlined. Nobody would destroy a laboratory responsible for such a cash return.

Signatories to the 1992 Convention on Biological Diversity have pledged to develop property rights for natural resources to help protect biodiversity, but there is a long way to go. Generally, governments only seem to recognize the environmental management services provided by natural ecosystems when, through negative impacts, they actually fail, causing such problems as desertification, floods and mudslides, "red tides" of toxic algae and coastal erosion.

Protecting biodiversity and the environmental services that ecosystems provide will require not only the creation of protected havens for wildlife, but a much more sophisticated management of entire landscapes, integrating ecological services within largely human-dominated environments. In heavily populated regions such as much of Europe, this is effectively the only viable approach. But increasingly it will also be true of tropical landscapes, where human rights often have to be integrated with environmental protection.

Land demands in the tropics mean that surviving natural forests can rarely be fenced off without damaging the livelihoods of people who harvest their fruit, nuts, medicinal plants and bushmeat. Many believe that such uses need to be promoted and sustained – along with other profitable activities from rubber-tapping to ecotourism, sustainable timber harvesting to trophy hunting – if the forests are to survive rather than being converted to other uses.

On a crowded planet, some protected areas will retain their place as reservoirs of biodiversity. But the hardest challenge – to preserve both species and the ecological services that sustain the Earth – will be to find room, and a profitable role, for nature in managed landscapes where people, too, can live and prosper.

Endnotes

POPULATION AND NATURAL RESOURCES

1. FAOSTAT, 2000.
2. Ibid.
3. WWF, *Living Planet Report 1999*, 1999.
4. Gleick, *Water in Crisis*, Oxford University Press, 1993.
5. WRI, *World Resources 1998-99*, 1999.
6. Abramouitz and Mattoon, *Paper Cuts: Recovering the Paper Landscape*, Worldwatch Institute, 1999.
7. Ibid.

Energy

1. Kete, *What Might a Developing Country Climate Commitment Look Like*, WRI, 1999.
2. Ibid.
3. Flavin, in *State of the World 1999*, Worldwatch Institute, 1999.
4. Ibid.
5. Ibid.
6. Goldemberg, *Guardian*, 29 October 1998.
7. Martin, *Shell World*, April 1999.
8. Pearce, *New Scientist*, May 1, 1999.
9. Brown, in *State of the World 2000*, Worldwatch Institute, 2000.
10. WHO, *Health and Environment in Sustainable Development*, 1997.
11. Sinton, *Energy Policy*, 26: 813, 2000.

Freshwater

1. Postel et al., *Science*, 271: 785, 1996.
2. Ibid.
3. Serageldin, quoted in *Population Reports*, 1995.
4. WRI, *World Resources 2000-2001*, 2000.
5. Gleick, *The World's Water*, Island Press, 1999.
6. Worldwatch Institute, *Vital Trends 1999-2000*, 2000.
7. Brown, *Beyond Malthus*, W.W. Norton, 1999.

Foodcrops

1. After Bender, *Environment*, 29(2): 10, 1997.
2. FAOSTAT, 2000.
3. Conway, *The Doubly Green Revolution*, Penguin, 1997.
4. Ibid.
5. Pretty, *Agricultural Systems 2000*, in press.
6. Conway, op. cit.
7. Brown, *Beyond Malthus*, W.W. Norton, 1999.
8. FAO, *Food for All*, 1996.
9. Parry, *Global Environmental Change*, 9: 551.
10. FAO, op. cit.

Meat and fish

1. US Department of Agriculture, *World Markets and Trends 1998*.
2. Steinfeld et al., *Livestock-Environment Interactions*, FAO, 1996.
3. Ehui, *2020 Vision*, IFPRI, March 1999.
4. IFPRI, *The World Food Situation*, 1997.
5. UNEP, *Global Environment Outlook 2000*, Earthscan, 1999.
6. Steinfeld, op. cit.
7. Robinson et al., *Science*, 284: 595, 1999.
8. WRI, *World Resources 1996-97*, 1997.
9. Advisory Committee on Fisheries Management, International Council for the Exploration of the Sea (ICES), 1999.
10. Brown, *Beyond Malthus*, W.W. Norton, 1999.
11. Nickerson, *Ecological Economics*, 29: 279, 1999.
12. Hinrichsen, *Coastal Waters of the World*, Island Press, 1998.

Forest products

1. Population Action International, *Forest Futures*, 1999.
2. FAO, *Forest Resources Assessment 1990*, 1995.
3. Population Action International, op. cit.
4. FAO, op. cit.

5. FAOSTAT, July 2000.
6. FAO, op. cit.
7. Sedjo, *Resources for the Future*, 1998.
8. Worldwatch Institute, *Vital Signs 1998*, 1998.
9. Calder, *The Blue Revolution*, Earthscan, 1999.
10. Dijk, *Assessment of Non-wood Forest Product Resources in Cameroon*, Tropenbos Foundation, 1998.
11. Robinson et al., *Science*, 284: 595, 1999.

International trade

1. Gornitz, *Climate Change*, 7: 285, 1985.
2. WTO Secretariat, *Trade and Environment Report*, October 1999.
3. Communication from Egypt to the WTO's High-Level Symposium on Trade and Development, March 1999.
4. Pretty, *Agricultural Systems 2000*, in press.
5. Gong, *China Daily*, December 1, 1999.

POPULATION AND LANDUSE

1. Richards, in Clark and Munn, *Sustainable Development of the Biosphere*, Cambridge University Press/IIASA, 1986.
2. Ibid.
3. Dean, in Tucker and Richards (eds), *Global Deforestation and the 19th Century World Economy*, Duke University Press, 1983.
4. Woodall, *Japan under Construction*, University of California Press, 1996.
5. O'Meara, *Reinventing Cities*, Worldwatch Institute, 1999; Robins, Suburbs: best of both worlds, *Resurgence*, January 2000.
6. Box, Conservation or greening, the challenge of post-industrial landscapes, *British Wildlife*, 3: 273, 1993.
7. Gibson, Brownfield red data: the values artificial habitats have for uncommon invertebrates, *Research Reports*, English Nature, 1998.
8. Dover, *To Feed the Earth*, WRI, 1987.
9. Pearce, *New Scientist*, November 27, 1993.

Croplands

1. Tilman, *PNAS* (Proceedings of the National Academy of Sciences of the USA), 96: 5995, 1999.
2. Ibid.
3. Vitousek et al., *Issues in Ecology*, Spring 1997.
4. Ibid.
5. Ibid.
6. Matson, *Science*, 277: 504, 1997.
7. WRI, *World Resources 1998-99*, 1999.
8. Ibid.
9. Pimentel, *Science*, 267: 1117, 1995.

10. Ibid.
11. Tilman, op. cit.
12. *The Potential of Agroecology to Combat Hunger in the Developing World*, IFPRI, 1998.

Pastures

1. Richards, in *The Earth as Transformed by Human Action*, Turner et al. (eds), Cambridge University Press, 1990.
2. FAOSTAT, July 2000.
3. UNEP, *Global Environment Outlook 2000*, Earthscan, 1999.
4. Conway, *The Doubly Green Revolution*, Penguin, 1997.
5. Steinfeld, *Livestock-Environment Interactions*, FAO, 1996.
6. Ibid.
7. Ibid.
8. Ibid.
9. International Livestock Research Institute (ILRI), *Livestock and Nutrient Transfer*, (www.cgiar.org/ilri/ factsheet).
10. Ibid.
11. de Haan et al., *Livestock and the Environment*, FAO, 1996.
12. Steinfeld, op. cit.
13. de Haan et al., op. cit.

Mineral extraction

1. Gardner and Sampat, *Mind over Matter*, Worldwatch Institute, 1998.
2. Jernelov and Ramel, *Ambio*, 27: 155, 1998.
3. UNEP, *Global Environment Outlook 2000*, Earthscan, 1999.
4. Gardner and Sampat, op. cit.

Migration and tourism

1. WRI, *World Resources 1998-99*, 1999.
2. Myers, *Environmental Exodus*, Climate Institute, 1995.
3. Homer-Dixon, *Population and Conflict*, International Union for

the Scientific Study of Population (IUSSP), 1994.
4. Brown, *Beyond Malthus*, W.W. Norton, 1999.
5. Myers, op. cit.
6. Ibid.
7. Töpfer, *Our Planet*, 10(1), UNEP, 1999.
8. Ibid.
9. Honey, *Environment*, 41(5): 4.

Urbanization

1. Girardet, *Connections*, Autumn 1995.
2. United Nations Population Fund (UNFPA), pers. comm.
3. Irwin, *UNESCO Courier*, June 1999.
4. WRI, *World Resources 1996-97*, 1997.
5. Ibid.
6. Satterthwaite, *An Urbanizing World*, United Nations Centre for Human Settlements, 1996.
7. Ibid.
8. Rees, *People and the Planet*, 5(2): 6, 1996.
9. Girardet, *Independent on Sunday*, April 14, 1996.
10. Chameides, *PNAS* (Proceedings of the National Academy of Sciences of the USA), November 1999.
11. *People and the Planet*, 5(2): 9, 1996.
12. Satterthwaite, op. cit.
13. Ibid.

POPULATION AND ATMOSPHERE

1. Brimblecombe, *The Big Smoke*, Methuen, 1987.
2. WRI, *World Resources 1998-99*, 1999.
3. Stoddard et al., *Nature*, 401: 575, 1999.
4. UNEP, *Global Environment Outlook 2000*, Earthscan, 1999.
5. Vitousek et al., *Issues in Ecology*, Spring 1997.
6. Carson, *Silent Spring*, Houghton Mifflin, 1962.
7. Colborn et al., *Our Stolen Future*, Little Brown, London, 1996.
8. AMAP, *Arctic Pollution Issues*, 1997.
9. UNEP, op. cit.
10. Ibid.
11. Houghton and Skole, in *The Earth as Transformed by Human Action*, Turner et al. (eds), Cambridge University Press, 1990.
12. Houghton et al., *Climate Change 1995*, Cambridge University Press, 1996.
13. WRI, *World Resources 1998-99*, 1999.
14. Rasmussen and Khalil, *Nature*, 332: 242, 1998.

Climate change

1. IPCC Working Group 1, *Third Assessment Report*, forthcoming.
2. WRI, *World Resources 1998-99*, 1999.
3. Ibid.
4. WRI, *World Resources 1994-95*, 1995.
5. Hadley Centre, *Climate Change and its Impacts*, 1999.
6. Houghton et al., *Climate Change 1995*, Cambridge University Press, 1996.
7. Hadley Centre, op. cit.
8. Ibid.
9. Sharp, *Lancet*, 347: 1612, 1996.

0. Rahmstorf, *New Scientist*, February 8, 1997.
1. Sinton et al., *Energy Policy*, 6: 813, 1998.
2. Reilly et al., *Nature*, 401: 49, 1999.
3. Worldwatch Institute, *Vital Signs 2000*, 2000.
4. IPCC Working Group 1, *Third Assessment Report*, forthcoming.
5. Pearce, *New Scientist*, November 29, 1997.

Air pollution

. Schwele, *Public Health Implications of Urban Air Pollution in Developing Countries*, Proceedings of the 10th World Clean Air Congress, 1995.
2. UNEP, *Global Environment Outlook 2000*, Earthscan, 1999.
3. Ibid.
4. World Bank, News Release, 96/68S, May 18, 1996.
5. Ibid.
6. Data on areas where critical loads are exceeded, RIVM, 1998.
7. Stoddard et al., *Nature*, 401: 575, 1999.
8. *Forest Condition Survey of Europe 1998*, United Nations Economic Commission for Europe (UNECE), 1999.
9. *Clear Water, Blue Skies: China's Environment in the New Century*, World Bank, 1997.
10. UNEP, op. cit.
11. *RAINS Asia: An assessment Model for Air Pollution in Asia*, report to World Bank, 1995.
12. AMAP, *Arctic Pollution Issues*, 1997.
13. *Science News*, 154: 374, 1998.
14. *The Indonesian Fires and Haze of 1997*, International Development Research Centre (IDRC), 1998.

POPULATION, WASTE AND CHEMICALS

1. *Technologies for the Abatement of Methane Emissions*, International Energy Agency Greenhouse (IEA) Gas R&D Programme, 1999.
2. European Topic Centre on Waste, http://www.etc-waste.int.
3. Cointreau-Levine, *Private Sector Participation in Municipal Solid Waste Services in Developing Countries*, World Bank, 1994.
4. EPA, *Characterization of Municipal Solid Waste in the United States: 1992 Update*, EPA/OSWAER, 1992.
5. Waste management in Ghana, *Warmer Bulletin*, 69, November 1999.
6. Lean et al., *Our Planet*, 10(4), UNEP, 1999.

Industrial chemicals

1. Smith, Introduction to contaminated land, *Environment 97*, 1997. On http://www.environment97.org/text/reception/r/techpapers/g22_biog-ab.htm.
2. Jacobson and Jacobson, *New England Journal of Medicine*, 335: 783, 1996.
3. AMAP Assessment Report: *Arctic Pollution Issues*, from Strosveien 96, PO Box 8100, Dep. N-0032, Oslo, Norway.
4. *The ENDS Report*, 285: 12, October 1998.
5. UNEP Chemicals, *Dioxin and Furan Inventories: National and Regional Emissions of PCDD/PCDF*, Geneva, May 1999.
6. *The ENDS Report*, 220: 11, May 1993.
7. Alcock and Jones, *Environmental Science and Technology*, 30: 3133, 1996.

8. Allanou et al., *Public Availability of Data on EU High Production Volume Chemicals*, European Chemicals Bureau, Ispra, Italy, 1999. On http://ecb.ei.jrc.it/Data-Availability-Documents/datavail.pdf.
9. Matthiessen, *Environmental Science and Technology*, 32(19): 460A, 1998.
10. *The ENDS Report*, 282: 50, July 1998.

Agrochemicals

1. FAO (Alexandratos, ed.), *World Agriculture: Towards 2010*, 1995.
2. WRI, *World Resources 1998-99*, 1999.
3. FAO, op. cit.
4. *The ENDS Report*, 260, September 1996.
5. *Nature*, 403: 80-84, January 2000.
6. *The ENDS Report*, 278: 9, March 1998.
7. Paerl, *Limnology and Oceanography*, 45: 1154-1165, 1997.
8. Czepiel et al., *Environmental Science and Technology*, 29(9): 2352-2356, 1995.
9. WRI, *World Resources 1998-99*, 1999.
10. FAO, *What is Integrated Pest Management?*, 1998.
11. *The ENDS Report*, 286: 9, March 1992.
12. Turnbull et al., *Journal of the Chartered Institute of Water and Environmental Management*, 11, 1997.

POPULATION AND ECOSYSTEMS

1. Clark and Munn, *Sustainable Development of the Biosphere*, Cambridge University Press, 1986.
2. Ibid.
3. WWF, *Living Planet Report 2000*, 2000.
4. Turner et al., *The Earth as Transformed by Human Action*, Cambridge University Press, 1990.
5. Ibid.
6. Ibid.
7. Moffat, *Science*, 279: 988, 1998.

Mountains

1. Denniston, *People and the Planet*, 5(1), 1996.
2. Price, *Unasylva*, 49: 3-12, 1998.
3. Denniston, op. cit.
4. World Bank, *World Development Report 1998*, 1998.
5. Denniston, op. cit.
6. Ibid.
7. Worldwatch Institute, *State of the World 1995*, 1995.
8. Hasnain, *Report of Working Group on Himalayan Glaciology*, International Commission on Snow and Ice, 1999.
9. Krajick, *Science*, 279: 1853, 1998.
10. International Federation of the Red Cross and Red Crescent Societies (IFRC), *World Disasters Report 1999*, 1999.
11. Calder, *The Blue Revolution*, Earthscan, 1999.

Forests

1. Lewin, *Science*, 226: 36, 1984.
2. Worldwatch Institute, *State of the World 1998*, 1998.
3. FAO, *Forest Resources Assessment 1990*, 1995.
4. Ibid.

5. Dobson, *Conservation and Biodiversity*, Scientific American Library, 1998.
6. FAO, op. cit.
7. WRI, *World Resources 1998-99*, 1999.
8. Department for International Development (UK), *Indonesia-UK Tropical Forest Management Programme*, London, 1999.
9. ITTO, *Guidelines for the Sustainable Management of Natural Tropical Forests*, 1990.

Deserts and drylands

1. UNCCD, *Fact Sheet 1: An Introduction to the UN Convention to Combat Desertification*, 2000.
2. Smith and Koala, *Desertification: Myth and Reality*, International Development Research Centre (IDRC), 1999.
3. Kerr, *Science*, 281: 633, 1998.
4. Thomas and Middleton, *Desertification: Exploding the Myth*, John Wiley, 1994.
5. UNEP, *World Atlas of Desertification*, Edward Arnold, 1992.
6. Western, *In the Dust of Kilimanjaro*, Island Press, 1998.
7. Jean-Marie Cour, *The Sahel* (report), Club du Sahel, 1998.
8. Middleton, *Research Paper 40*, University of Oxford School of Geography, 1986.
9. Tiffen et al., *More People Less Erosion*, John Wiley, 1994.
10. Ibid.
11. Harrison, *The Greening of Africa*, Paladin, 1987.
12. Mortimore, *Adapting to Drought*, Cambridge University Press, 1989.
13. Worldwatch Institute, *State of the World 1984*, 1984.

Freshwater wetlands

1. Dugan, *Wetlands in Danger*, Mitchell Beazley, 1993.
2. Moser, Wetlands International, quoted in *New Scientist*, March 30, 1996.
3. Barbier et al., *Economic Valuation of Wetland Benefits*, International Institute for Environment and Development (IIED), 1991.
4. Roush, *Science*, 276: 1029, 1997.
5. EPA, *Wetlands and Nature*, 1999.
6. Young, *Environmental Science and Technology*, 30: 292A, 1996.
7. Crivelli and Pearce, *Characteristics of Mediterranean Wetlands*, Tour du Valat, 1994.

Mangroves and estuaries

1. Choudhury, *World Forestry Congress*, 6, topic 38.6, 1997.
2. Hinrichsen, Coasts in crisis, *Issues in Science and Technology*, Summer 1996, AAAS.
3. Ibid.
4. Choudhury, op. cit.
5. Nickerson, *Ecological Economics*, 29: 279, 1999.
6. Hinrichsen, op. cit.
7. Cohen, *Science*, 278: 1209, 1997.
8. *Economist*, May 23, 1998.
9. Bryant et al., *Coastlines at Risk*, WRI Indicator Brief, 1995.
10. Sunghui and Hodgkiss, *Harmful Algae News*, (18), UNESCO, 1999.
11. Harwood, *Nature*, 393: 17-18, 1998.
12. Butler, Commonwealth Scientific and Industrial Research Organization (CSIRO), reported by Reuters, March 28, 2000.

13. Meinesz, EU International Seminar on *Caulerpa Taxifolia*, Nice, 1994.
14. Hecht, *New Scientist*, February 21, 1998.
15. Pearce, *New Scientist*, November 6, 1999.

Coral reefs

1. Bryant et al., *Reefs at Risk*, WRI, 1998.
2. Ibid.
3. Ibid.
4. Ibid.
5. Shinn, Coral mortality and African dust, *Proceedings of Oceanographic Society (US)*, 1996.
6. Kleypas, *Science*, 284: 118, 1999.
7. Pearce, *Our Planet*, 10(3), UNEP, 1999.
8. Seaweb, Pollution, climate change threaten world's coral reefs, *Ocean Update*, 1999.
9. Sheppard, *Chagos Islands* (report), UK Foreign Office, 1999.
10. Costanza, *Nature*, 387: 253, 1997.
11. Bryant et al., op. cit.

Regional seas

1. Jeftic, *UNEP Regional Seas Reports No 132*, 1990.
2. Platt, *Dying Seas*, Worldwatch Institute, 1995.
3. Weber and Gradwohl, *Wealth of the Oceans*, W.W. Norton, 1995.
4. Malakoff, *Science*, 281: 190, 1998; Moffat, *Science*, 279: 988, 1998.
5. UNEP (Heywood, ed.), *Global Biodiversity Assessment*, 1995.
6. Hinrichsen, *Coastal Waters of the World*, Island Press, 1998; UNEP, *Global Environment Outlook-1*, Oxford University Press, 1997.
7. *Economist*, May 23, 1998.
8. Mulvaney, *E Magazine*, 9, Jan/Feb 1998.

Oceans

1. Snelgrove and Madin, *Oceanus*, Fall 1995.
2. Olsgard and Gray, *Marine Ecology Progress Series*, 1995.
3. Holmes, *New Scientist*, March 1, 1997.
4. IPCC Working Group 1, *Third Assessment Report*, forthcoming.
5. Ibid.
6. Broecker, *Science*, 278: 1582, 1997.
7. IPCC, op. cit.
8. Nicholls et al., *Global Environmental Change*, 9: 589, 1999.

Polar regions

1. Stone et al., *Arctic Pollution Issues*, AMAP, Oslo, 1997.
2. Ibid.
3. UNEP, *Global Environment Outlook 2000*, Earthscan, 1999.
4. IPCC Working Group 1, *Third Assessment Report*, forthcoming.
5. Ibid.
6. Malloy et al., *PNAS (Proceedings of the National Academy of Sciences of the USA)*, 94: 1258, 1997.

POPULATION AND BIODIVERSITY

1. Service, *Science*, 275: 1740, 1997.
2. Rosenzweig, *Science*, 284: 276, 1999.
3. De Leo and Levin, *Conservation Ecology*, 1: 3, 1997.
4. Balick and Cox, *Plants, People and Culture*, Scientific American Library, 1996.
5. Myers, *The Sinking Ark*, Pergamon, 1979.
6. *Agro-ecology: Creating the Synergism for Sustainable Agriculture*, UNDP, 1995.
7. Wilson, Threats to biodiversity, *Scientific American*, September 1989.
8. *Managing Global Genetic Resources*, National Academy of Sciences of the USA, 1992.
9. Rosenthal and Grifo, *Biodiversity and Human Health*, Island Press, 1997.
10. Shand, *Human Nature*, Rural Advancement Foundation International (RAFI), 1997.
11. Wilson, *The Diversity of Life*, Harvard University Press, 1992.
12. UNEP (Heywood, ed.), *Global Biodiversity Assessment*, 1995.
13. United Nations Population Fund (UNFPA), *Population and Sustainable Development: Five Years after Rio*, 1997.

Species

1. Bryant, *Biodiversity and Conservation*, hypertext book, 1997.
2. WRI, *A History of Extinction*, 1992.
3. World Conservation Monitoring Centre, *Global Biodiversity: Status of the Earth's Living Resources*, Chapman and Hall, 1992.
4. World Conservation Monitoring Centre, Biodiversity Series No. 8, *Freshwater Biodiversity: A Preliminary Global Assessment*, 1998.
5. IUCN, *1996 Red List of Threatened Animals*, 1996.
6. UNEP (Heywood, ed.), *Global Biodiversity Assessment*, 1995.
7. Tuxill, *Nature's Cornucopia*, Worldwatch Institute, 1999.
8. Shand, *Human Nature*, RAFI, 1997.
9. FAO, *Plant Genetic Resources*, 1993.
10. Shand, op. cit.
11. Cohen, *Science*, 276: 1329, 1997.

Ecosystems and conservation

1. Myers, *Nature*, 403: 853, 2000.
2. Harrison, *The Third Revolution*, Penguin, 1993.
3. Myers, op. cit.
4. Nabham and Buchmann, *Nature's Services*, Island Press, 1997.
5. Salati, *The Geophysiology of Amazonia*, John Wiley, 1987.
6. Daily et al., *Issues in Ecology 2*, Ecological Society of America, 1997.
7. Jenkins, *Madagascar: An Environmental Profile*, World Conservation Monitoring Centre, 1987.

Part 3: Case studies

The Northern Andes ecoregion

HE NORTHERN ANDES ecoregion, extending from Venezuela to northern Peru, contains an exceptionally diverse set of landscapes. Its rugged topography, extreme climatic variation, geologic and biogeographic history have created a unique collection of habitats found nowhere else on Earth.

The montane forests and meadows of the region nurture a rich complex of species, including many that are endemic. Some of the more well-known representatives of local fauna are the spectacled bear, the puma and the Andean tapir. The biota of the Northern Andean paramos is equally outstanding. These unique high altitude grasslands developed in altitudinal isolation, leading to an exceptional degree of biological diversity. It has been estimated that up to 60 percent of this ecosystem's approximately 3 000 to 4 000 species of vascular plants may be endemic.

Intense pressures from urbanization, logging, grazing and land conversion threaten the Northern Andes ecosystem. As habitats are destroyed, animal and plant populations decrease, and many species eventually become extinct. Since habitat loss is highly correlated with the intensity of human population and activities, a map showing the location of people and their economic activities provides a close approximation to a map of threats to biodiversity. By mapping demographic and related variables, WWF can strategize conservation action across an ecoregion. These maps help target operations in regions where threats co-occur with important biological phenomena. Areas with relatively little threat are prime candidates for new reserves or wildlife corridors between reserves.

Population growth is a useful indicator of current and future threat to biodiversity as high growth rates are indicative of an increase in consumption and the exploitation of natural resources. Consequently, habitat and species are adversely affected. Conversely, depopulation of an area (negative growth) can support biodiversity if previously exploited lands are left to grow back to a natural state. Examining these patterns of growth can help WWF detect where threats to biodiversity will continue to rise in the near term. Current statistics for the Northern Andean countries show positive growth rates throughout yet growth is significantly lower in the Andean mountains than in adjacent forest lowlands. In large part, this is because landless peasants have been moving to the coast or are attracted to oil or mining developments in the

POPULATION GROWTH RATES IN THE NORTHERN ANDES ECOREGION, 1990s

Less than 0%
0-1%
1-2%
2-4%
4-6%
More than 6%

Northern Andean montane forest

Northern Andean paramos

Source: WWF-Colombia; CIAT.

Amazon. The Ecuadorean canton of Pichincha is the only Andean political unit with a growth rate over 2 percent. This canton could be losing habitat at an alarming rate.

Population statistics are often only available for large administrative units such as counties or *municipios*. Such coarse resolution makes it difficult to associate population patterns with particular sites of interest. Human populations tend to concentrate in cities or towns or locate near roads or other transportation routes. Future human populations are more likely to settle in these relatively accessible areas as well. Therefore, mapped layers of roads and towns can indicate probable population densities at finer scales than entire counties. The maps on this page, the result of a market accessibility model based on town and road locations, approximate the distribution of human populations and their activities in the Northern Andes. The model uses time value as a surrogate for accessibility to each location throughout the ecoregion. Topography and the networks of roads, rivers and streams were all used to calculate the results. On the maps, higher values indicate low accessibility (high travel time requirement), while lower values indicate high accessibility (low travel time requirement).

In spite of the threat that they present to the natural environment, roads and other transportation corridors often provide a positive social function. Better access to urban centers and markets leads to diversification of rural economies by opening up markets to villagers who want to sell labor, artisan products or agricultural produce. In some cases, increased access to towns allows rural people to participate in a wage economy, potentially reducing the need to exploit local resources. It is more likely, however, that increased access to urban centers combined with close proximity to those centers can lead to higher levels of habitat degradation as a result of cash cropping, logging and other economic opportunities introduced by market integration. Therefore, priority areas for conservation will have a better chance of remaining intact if they are located in relatively inaccessible sites. The accessibility model provides a useful viability indicator for locating these sites, which have the potential to function as buffer zones, wildlife corridors and protected areas. Meanwhile, taking areas of high biological diversity into account when planning for additional infrastructure will help minimize the impact of social infrastructure on existing parks and wilderness areas while supporting human development needs.

ACCESSIBILITY IN THE NORTHERN ANDES, 2000

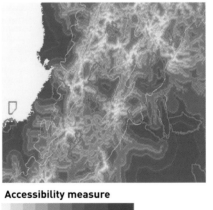

Accessibility measure

High   Low

Northern Andes ecoregion

Protected area

Source: WWF-Colombia; CIAT.

Canaima National Park, Venezuela

THE IMPACTS of population and population growth can vary widely, depending on the activities of the people involved and the nature of the environmental setting in which they live. A good example of this is Canaima National Park in Venezuela.

Covering about 30 000 square kilometers in the state of Bolívar in southeastern Venezuela, Canaima National Park is a place of spectacular natural beauty. Although known best as the home of Angel Falls, the world's tallest, and dozens of tall rock *mesas* called *tepuys* that rise dramatically out of the surrounding flat lands, Canaima contains a wide array of biological resources in the forests that still cover much of the park. It is also the home of thousands of Pemón, an indigenous people who have resided in this portion of northern South America for 200 to 300 years.

For generations, the Pemón have relied primarily on shifting cultivation, or swidden agriculture, for their livelihood. Swidden agriculture involves growing crops in small plots that are cleared of forest through a combination of cutting and burning foliage. Each plot is used for a short period of time, after which the Pemón abandon it to allow the forest to regenerate and soil nutrients to

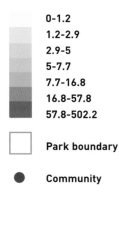

POPULATION DENSITY NEAR CANAIMA NATIONAL PARK, 2000

Population density per square kilometer

0-1.2
1.2-2.9
2.9-5
5-7.7
7.7-16.8
16.8-57.8
57.8-502.2

Park boundary

Community

Source: OCEI.

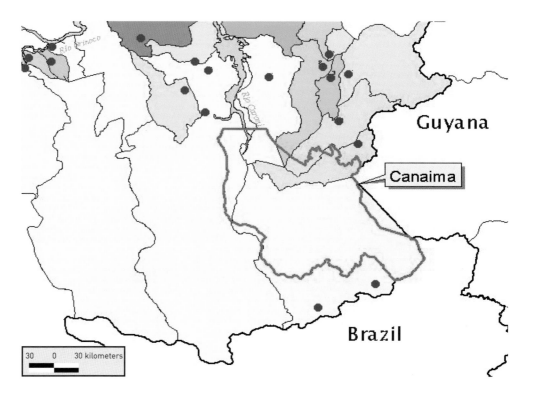

recover. Unfortunately, in recent years forest regeneration has declined dramatically, and much of the area cleared by the Pemón has become grasslands instead – areas that are not suitable for agriculture because of their lack of soil nutrients. Researchers blame much of this transition on population growth.

Nearly all of the human residents of Canaima are Pemón. Population tends to be widely dispersed in small villages, usually located on the edge of dense stands of forest. Due to this dispersed settlement pattern, population density in Canaima and its surrounding area is quite low – so low that population-related problems at first glance seem unlikely. But population has been growing rapidly in recent years, for two main reasons. One is natural increase, where the number of births exceeds the number of deaths – in the case of Canaima, due largely to improved health care saving more lives. The other is in-migration, mainly by other Pemón relocating from the nation of Guyana east of the park, due largely to uncertainty about their future under the government of that country. The result has been extremely high rates of population growth throughout much of Canaima, a trend expected to continue in coming decades.

What are the impacts of this population growth? Although population densities remain low, they are increasing. The swidden agriculture that the Pemón practice is sustainable only for extremely sparse populations, where continual relocation of plots is possible to allow the recovery of forest and soil nutrients.

When population density increases, plots are used for longer periods and recovery times are reduced. Moreover, denser populations mean more fires to clear land, increasing the risk that forest not being cleared will be affected when fires get out of control. In the absence of adequate base nutrients to begin forest regrowth, and with less and less forest to serve as a source of seed due to lack of regeneration or inadvertent burning, grasslands become established. Thus, in delicate ecosystems such as those found in Canaima, even slight increases in population density can lead to an imbalance in the cycle of life under certain conditions. Such situations point up the real importance of understanding not only how many people occupy an area, but what they are doing and how those activities affect their natural surroundings.

AVERAGE ANNUAL POPULATION CHANGE, 1990–2000

Average annual change

- Less than −4.8%
- −4.8–0.0%
- 0.0–1.0%
- 1.0–2.0%
- 2.0–4.0%
- 4.0–6.5%
- More than 6.5%

☐ Park boundary

● Community

Source: OCEI.

The Nature Conservancy®

Population and hydrology in the Dominican Republic

T HE DOMINICAN REPUBLIC occupies the eastern part of the island of Hispaniola in the Caribbean Sea. Covering nearly 50 000 square kilometers, this island nation encompasses a broad array of environmental zones, from the pine-covered slopes of the highest peak in the Caribbean to dense webs of mangroves along large stretches of its coasts.

Much of the surface of the Dominican Republic today is dominated by agriculture, practiced on a small scale by the native Taino Indians when Christopher Columbus arrived there in 1492, but now much more extensive. Known especially for its sugar production, the Dominican Republic also produces coffee, cocoa and rice, along with other crops of lesser importance and livestock. In recent decades, tourism and manufacturing have come to dominate the economy.

The demography of the Dominican Republic has changed considerably since the arrival of Europeans in the 15th century. Disease and maltreatment, both from the Spanish, virtually eradicated the indigenous population by the early 1500s. In response the Spanish brought slaves from Africa to replace the indigenous peoples as a source of labor. Due primarily to continuing in-

POPULATION CHANGE IN THE DOMINICAN REPUBLIC, 1981-93

Average annual change

- Less than −5%
- −5 − −3%
- −3 − −1%
- −1 - 0%
- 0 - 1%
- 1 - 2%
- 2 - 4%
- 4 - 7%
- 7 - 10%
- More than 10%
- id

∿ Protected area

Source: ONE.

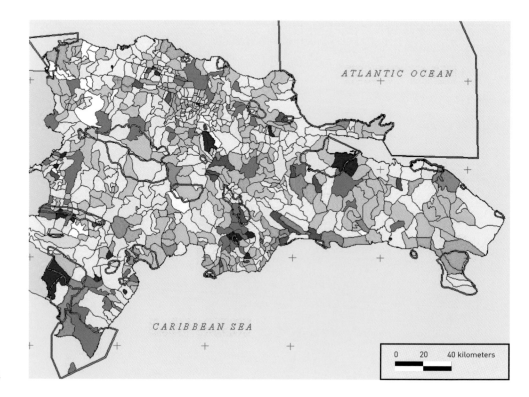

migration, the population began to grow – slowly at first, then more rapidly. By the time of its first systematic census in 1920, roughly 890 000 people lived in the Dominican Republic. Steady population growth occurred over the ensuing seven decades, resulting in a total population of about 7.3 million in 1993, the date of the most recent census. Natural increase, augmented by slight in-migration, has fuelled this population growth. Between the most recent two censuses of 1981 and 1993, population was still growing on average at a rate of 2.3 percent per year. But the most note-worthy characteristic of the country's demographic change in the past three decades has been internal migration, primarily from rural areas to cities, leading to dramatic shifts in the geographic distribution of people in this island nation.

As home to more than 30 national protected areas, the conservation of the natural environment is a major consideration in the Dominican Republic. One of the most important components of con-servation is freshwater, most of which originates as rainfall in the central mountain chain that runs east-west across Hispaniola. Fulfilling demands for domestic use in major cities along the coast, freshwater also plays a key role in maintaining all ecosystems on the island and contributes to var-ious economic activities, most notably agriculture. The more than 100 major watersheds in the Dominican Republic can be classified as to their general condition through an examination of satel-lite imagery to measure the amount of vegetation disturbance in each. Comparing these levels of disturbance to population levels reveals a general correlation between the number of people res-iding in a watershed and its condition – that is to say, the watersheds in poorest condition tend to be those with the largest populations. However, this association is not perfect. In some cases, heavily disturbed watersheds contain fewer people, while in other cases watersheds with minimal distur-bance contain high populations. The former condition tends to occur in areas of high agricultural activity, the latter in areas with less agricultural activity and populations concentrated in a few main settlements. Through the further study of how humans and human activity are spatially distributed across the Dominican Republic, researchers and government planners can better understand how people affect freshwater and how this key resource can be conserved and used more wisely in this small island nation.

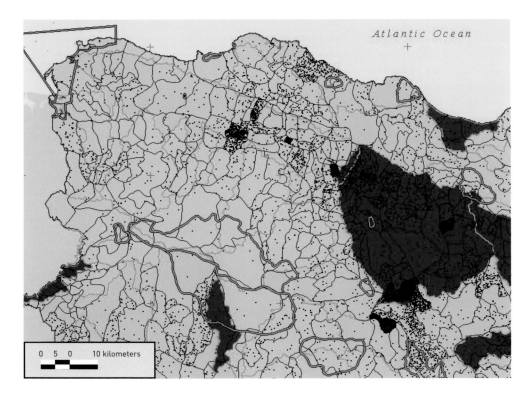

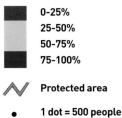

WATERSHED DISTURBANCE AND TOTAL POPULATION IN THE DOMINICAN REPUBLIC, 1993 (DETAIL)

Proportion of watershed disturbed

- 0-25%
- 25-50%
- 50-75%
- 75-100%

∿ Protected area

• 1 dot = 500 people

Source: ONE; Ministry of Territorial Organization, Dominican Republic.

The Eastern Himalayas

POPULATION DENSITY IN THE EASTERN HIMALAYAS

Population density per square kilometer

Less than 10
11-25
26-50
51-100
101-200
201-300
301-400
401-500
501-1 000
1 000-2 000
More than 2 000

Source: National census data; CIESIN.

FEW PLACES ON EARTH can match the breathtaking splendor of the Himalayas. The towering peaks and secluded valleys of this mountain range form a 2 400-kilometer barrier separating the lowlands of the Indian subcontinent from the high, dry Tibetan Plateau.

Stretching from lush moist forests in the south to towering snowcapped peaks in the north, the Himalayas feature an astonishing variety of animals and plants. The Eastern Himalayas, located in the rugged mountain terrain of Nepal, Bhutan and northeast India, are a conservation priority for WWF. These ecoregions consist of some of the world's most diverse temperate forests, the world's tallest grasslands with the highest densities of tigers and rhinos in Asia, and alpine meadows rich in plant and animal life. The ecoregions are globally outstanding because they support habitats that protect many of the world's rarest animals, including greater one-horned rhinos, Asian elephants, golden langurs, tigers, takins, red pandas and snow leopards.

Population density and continuing rapid population growth are among the most significant pressures influencing the intensity of land and resource use. In turn, negative patterns of land use contribute directly to the decline of local habitats and species. In an effort to clarify the distribution and intensity of negative pressures associated with humans and their activities, WWF has mapped several population variables across the Eastern Himalayan region. By overlaying these variables with habitat or species data onto one map, high biodiversity regions under the greatest threat from population pressures are revealed. Focused conservation action needs to occur when these areas contain unique and irreplaceable species or habitats.

The major human activities that threaten biodiversity in the Eastern Himalayas are agricultural conversion, overuse of forest resources, hunting and overgrazing. The intensity of many of these human induced pressures is positively correlated with population density, which follows a steep,

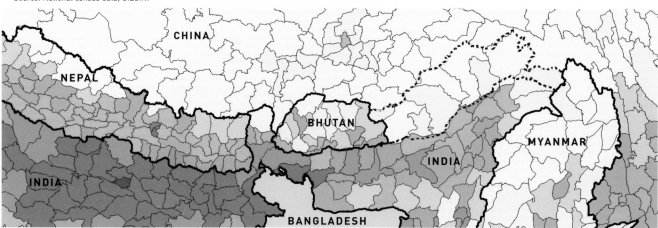

positive gradient from east to west and from north to south. The highest densities are reached in the Tarai, a grassland in the south of Nepal, Bhutan, and the Indian states of Sikkim and Arunachal Pradesh. Up until the mid-1950s this region was populated only by Tharus, an ethnic group with genetic immunity to malaria. Once malaria was brought under control, the Tarai's rich agricultural land attracted migrants from both the mountainous north and Indian plains to the south. The subsequent growth in people and agriculture since the 1950s is mirrored by the decline in forests, natural grasslands and their wild inhabitants.

A more direct link between humans and habitat can be made by combining human density and remaining forest figures into one ratio. People in the Eastern Himalayas depend upon the forests for timber, fuelwood, grazing, foraging, sub-canopy plantations of cardamom, and many other uses. At the same time, the forest represents important habitat for the majority of the region's fauna. Mapping the area's forest to person ratio indicates the relative level of pressure human population exerts on habitat. The lower the ratio, the less forest available per person and the higher the pressure on habitat. All of Nepal shows a great deal of pressure on remaining forests, leaving a threatening situation for protected areas which may be the only source of forest products for the local population. The further east in the ecoregion, the more forests are left, with especially high values in Arunachal Pradesh and Myanmar. The forests in these high value regions are most certainly in better condition with more intact species assemblages.

Population growth in the Eastern Himalayas averages 2.1 per cent per year with a maximum of 4.83 per cent in the Kailali district in Nepal. The doubling time for 2.1 per cent is approximately 33 years, while the doubling time for 4.83 is just over 14 years. The short doubling time underscores the fact that slowing population growth is desirable from both human and ecological standpoints.

Birth rate is one of the factors that control growth rate. A practical measure of birth rate is total fertility, which measures the average number of children that women would have, assuming that these women had children at the average rate for each period in their lives. Statistics from Nepal show that, in recent years, the total fertility rate is declining. Growth in both the urban and rural environment can be influenced to decline by increasing access to health facilities and raising the female literacy rate. WWF is encouraging activities that will help accelerate progress in these two areas.

Biologists agree that, due to the limited effectiveness of small, isolated protected areas, conservation must occur in areas inhabited by people. However, in doing this, potential conflicts between human development and conservation will increase, as will the need for innovative solutions to address both elements. Demographic maps give WWF a good indication of where pressure on habitat and species is most acute. WWF is reallocating much of its efforts to areas where high human pressure and recognized biological importance coincide. Within these areas, WWF is seeking and applying strategies to help foster behavior and attitudes that will better serve conservation goals.

TOTAL FERTILITY RATE IN NEPAL

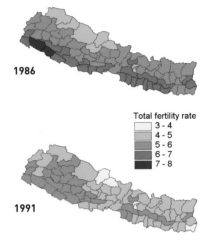

1986

Total fertility rate
- 3 - 4
- 4 - 5
- 5 - 6
- 6 - 7
- 7 - 8

1991

Source: Central Bureau of Statistics, Nepal.

FOREST TO PEOPLE RATIO IN THE EASTERN HIMALAYAS

Forest to people ratio

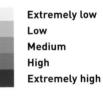

- Extremely low
- Low
- Medium
- High
- Extremely high

Source: National census data; CIESIN; USGS.

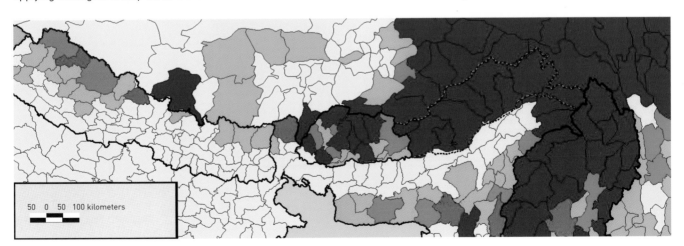

50 0 50 100 kilometers

Population trends and the environment in Madagascar

THE ISLAND OF MADAGASCAR is a living laboratory of evolution. More than 150 million years ago, the widening Mozambique channel split Madagascar off from Africa and created the world's fourth largest island, covering more than 587 000 square kilometers.

An astonishing 98 percent of Madagascar's land mammals, 92 percent of its reptiles, 68 percent of its plants and 41 percent of its breeding bird species exist nowhere else on Earth. Madagascar boasts two thirds of the world's chameleons and 50 species of lemur, which are unique to the island. The dry and spiny forests are one of the many fascinating subregions of the island. Within this landscape, rare species of tortoise, including the radiated and angonoka tortoises, inch their way across the ancient landscape. Other residents include Verreaux's coua, part of a sub-family of cuckoo-like birds, and the sicklebill vanga. The spiny desert is also known for its plant species. Here, forests of Didiereaceae, a unique plant family with no obvious affinity to any other, mix with endemic *Euphorbia* species. Sifakas, ringtails and other lemurs lounge in these unusual woody succulents.

The future of these remarkable plants and animals is far from secure. Massive deforestation has taken place since the 1970s. Only a fragment of the island's original forest cover remains and over 300 species of its plants and animals are threatened with extinction. The plight of the human population is also grim. With an average per-capita income of US$216 a year and a foreign debt that nearly equals its gross national product, the island is ranked amongst the poorest nations in the world.

POPULATION GROWTH AND FEMALE LITERACY

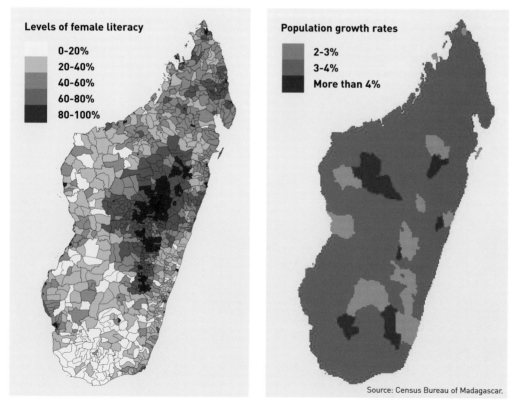

Levels of female literacy

- 0-20%
- 20-40%
- 40-60%
- 60-80%
- 80-100%

Population growth rates

- 2-3%
- 3-4%
- More than 4%

Source: Census Bureau of Madagascar.

Madagascar's exploding population exacerbates its economic stress. The island's average population growth rate ranks among the highest in Africa at 2.8 percent per year. The population of around 14.1 million is expected to double by 2025. Since in-migration is negligible, population growth is driven by high fertility rates. In turn, poverty and a lack of reproductive health facilities contribute to the high fertility rate. Research has also shown a clear correlation between fertility and women's access to education. This is significant for Madagascar as over 40 percent of the female population over the age of 15 is illiterate. Female literacy is exceptionally low in the spiny forest but higher in the central highlands in and around the capital, Antananarivo.

Understanding the significant relationships between population growth, fertility and literacy in Madagascar is important for those concerned with protecting the island's biological diversity. First, it suggests the need for fine-scale investigation into how specific demographic trends in and around important biological sites affect wild species and habitat. The results of these investigations could spur partnerships between conservation organizations, local agencies and communities. An effort to depress fertility through education may benefit natural spaces as well as improve the prospects for Madagascar's younger generations.

LIVESTOCK AND THE ENVIRONMENT

To the Malagasy people, cattle have great cultural, spiritual and economic significance. As bargaining chips for exchanges including brides and personal property, cattle are a form of wealth, pride and financial security. The cattle culture is especially strong in central and southern Madagascar. Unfortunately, too many cattle on too little land have disastrous effects on natural habitat. Heavy grazing as well as slash-and-burn agriculture cause severe erosion even where human populations are comparatively sparse. The soils of western Madagascar have been degraded to the point where the native dry forests and thickets seem unable to regenerate. Exotic weeds are becoming more and more prevalent in the resulting savannah-like landscape. Needless to say, native fauna is disappearing at a startling rate.

The study of the spatial pattern of human and livestock demographic trends can help explain the current state of Madagascar's natural environment. Understanding the intricacies of human-environment relations is a prerequisite for protecting the island's environment for both people and wildlife. By assessing the human pressures associated with environmental degradation, WWF and its partners hope to understand and ultimately to stem threats to ancient and diverse habitats.

Source: GLASOD/UNEP-GRID;
Census Bureau of Madagascar.

LAND DEGRADATION AND LIVESTOCK DENSITY

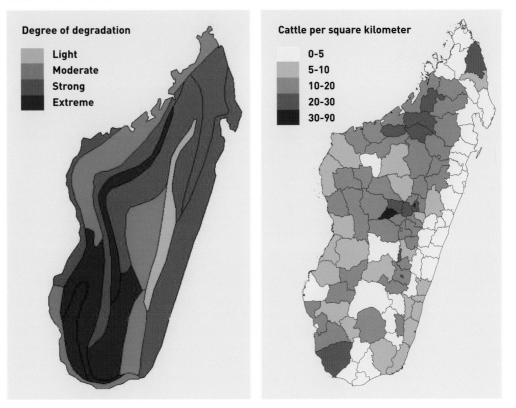

Degree of degradation

Light
Moderate
Strong
Extreme

Cattle per square kilometer

0–5
5–10
10–20
20–30
30–90

The Nature Conservancy®

Population and conservation in the Sonoran Desert

F EW AREAS in North America can match the challenges to conserving the natural environment that have accompanied human population growth and development in the Sonoran Desert. The biological resources in this region comprise a broad array of plant and animal species, many found nowhere else in the world. But the threats to the survival of these resources are considerable, with population growth and development in the Sonoran Desert over the past half-century occurring at rates rarely matched anywhere on the North American continent.

Located in the states of Arizona and California in the southwestern United States, and in the states of Baja California and Sonora in northwestern Mexico, the Sonoran Desert covers about 222 700 square kilometers. As with all deserts, it receives minimal precipitation – as little as 100 millimeters annually in its driest sections. But despite this aridity, the Sonoran Desert contains remarkably high biological diversity. Available evidence indicates the presence of about 130 species of mammals, 20 of amphibians, nearly 150 of reptiles, about 25 of fish, and at least 500 species of birds. Plant diversity is marked as well; the state of Sonora alone contains at least 20 percent of Mexico's plant species. In terms of the number of life forms and the variety of ecological communities, the Sonoran has been called the richest desert in North America.

As often is the case, the species in the Sonoran Desert that has come to dominate all others is human beings. Human occupation began about 11 000 years ago, when prehistoric hunter-gatherers entered the region. Although some indigenous peoples eventually developed elaborate irrigation systems, providing an adequate agricultural foundation for sedentary settlements, total population in the Sonoran Desert remained of the order of a few tens of thousands until European contact in the 16th century. For several reasons, most notably its remote location and its arid natural environment, population grew slowly during the ensuing four centuries of Hispanic and Anglo-American occupation. But late in the 19th century, the connection of this remote region to other areas by road and rail, and the emergence of large-scale projects to control water, provided the foundation for considerable population growth. This growth began in earnest after the Second World War. By 1970 the population of the Sonoran Desert had reached nearly 2.3 million people and was growing at a rate in excess of 4.0 percent annually; by 1995, regional population was nearly 5.5 million, and still growing at a rate of 3.0 percent per year.

The vast majority of current population in the Sonoran Desert occurs in and around urban areas. Some cities have grown quite large. For example, in the Mexican portion of the region, the cities of Mexicali and Hermosillo both currently contain more than half a million people, while in the United States portion of the region, metropolitan Phoenix contains about 2.5 million people and metropolitan Tucson another half-million. In 1990, the most recent year for which we have reliable data for the entire region, more than 88 percent of the Sonoran Desert's inhabitants lived in 40 communities containing 10 000 people or more. Although concentrated population tends to concentrate impacts to the natural environment, in the Sonoran Desert sprawl serves to disperse impacts around the urban centers. Moreover, the modern technology that has enabled the development of large concentrations of population also serves to deplete surface and subsurface water supplies far beyond the geographic limits of these cities, causing enormous environmental impacts.

Although an excess of births over deaths has contributed to the population increase in the Sonoran Desert, the majority of population growth has been due to migration. Between 1985 and 1990, for instance, in several United States counties and Mexican *municipios* in the region more than 20 percent of the population aged five years and older had relocated from another state or country – the total for the desert in excess of 650 000 in that short period alone. The reasons for this high rate of migration vary between the two countries, but seem to share a common foundation in economic opportunity. In the Mexican part of the Sonoran Desert, many people have relocated from other parts of the country to areas close to the border to take advantage of potential employ-ment – primarily to work in manufacturing plants called *maquiladoras*, and to a lesser extent to work in the Borderlands cities and in coastal resorts. In the United States portion of the region, growth in the Sonoran Desert has been part of a larger phenomenon of growth throughout the Sun Belt, a combination of relocation for retirement coupled with economic growth in manufacturing, the tourism industry, and to support the growing population of retirees.

A recent conservation plan developed by The Nature Conservancy and partner organizations identified 100 landscape-scale conservation sites and about 30 smaller conservation sites in the Sonoran Desert. Many of these sites are in areas of sparse population and minimal population growth. Others, unfortunately, lie in areas of dense and growing population, or in the path of likely growth. What the future holds for these sites depends in large part on the direction of future pop-ulation change and development and, in particular, on efforts to guide development in a way that uses scarce resources wisely and minimizes the damage done to the natural environment.

POPULATION AND CONSERVATION IN THE SONORAN DESERT REGION, 1990

Population density per square kilometer

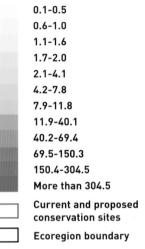

0.1-0.5
0.6-1.0
1.1-1.6
1.7-2.0
2.1-4.1
4.2-7.8
7.9-11.8
11.9-40.1
40.2-69.4
69.5-150.3
150.4-304.5
More than 304.5

Current and proposed conservation sites

Ecoregion boundary

Source: US Bureau of the Census; INEGI.

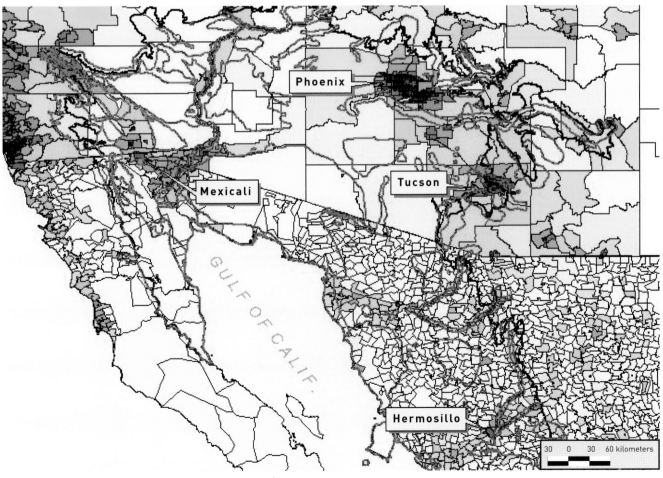

Index

Sources

AAAS American Association for the Advancement of Science http://www.aaas.org

de Sherbinin and Dompka Markham (eds), *Water and Population Dynamics: Case Studies and Policy Implications*, AAAS, IUCN, Population Reference Bureau, USAID and University of Michigan Population and Environment Fellows Program, Washington DC, 1998

Dompka Markham (ed.), *Human Population, Biodiversity and Protected Areas: Science and Policy Issues*, AAAS, Washington DC, 1996

AMAP Arctic Monitoring and Assessment Programme http://www.amap.no/

Rekacewicz and Bournay, Major Areas of Oil and Gas Development and Potential Development in the Arctic, Oslo, 1998

Rekacewicz and Bournay, Total and Indigenous Populations of the Arctic, by Arctic Area of each Country, Oslo, 1998

BP http://www.bp.com

BP Amoco Statistical Review of World Energy 2000 (and earlier years), UK, 2000, also at http://www.bp.com/worldenergy

CBP Chesapeake Bay Program http://www.chesapeakebay.net

Water Quality Database, Annapolis, Maryland, 2000

CDIAC Carbon Dioxide Information Analysis Center, Oak Ridge National Laboratory (US) http://cdiac-esd.ornl.gov/

Brenkert, Carbon Dioxide Emission Estimates from Fossil-Fuel Burning, Hydraulic Cement Production, and Gas Flaring for 1995 on a One Degree Grid Cell Basis, CDIAC, Oak Ridge, Tennessee, 1998

Olson, Watts and Allison, Major World Ecosystem Complexes Ranked by Carbon in Live Vegetation, CDIAC, Oak Ridge, Tennessee, 1985

CEFIC European Chemical Industry Council http://www.cefic.org/

Census Bureau of Madagascar Some data at http://www.ons. dz/unfpa/pmappl/madatlas.htm

Central Bureau of Statistics (Nepal)

CGIAR Consultative Group on International Agricultural Research http://www.sgrp.cgiar.org

Choudhury World Forestry Congress, 6, topic 38.6, 1997

CIAT International Center for Tropical Agriculture http://www.ciat.cgiar.org/

CIESIN Center for International Earth Science Information Network http://www.ciesin.org

CIESIN, IFPRI and WRI, Gridded Population of the World (GPW), ver. 2, CIESIN, Columbia University, Palisades, New York, 2000, http://sedac.ciesin.org/plue/gpw

CITES Convention on International Trade in Endangered Species of Wild Fauna and Flora http://www.cites.org

http://international.fws.gov/ global/citesnew.html

Dobson, *Conservation and Biodiversity*, Scientific American Library, 1998

EC European Commission http://europa.eu.int/comm/

Allanou, Hansen and van der Bilt, *Public Availability of Data on EU High Production Volume Chemicals*, European Commission, Joint Research Centre, Institute for Health and Consumer Protection, European Chemicals Bureau, Italy, 1999, http://ecb.ei.jrc.it/Data-Availability-Documents/ datavail.pdf

EEA European Environment Agency http://www.eea.eu.org

Environment in the European Union at the Turn of the Century, Environmental Assessment Report No. 2, Luxembourg, 1999

EEA and UNEP, *State and Pressures of the Marine and Coastal Mediterranean Environment*, Luxembourg, 1999

EPA United States Environmental Protection Agency http://www.epa.gov/

Office of Solid Waste and Emergency Response, *Characterization of Municipal Solid Waste in the United States: 1992 Update*, Washington DC, 1992

ESRI Environmental Systems Research Institute, Inc. (US) http://www.esri.com

ArcAtlas: Our Earth, ESRI, Redlands, California, 1996

Fairplay Fairplay Publications Limited http://www.fairplay.co.uk

Fairplay Ports Guide, Surrey, UK, 2000, http://www.portguide.com/

FAO Food and Agriculture Organization of the United Nations http://www.fao.org

FAOSTAT database http://apps.fao.org

State of the World's Forests 1999 (and earlier years), FAO, Rome, 1999

The State of Food Insecurity in the World, FAO, Rome, 1999

Food for All, FAO, Rome, 1996

Dimensions of Need: An Atlas of Food and Agriculture, FAO, Rome, 1995

Alexandratos (ed.), World Agriculture: Towards 2010, FAO and John Wiley & Sons, Chichester, UK, 1995

FASE Foundation for Advancements in Science and Education http://www.fasenet.org/

Fase Research Report, Spring 1996

GLASOD/UNEP-GRID Global Assessment of Human-induced Soil Degradation / United Nations Environment Programme Global Resource Information Database http://www.grid.unep.ch/datasets/gnv-data.html

Oldeman, Hakkeling and Sombroek, World Map of the Status of Human-induced Soil Degradation: An Explanatory Note, International Soil Reference and Information Centre, Wageningen, Netherlands, 1990

Gold Institute, The http://www.goldinstitute.org

Data supplied by Gold Fields Mineral Services Ltd, UK

Hadley Centre Hadley Centre for Climate Prediction and Research, Meteorological Office (UK) http://www.meto.govt.uk/sec5/sec5pg1.html

HadCM3, Hadley Centre, London, UK, 1998

Harvard School of Public Health, Division of Environmental Science and Engineering, and the Center for Health and the Global Environment http://www.med.harvard.edu/chge/

Epstein and Sherman, Global Precipitation Anomalies and Associated Disease Outbreaks, Harvard School of Public Health, Cambridge, Massachussetts, 1999

IAATO International Association of Antarctica Tour Operators http://www.iaato.org

ICLARM International Center for Living Aquatic Resources Management http://www.cgiar.org/iclarm/

IFPRI International Food Policy Research Institute http://www.ifpri.cgiar.org/index1.asp

IIASA International Institute for Applied Systems Analysis http://www.iiasa.ac.at/

Leemans and Cramer, The IIASA Database for Mean Monthly Values of Temperature, Precipitation and Cloudiness of a Global Terrestrial Grid, IIASA, Laxenburg, Austria, RR-91-18, 1991

Independent Commission on Population and Quality of Life

Harrison, Carrying Capacity in Relation to Production and Consumption Patterns, Independent Commission on Population and Quality of Life, Paris, 1994

INEGI Instituto Nacional de Estadística, Geografía e Informática (National Institute of Statistics, Geography and Informatics) (Mexico) http://www.inegi.gob.mx

IPCC Intergovernmental Panel on Climate Change http://www.ipcc.ch/

ISEL Institute of Shipping Economics and Logistics http://www.isl.uni-bremen.de/

Shipping Statistics Yearbook, Bremen, Germany, 1998

ISME International Society for Mangrove Ecosystems

Spalding et al. (eds), World Mangrove Atlas, ISME/WCMC/ITTO, 1997

ITOPF The International Tanker Owners Pollution Federation Limited http://www.itopf.com

ITOPF Past Spill Statistics, http://www.itopf.com/stats.html

ITTO International Tropical Timber Organization http://www.itto.org.jp

IUCN IUCN–The World Conservation Union http://www.iucn.org

1996 IUCN Red List of Threatened Animals, IUCN, Geneva, 1996

McNeely et al., Conserving the World's Biological Diversity, IUCN, Gland, 1990

Jones et al. Jones, Osborn and Briffa, Climatic Research Unit, University of East Anglia, and Parker, Hadley Centre (UK) http://cdiac.esd.ornl.gov/trends/temp/jonescru/jones.html

Lloyds Register http://www.lr.org

World Fleet Statistics, London, UK, 1999

Meadows et al. Meadows, Donella et al., Beyond the Limits, Earthscan Publications, 1992

Met. Office The Meteorological Office (UK) http://www.met-office.gov.uk/

Climate Change and its Impacts, 1993, http://www.met-office.gov.uk/sec5/CR_div/pubs/brochures/B1999/contents.html

Ministry of Territorial Organization (Dominican Republic)

NADP/NTN National Atmospheric Deposition Program/National Trends Network (US) http://nadp.sws.uiuc.edu/

Sulfur Concentration 1999, NADP/NTN, Champaign, Illinois, 2000

NASA National Aeronautics and Space Administration (US) http://www.nasa.gov

SeaWiFS Project, Sea-viewing Wide Field-of-view Sensor (SeaWIFS), Distributed Active Archive Center, Goddard Space Flight Center, Goddard, Maryland, 1998, under the auspices of NASA, http://seawifs.gsfc.nasa.gov/SEAWIFS.html

National Census Data Central Statistical Office of the Ministry of Planning, Bhutan; Central Bureau of Statistics, Nepal

Nature Conservancy, The http://www.tnc.org

NOAA National Oceanic and Atmospheric Administration (US) http://www.noaa.gov/

National Geophysical Data Center, Digital Relief of the Surface of the Earth, NOAA, Boulder, Colorado, 1988, http://www.nodc.noaa.gov/

Ocean Climate Laboratory, Global Plankton Database, National Oceanographic Data Center, NOAA, 1998, http://www.nodc.noaa.gov/OC5/RESEARCH/PLANKTON/plankton.html

Operational Significant Event Imagery, http://www.osei.noaa.gov/

NSIDC National Snow and Ice Data Center (US) http://nsidc.org/

DMSP SSM/I Brightness, Temperatures and Sea Ice Concentration Grids for the Polar Regions, 1987 - present, NSIDC Distributed Active Archive Center, University of Colorado at Boulder, 1999, digital data available from nsidc@kryos.colorado.edu

OCEI Oficina Central de Estadística e Informática (Central Office of Statistics and Informatics) (Venezuela) http://www.ocei.gov.ve

OECD Organisation for Economic Co-operation and Development http://www.oecd.org/

OECD Environmental Data Compendium 1999, ENV/EPOC/SE(98)2/FINAL

Environmental Indicators, OECD, Paris, 1998

ONE Oficina Nacional de Estadística (National Office of Statistics) (Dominican Republic) http://www.one.gov.do

ORNL Oak Ridge National Laboratory (US) http://www.ornl.gov/gist/

Geographic Information Science and Technology (GIST) Group data, ORNL, 1998, featured in Dobson, Bright, Coleman, Durfee and Worley, LandScan: a global population database for estimating populations at risk, *Photogrammetric Engineering & Remote Sensing*, 66(7): 849-857, 2000

PopMap An Information and Decision Support System for Population Activities http://www.un.org/Depts/unsd/softproj/software/popmap.htm

Population Action International http://www.populationaction.org/

Gardner-Outlaw and Engelman, *Sustaining Water, Easing Scarcity: A Second Update*, Population Action International, 1997

Ramsar Bureau Bureau of the Convention on Wetlands of International Importance Especially as Waterfowl Habitat http://www.ramsar.org

RIVM National Institute of Public Health and the Environment (Netherlands) http://www.rivm.nl/

Klein Goldewijk, A History Database of the Global Environment: HYDE, RIVM, Bilthoven, the Netherlands, 2000, http://www.rivm.nl/env/int/hyde

SCAR Scientific Committee on Antarctic Research http://www.scar.org

Stations of SCAR Nations Operating in the Antarctic, Cambridge, UK, 1999

British Antarctic Survey, Antarctic Protected Areas, SCAR, Cambridge, UK, 1999, http://www.antarctica.ac.uk

British Antarctic Survey, Antarctic Digital Database, ver. 2.0, SCAR, Cambridge, UK, 1998, http://www.antarctica.ac.uk

Simon, *The Ultimate Resource 2*, Princeton University Press, New Jersey, 1996

STATBASE UK National Statistics Online http://www.statsbase.gov.uk/statbase/mainmenu.asp

Times Times Books Group Ltd

The Times Atlas of the World, Comprehensive Edition, Times Books Group Ltd, London, UK, 1999

UN United Nations http://www.un.org

United Nations Statistics Division http://www.un.org/Depts/unsd/global.htm

World Cities Population Database, UN, New York, 1999

Kyoto Protocol to the United Nations Framework Convention on Climate Change, Article 3, Annex B, UN, New York, 1997, http://www.unfccc.de

NDP United Nations
evelopment Programme
ttp://www.undp.org/

*uman Development Report
999*, UNDP, 1999

NEP United Nations
nvironment Programme
ttp://www.unep.org

NEP ENTRI Query System,
ttp://www.ciesin.org/harvest/
rokers/entri2/query.html

ur Planet 11(2), 2000 (and
arlier issues), also at
ttp://www.ourplanet.com

*lobal Environment Outlook
)00*, Earthscan Publications Ltd
r and on behalf of UNEP, 1999

*roduction and Consumption of
zone Depleting Substances
986-1998*, Ozone Secretariat,
NEP, 1999

orld Atlas of Desertification,
nd edition, Arnold, London, UK,
397 (and 1992)

eywood (ed.), *Global
iodiversity Assessment*,
ambridge University Press for
NEP, Cambridge, UK, 1995

NEP/GRID-Arendal
ttp://www.grida.no/

iternational Permafrost
ssociation, Circum-arctic Map
Permafrost and Ground-Ice
onditions, ver. 1.0, 1998, http://
ww.grida.no/prog/polar/ipa/

NEP-WCMC The UNEP World
onservation Monitoring Centre
ttp://www.wcmc.org.uk

rotected Areas Database

Groombridge and Jenkins,
*Global Biodiversity: Earth's
Living Resources in the 21st
Century*, World Conservation
Press, Cambridge, UK, 2000

Information Services and the
Protected Areas Unit, Protected
Areas of the World, ver. 1.1,
WCMC, Cambridge, UK, 1997

UNESCO United Nations
Educational, Scientific and
Cultural Organization
http://www.unesco.org

World Heritage Centre, World
Heritage Sites, Paris, 2000

UNFPA United Nations
Population Fund
http://www.unfpa.org

UNHCR United Nations High
Commissioner for Refugees
http://www.unhcr.org

1999 Statistical Overview,
UNHCR

UNICEF United Nations
Children's Fund
http://www.unicef.org

*The State of the World's
Children 2000*, also at
http://www.unicef.org/sowc00/

UNPD United Nations
Population Division
http://www.un.org/esa/
population/pop.htm

*World Population Prospects:
The 1998 Revision*, UN, New
York, 1999, data also available at
http://apps.fao.org

*Urban Agglomerations, 1950-
2015 (The 1996 Revision)*,
UNPD, 1997

Department for Economic and
Social Information and Policy
Analysis, *International Migration
Policies*, UNPD, 1995

Annual Populations, 1994

USAID US Agency for
International Development
http://www.usaid.gov

US Bureau of the Census
http://www.census.gov

USGS US Geological Survey
http://usgs.gov/

Mineral Commodity Summaries,
February 2000

Global Land Cover
Characteristics Data Base, ver.
1.2, EROS Data Center, Sioux
Falls, South Dakota, 1998, http://
edcdaac.usgs.gov/glcc/glcc.html

WHO World Health Organization
http://www.who.int/

WMO World Meteorological
Office http://www.wmo.ch

World Bank, The
http://www.worldbank.org

*World Development Indicators
2000* (and earlier years), World
Bank, Washington DC, 2000, print
and CD-ROM versions, some
data at http://www.worldbank.
org/data/edi2000/index.htm

World Energy Council
http://www.worldenergy.org/
wec-geis/

World Tourism Organization
http://www.world-tourism.org

*Yearbook of Tourism Statistics
1999*, Madrid

Worldwatch Institute
http://www.worldwatch.org

World•Watch, March/April 2000

WRI World Resources Institute
http://www.wri.org/

WRI, UNEP, UNDP, World Bank,
World Resources 2000-2001
(and earlier years), WRI,
Washington DC, 2000, print and
CD-ROM versions, some data at
http://www.wri.org/facts/
data-tables.html

Bryant et al., *Reefs at Risk*,
WRI/ICLARM/WCMC/UNEP,
Washington DC, 1998

WSP–USDA World Soil
Program, United States
Department of Agriculture
http://www.usda.gov

WSP, Global Cropland
Degradation, USDA, Washington
DC, 1999

WTO World Trade Organization
http://www.wto.org

Trade Statistics: World Trade
Overview and Long-term Series

WWF World Wide Fund For
Nature http://www.panda.org

Living Planet Report 2000,
WWF, Gland, 2000

Myers, *The Wild Supermarket*,
WWF, Switzerland, 1986

WWF-Colombia World Wide
Fund For Nature Programme
Office, Colombia
http://www.andesdelnorte.net

WWF-US World Wildlife Fund
http://www.worldwildlife.org

COUNTRIES OF THE WORLD

Svalbard
(Nor.)

AND

RUSSIAN FEDERATION

ARMENIA
AZERBAIJAN

KAZAKHSTAN

MONGOLIA

DEMOCRATIC
PEOPLE'S REPUBLIC
OF KOREA

UZBEKISTAN KYRGYZSTAN

TURKMENISTAN

TAJIKISTAN

JAPAN

Madeira
Port.)

IRAQ

ISLAMIC
REPUBLIC
OF IRAN

AFGHAN-
ISTAN

CHINA

REPUBLIC
OF KOREA

ALGERIA

LIBYAN ARAB
JAMAHIRIYA

EGYPT

KUWAIT

STERN
AHARA

SAUDI
ARABIA

OMAN

PAKISTAN

NEPAL

BHUTAN

TAIWAN PROVINCE
OF CHINA

MAURITANIA

MALI

NIGER

CHAD

ERITREA

YEMEN

SUDAN

BANGLADESH

INDIA

MYANMAR

LAOS

NEGAL
A

BURKINA
FASO

NIGERIA

DJIBOUTI

THAILAND

VIETNAM

PHILIPPINES

AU GUINEA

EONE

GHANA

CENTRAL
AFRICAN
REPUBLIC

ETHIOPIA

CAMBODIA

BRUNEI
DARUSSALAM

PALAU

LIBERIA

CÔTE D'IVOIRE

CAMEROON

SOMALIA

SRI
LANKA

MALDIVES

MALAYSIA

TOGO

BENIN

GABON

RWANDA
UGANDA

KENYA

SINGAPORE

INDONESIA

PAPUA NEW
GUINEA

EQUATORIAL GUINEA

TOME AND PRINCIPE

CONGO

DEMOCRATIC
REPUBLIC
OF CONGO

BURUNDI

UNITED REPUBLIC
OF TANZANIA

SEYCHELLES

SOLOMON
ISLANDS

ANGOLA

ZAMBIA

MALAWI

COMOROS

VANUATU

ZIMBABWE

BOTSWANA

MOZAMBIQUE

MADAGASCAR

MAURITIUS

Réunion (Fr.)

FIJI

NAMIBIA

New Caledonia
(Fr.)

AUSTRALIA

SWAZILAND

REPUBLIC
OF SOUTH
AFRICA

LESOTHO

NEW
ZEALAND

Conversion tables

How to use the conversion tables:

centimeter		inch
2.54	**1**	0.39

Read the number in the center column. Look left to convert imperial to metric, and look right to convert metric to imperial.
In this case:
1 inch = 2.54 centimeters
1 centimeter = 0.39 inches

Numbers
Million = 1 000 000
Billion = 1 000 000 000
Trillion = 1 000 000 000 000

Distance
10 millimeters (mm) = 1 centimeter (cm)
100 centimeters = 1 meter (m)
1 000 meters = 1 kilometer (km)

meter		yard		kilometer		mile
0.9144	**1**	1.0936		1.6093	**1**	0.6214
1.8288	**2**	2.1872		3.2187	**2**	1.2427
2.7432	**3**	3.2808		4.8280	**3**	1.8641
3.6576	**4**	4.3744		6.4374	**4**	2.4855
4.5720	**5**	5.4680		8.0467	**5**	3.1069
9.1440	**10**	10.936		16.093	**10**	6.2140
45.720	**50**	54.680		80.467	**50**	31.069
91.440	**100**	109.36		160.93	**100**	62.140
914.40	**1 000**	1 093.6		1 609.3	**1 000**	621.40

Area
100 square millimeters (mm²) = 1 square centimeter (cm²)
10 000 square centimeters = 1 square meter (m²)
10 000 square meters = 1 hectare (ha)
100 hectares = 1 square kilometer (km²)

hectare		acre		square kilometer		square mile
0.4047	**1**	2.4710		2.590	**1**	0.3861
0.8094	**2**	4.9421		5.180	**2**	0.7722
1.2141	**3**	7.4131		7.7699	**3**	1.1583
1.6187	**4**	9.8842		10.36	**4**	1.5444
2.0234	**5**	12.355		12.95	**5**	1.9305
4.0470	**10**	24.710		25.90	**10**	3.8610
20.234	**50**	123.55		129.50	**50**	19.305
40.470	**100**	247.10		259	**100**	38.610
404.70	**1 000**	2 471		2 590	**1 000**	386.10

Volume
1 000 cubic millimeters (mm³) = 1 cubic centimeter (cm³)
1 000 000 cubic centimeters = 1 cubic meter (m³)
1 000 000 000 cubic meters = 1 cubic kilometer (km³)

cubic meter		cubic foot		liter		gallon (US)
0.0283	**1**	35.315		3.7853	**1**	0.2642
0.0566	**2**	70.629		7.5706	**2**	0.5284
0.0849	**3**	105.94		11.356	**3**	0.7925
0.1133	**4**	141.26		15.141	**4**	1.0567
0.1416	**5**	176.57		18.926	**5**	1.3209
0.2830	**10**	353.15		37.853	**10**	2.6420
1.4160	**50**	1 765.7		189.26	**50**	13.209
2.8300	**100**	3 531.5		378.53	**100**	26.420
28.300	**1 000**	35 315		3 785.3	**1 000**	264.20

1 US gallon = 0.8327 UK gallons
1 UK gallon = 1.2009 US gallons
1 barrel of oil = 159 liters = 42 US gallons = 35 UK gallons

Weight
1 000 milligrams (mg) = 1 gram (g)
1 000 grams = 1 kilogram (kilo)
1 000 kilograms = 1 metric ton (ton)

kilogram		pound (lb)
0.4536	**1**	2.2046
0.9072	**2**	4.4092
1.3608	**3**	6.6139
1.8144	**4**	8.8185
2.2680	**5**	11.023
4.5360	**10**	22.046
22.680	**50**	110.23
45.360	**100**	220.46
453.60	**1 000**	2 204.6

Energy
1 metric ton of oil equivalent (mtoe) =
approximately
1.5 tons hard coal
3 tons lignite
1.23 tons liquid natural gas
1 111 cubic meters natural gas

For Reference

Not to be taken from this room